MENTAL GYMNASTICS

JEAN M. SHAW

MARY JO PUCKETT CLIATT

University of Mississippi

Prentice-Hall, Inc. Englewood Cliffs, New Jersey 07632

SHAW, JEAN M.
  Mental gymnastics.

  Bibliography: p.
  Includes index.
  1. Creative thinking (Education) 2. Creative
activities and seat work. I. Cliatt, Mary Jo Puckett.
II. Title
LB1062.S48 1984   370.15'7   83-9177

Editorial/production supervision
  and interior design: Barbara Kelly Kittle
Cover design: George Cornell
Manufacturing buyer: Ron Chapman

Printed in the United States of America

10 9 8 7 6 5 4 3 2 1

ISBN 0-13-575928-5

Prentice-Hall International, Inc., London
Prentice-Hall of Australia Pty. Limited, Sydney
Editora Prentice-Hall do Brasil, Ltda., Rio de Janeiro
Prentice-Hall Canada Inc., Toronto
Prentice-Hall of India Private Limited, New Delhi
Prentice-Hall of Japan, Inc., Tokyo
Prentice-Hall of Southeast Asia Pte. Ltd., Singapore
Whitehall Books Limited, Wellington, New Zealand

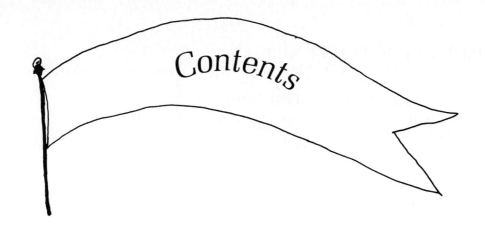

Contents

7 ACTIVITIES FOR SOCIAL STUDIES 124

8 ACTIVITIES FOR ART 154

ACTIVITIES FOR MUSIC 188

EVALUATION 215

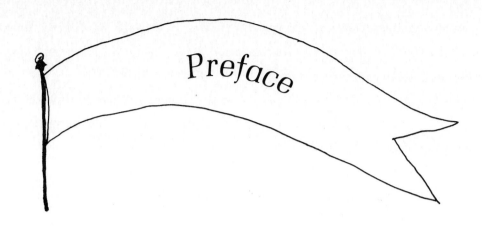

Preface

We are living in a period of rapid change. Ideas that are valid and pertinent today are likely to be obsolete tomorrow. Because facts and technology change so rapidly, we can no longer depend on pulling adequate solutions to problems from a pool of information. Even the types of problems we encounter have become more complicated; thus, we must learn how to think rather than what to think.

The increasing number of problems in the world today indicates the need for the fostering of creative thinking abilities to help us solve our problems. Divergent thinking is a tool for helping us cope with those we encounter every day. No longer are there simple methods of generating less obvious solutions, and of comparing alternative solutions.

In spite of the importance of developing divergent thinking skills, teachers in many classrooms still stress convergent thinking. Perhaps they don't know how to ask divergent thinking questions. Maybe they never dealt with divergent thinking themselves. Perhaps teachers don't think that divergent thinking will fit into their curriculum, or they don't think that they have enough time to teach divergent thinking skills in the classroom. To help teachers, Mental Gymnastics offers simple and effective ways to incorporate divergent thinking in the classroom. At the same time, this book helps teachers, themselves, to think more divergently. Using divergent thinking in the classroom isn't hard; it's just a different orientation. Becoming competent at divergent thinking does take practice. When divergent thinking is used in the classroom, classrooms come alive, because divergent thinking is fun and challenging.

Mental Gymnastics is intended as a sourcebook for inservice and preservice teachers of elementary and junior high school students. It will be of special interest to teachers of the gifted. The book could also be used to help educators develop curriculum, and in classrooms to promote interaction among students. Additionally, this book might be utilized by parents, camp directors, school supervisors, or others who deal with the cognitive and affective development of young people.

This book includes over 500 classroom activities that encourage teachers and their students to explore many aspects of the divergent thinking process. The chapters of the book include activities for the following curricular areas: language arts, math, science, social studies, art, and music. An introductory chapter provides the reader with background information on divergent thinking.

Chapter three, "Readings and Research," overviews the voluminous educational and psychological literature on divergent thinking. Mental Gymnastics also includes a chapter on successful management of divergent thinking activities in the classroom. The book concludes with a chapter to help teachers evaluate their progress in using divergent thinking.

Each curriculum chapter offers the reader an overview of the content, skills, and processes for that curricular area. The bulk of the chapter features scores of activities for large and small groups and dozens more suited for individual students. Large group activities let everyone put ideas together and build on each other's thoughts. Small group activities provide for much interaction and "hands-on" work; every member of a small group can get in on the action. Individual activities provide opportunities for independent creative thinking. Some individual activities can be used in the classroom; others can be used for unique homework assignments. Some of the small group and individual activities are intended to be teacher-directed; others are presented in a form so they can be used independently by students. Each curriculum chapter begins with brief exercises to start adults thinking divergently and concludes by suggesting ways teachers can apply their own divergent thinking skills in the classroom. All of the activities in Mental Gymnastics stress active involvement. They utilize many presentational forms such as speaking, drawing, acting, and writing.

We wish to thank many people for helping us with this book. Our students constantly inspired us and gave us new ideas as they experimented with divergent thinking. We are grateful to our friend, Lynne Murchison, for the many hours she spent helping us edit and refine our writing. We thank our typists, Janet Goodman, Billie Sue Gunter, Rae Pitcock, and Helen Richardson for the hard work that they have put into this book. We appreciate the support of our department chairman, Robert W. Plants, and our dean, S.A. Moorhead. Our editor, Ted Jursek, gave us the idea for the title of this book. We have had lots of fun developing our theme from his title. We are grateful to our families for their constant loving support and the suggestions they offered. The ideas that Vicki and Billy gave us from a young person's point of view were especially helpful. Our "Andy" character is based on a real, active dog, Mickthea Andrew Grant. He watched with great curiosity as we developed almost every line and sketch of this book.

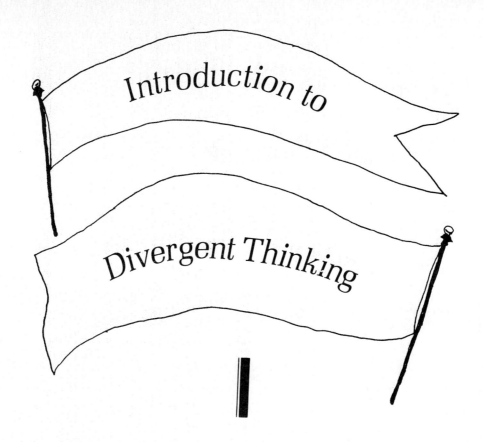

Introduction to Divergent Thinking

These days people are interested in keeping fit. They carefully eat the right foods. Some use the strategies of eating natural foods, avoiding those high in cholesterol, or counting every calorie. Many people supplement their diets with vitamins. Others eschew "junk" foods and other foods that add little nutritional value to their regimens.

Some individuals who are interested in the physical fitness aspect of health carefully plan exercises to be pursued on a regular basis. Body exercise is a worthy endeavor because our muscles have a tendency to become flabby. They need to be toned up and developed. People have different body areas that go to pot. Some have sagging bellies; some have double chins; still others have flabby legs. To find the flabby or weak area in your body, just try a new type of exercise and see what areas ache the most the next day. This experiment will give you a good indication of areas in your body that need toning up.

Just as your body needs exercise to keep fit, your mind also needs exercise. For most people the area of the mind that is the least developed is the divergent thinking area. Only a small minority of people use this area consistently and profitably. You cannot see your mind. Sometimes you don't even know it's not in shape, but it is one area that if toned up could work to benefit both you and those around you. It can bring fun and excitement to your life and add new dimensions to your personality. It can give you clues to solving problems that normally defy solution. Becoming proficient at divergent thinking could prove to be profitable in more tangible ways; it could even make some money for you. Divergent thinking

1

is a dimension that will enrich your life. You will find you can't do without it once it is tried and developed.

DIVERGENT THINKING MIND STRETCHERS

But what is this type of mental exercise called divergent thinking? Before we attempt to define it, let's explore a few examples. Take several minutes to think about these questions. You may want to talk aloud to yourself about them.

1. If you could be any place you wanted right now, where would you be? Imagine yourself there. What are you doing? Who is with you? Describe the surroundings. Now choose another place to be. Decide what you'll wear. Plan what you'll do for the day.

2. What gripes do you have about the latest fashions? Pretend you are a successful fashion designer. What would you change about current fashions? Create a new garment or accessory. Be daring or conservative, exotic or practical, but make your creation fit your personality.

3. Think about your place of work. If you were the boss, how would you change things? Remember you must be a responsible boss, making practical and workable decisions. Think of ways to initiate your ideas or changes.

Although the previous exercises may appear to be frivolous, they exercise a part of your brain that probably seldom is used. Remember that many people are tempted to give up body exercises on the first few tries, but when they stick with them they are rewarded with trim bodies and a feeling of achievement. The divergent thinking exercises above are intended to start your program of mental gymnastics. Working through exercises such as these is fun and beneficial. These exercises expand your mind and your ability to think divergently.

Now that you've done some divergent thinking, let's explore some definitions. Divergent thinking is the generation of many appropriate responses to a question or problem. It is the ability to think creatively,[1] to depart from a set course or norm,[2] and to move to a variety of new and unique responses.[3]

TYPES OF THINKING

Let's compare divergent thinking with some other kinds of thinking. Convergent thinking involves generating one acceptable solution or answer to a problem or question. In convergent thinking, people start with a problem and move toward one correct answer. Convergent thinking usually involves memorizing and using facts, interpreting data, and developing appropriate vocabulary usage. Teachers employ convergent thinking when they ask their students to match words with definitions, to memorize arithmetic facts, or to diagram sentences.

Another kind of thinking is evaluative thinking. In evaluative thinking, people make judgments according to standards they have set.[4] Evaluative thinking involves first setting standards, then determining how closely ideas meet those standards.[5] For instance, you use evaluative thinking when you appraise a menu and select foods that fit both your personal taste and your pocketbook. When you choose a living place, you establish such standards as closeness to work or shopping, price, demands for upkeep, or type of neighborhood to help you make your decision.

While convergent thinking involves settling on one correct answer, divergent thinking explores many possible answers or ways of arriving at answers. Although evaluative thinking is different from divergent thinking, it uses an element of divergent thinking in developing standards. For example, in buying a car, economy and ease of handling may determine your choice. Other people might set completely different standards based on status, color, and interior style more than other factors.

Now here's a little mental workout to test your ability to differentiate between the three types of thinking we've just described. Can you identify each of the following problems as

---

[1]Cliatt, Shaw, and Sherwood, Child Development, December, 1980, pp. 1061–64.

[2]American Heritage Dictionary of the English Language, p. 384–85.

[3]King-Stoops, The Child Wants to Learn, p. 54–55.

[4]Sanders, Classroom Questions, p. 3.

[5]Bloom, Taxonomy of Education Objectives, p. 185.

convergent, divergent, or evaluative thinking? Fill in the blanks at the left with the correct answer.

_____ 1. You're going on a weekend vacation. You need to decide whether to take the kids or leave them at home.

_____ 2. You want to plan a party for six people.

_____ 3. You need to get to the grocery store by the shortest possible route.

_____ 4. You bake a loaf of bread using your mom's favorite recipe.

_____ 5. It's midnight and you're on page 400 of an exciting novel. You must decide whether to finish the book or turn out the light and get to sleep.

_____ 6. You compose a poem to honor a loved one.

_____ 7. You plan which vegetables you'll plant in your spring garden.

_____ 8. You want to spruce up your wardrobe but have no money for new clothes. Think of different ways to combine the clothes and accessories you already have.

How do you think you did? Use our "Check Yourself" answers at the end of this chapter to see if you answered correctly.

Divergent Thinking in the Classroom

Divergent thinking is important because we are living in a period of rapid change. Ideas that are valid and pertinent today are likely to be obsolete tomorrow. The types of problems we encounter have become more complicated than in the past. No longer are there simple or obvious solutions to all of our problems. Rather, we need methods of generating less obvious solutions and of comparing alternative solutions. Possible solutions are conceived through the divergent thinking process. Then evaluative thinking helps us to judge their appropriateness.

In many classrooms, teachers stress convergent thinking. Both children and teachers are lulled to sleep with boredom as a result. Students maintain an outward pretense of thinking while their minds are 100 kilometers away. Thus, they establish slovenly mental habits. But just insert a divergent thinking question or two into a classroom discussion and wandering minds will pay attention. Divergent thinking is a motivator.

Divergent thinking develops mental competence in people and thus improves their feelings of adequacy. When people feel good about themselves, they have the confidence to approach more difficult problems. It's like a spiral. Effort leads to achievement, achievement builds confidence, and confidence encourages us to strive toward even greater achievements. Thus, we become more proficient.

People of all ages and levels of sophistication can and should participate in divergent thinking activities. Ask some three-year-olds to help you think of lots of things that make noises. Talk to some fourth graders about the many different ways to play with a ball. Ask a group of college students their ideas about building a better society in the future. Encourage a group of adults in the business world to share their perspectives about solutions to the energy crisis. You might be surprised at the number and variety of answers you receive. You'll probably be impressed when you notice how much people enjoy interacting, sharing ideas, and building on the ideas of others.

Divergent thinking can be one of the highest levels of thinking. Divergent thinking is a vital part of synthesis. In terms of quality and complexity, Bloom[6] places synthesis second only to evaluative thinking. As our diagram[7] shows, divergent thinking builds on the levels of thinking below it. Great people throughout the ages have utilized divergent thinking. Creative thinkers such as Copernicus, Galileo, Pasteur, Picasso, and Stravinsky pursued nontraditional thinking and discovered solutions, formulated theories, and invented products that changed and influenced future work in their fields. Their use of divergent thinking changed the course of history and still has a great impact on our lives today.

Important as this skill is, it is little stressed today in schools. Few children are systematically trained in divergent thinking. In fact, most educators place little value on creative thinking. However, if more emphasis were placed on divergent thinking, we might produce students with the skill and confidence to equal and perhaps even surpass the accomplishments of the great thinkers of the past—thinkers who could find creative solutions to the problems that confound us in our world today.

We hope you agree that divergent thinking is important. But is it practical in a classroom? Let's compare two versions of the same lesson. One employs the traditional method of convergent thinking. The second is based on divergent thinking. Imagine yourself in a third-grade classroom in which the teacher is conducting a science lesson on the sense of touch.

Convergent Lesson	Divergent Lesson
Teacher: What sense are you using when you feel something?	Teacher: What are some ways you use your body to find out about things?
Ken: Touch.	Jon: Well, you look at things.
Teacher: What do you feel with? Lisa?	Suzy: You can talk and hear things.

---

[6]Bloom, pp. 162-184.

[7]We have used the term "memory" to replace Bloom's term "knowledge" because memory is a good descriptor of the intellectual activity to which Bloom refers.

Convergent Lesson

Lisa: Your hands.

Teacher: Your hands. Right. If you couldn't see, your hands could still tell you a lot about the world around you. Go ahead. Close your eyes. Find the desk in front of you. Does it feel rough or smooth?

Class: Smooth.

Teacher: Is it warm or cool?

Class: Cool.

Teacher: Now, feel around the edge of your desk. What shape is it, Judy?

Judy: Square.

Teacher: Keep feeling, Judy. Are all four sides the same length?

Judy: Well, no.

Teacher: When two sides are longer than the other two, what shape is it?

Carmen: A rectangle!

Teacher: Yes. Everybody feel the rectangle . . . two long sides and two shorter ones. I have some things up here, and I want you to feel them. Billy, you be first. Here, let me put this blindfold on you, okay? Choose an object. (Billy picks a piece of sandpaper.) Is it rough or smooth?

Billy: Rough.

Teacher: Are both sides the same?

Billy: Well, one side is rough and one's smooth.

Teacher: What shape is it?

Billy: A circle.

Teacher: Is it thin or thick?

Billy: Uh . . . pretty thin.

Teacher: Good, Billy! Who wants to be next? OK, Ora Mae, it's your turn. Here's the blindfold.

(Ora Mae picks a small rubber ball.)

Teacher: What's the shape of your object?

Ora Mae: Well, it's round. It's a ball.

Teacher: Is it rough or smooth?

Ora Mae: It's smooth. Look, you can squeeze it.

Divergent Lesson

Marshall: I just heard a siren outside. I'll bet there's a fire. Maybe it's coming to this school!

(Laughter)

Teacher: Yes, we tell a lot by seeing and hearing things. Can you think of other ways to find out about things?

Kevin: You can taste things to see if they're good.

Joanne: Well, if you were blind, you'd feel things.

Teacher: There are lots of ways to find out about things. Let's talk about feeling and touch. There are many ways to feel things. Can you think of some? Marshall?

Marshall: We feel with our hands.

Teacher: What if you didn't have hands? Could you still feel things? Ruby?

Ruby: When I take off my shoes, I can feel with my feet.

Teacher: Good. Can you think of another way?

Ruby: Well, you could even feel it with your elbow!

Gladys: And your tongue!

(Several more body parts are suggested.)

Teacher: OK. We can feel with many different body parts. Close your eyes. Right at our desks, what could we feel? Emily?

Emily: I can feel the pencil tray.

Vickie: Well, somebody put gum under my desk. I can feel it.

Teacher: Scott?

Scott: I don't know.

Teacher: Well, try the sides.

Scott: I don't know. Well, it's flat.

Teacher: Good, Scott. Now, I have some things up here, and I want you to feel them. Billy, you be first. Here, let me put this blindfold on you, OK? Choose an object. (Billy picks a piece of sandpaper.) How does it feel to you?

Billy: Well, it's rough.

Teacher: Can you think of some other things to tell me about it?

Convergent Lesson

Teacher: Yes, but tell me what size it is. Is it big or little?

Ora Mae: It's pretty small.

Teacher: Fine. Khee, do you want to be next?

(Khee comes up, gets blindfolded, and picks a brick.)

Teacher: Khee, is your object heavy or light?

Khee: Heavy!

Teacher: Is it rough or smooth?

Khee: Well, it's rough.

(The children continue to take turns feeling objects and responding to the teacher's questions.)

Divergent Lesson

Billy: It's got little bumps all over it.

Teacher: All over it?

Billy: Well, not here. The bottom is smooth.

Teacher: What does it remind you of?

Billy: It's sandpaper. It reminds me of the sandpaper me and dad used when we refinished the table.

Teacher: Good, Billy! Who wants to be next? OK, Ora Mae, it's your turn.

(The children continue to take turns feeling objects and responding to the teacher's questions.)

Let's compare the two lessons. There were several similarities. Both teachers elicited responses from the children. Both asked questions pertinent to the subject. Both used concrete objects and experiences to involve the children in their lessons.

The main difference between the two lessons was the type of questions used. In the convergent thinking lesson, the teacher gave little room for choice; he seemed to expect one specific answer. When Ora Mae digressed, mentioning that she could squeeze the ball, the teacher brought her right back to the topic he had in mind. In the divergent thinking lesson, the teacher asked questions that had many possible answers. In fact, he encouraged the children to think of many possible answers. Thus, the children thought of many different ways to touch objects rather than just the conventional way of touching with their hands. The children were encouraged to examine and describe many characteristics of the objects they felt rather than only those suggested by the teacher. The first lesson was close-ended; the second lesson was open-ended.

BUILDING YOUR MIND POWER

To prepare you to use divergent thinking in the classroom, get yourself in shape. Pick one of the exercises that follow for each day of next week. Just as you have to start slowly to work up to a five-kilometer jog, you'll probably have to build up your proficiency in divergent thinking. Your seventh day of mental gymnastics should be far easier and more productive than the first day. As you select a "mind builder" for each day, let your mind wander and stretch to think of as many different answers as possible.

1. Suppose you've just inherited five thousand dollars. What might you do with it?

2. Children are fighting in your classroom or home. What are some possible solutions to the problem?

3. Plan an exotic meal--one that is different from your ordinary menu.

4. When you woke up this morning, you found that you had turned into a dragon! How might people around you react?

5. Copy a square like this one onto scratch paper. What can you add to it to turn it into something different? How many different things can you make from it?

6. Are you "arts 'n' craftsy"? Spend a minute or two and cut out several dozen triangles from paper. Now arrange your triangles in groups of seven to make as many different shapes or designs as you can.

7. Let's take off. Suppose you could fly under your own power (not in any kind of plane). What are some of your problems? What advantages do you have now?

8. Serious business . . . what are some viable solutions to the problems caused by inflation?

9. Is thinking about inflation on a nationwide level too much for you? What are some possible solutions for your family?

10. Think of several advertising slogans for the "better mousetrap" that you have built.

Check Yourself

Here are the answers to the mental workout on page 4. Numbers 1, 5, and 7 involve evaluative thinking because they require that you make judgments based on standards you develop. Numbers 3 and 4 are convergent thinking problems. They have only one good answer or method of arriving at the solution. Because they have many possible answers, numbers 2, 6, and 8 are divergent thinking problems.

Readings and Research in Divergent Thinking

2

USING OUR BOOK

You may find several different ways to use this book. You might wish to go through it chapter by chapter, working the exercises and trying many of the activities in your classroom. Perhaps you would enjoy starting with only one chapter in practicing divergent thinking techniques with your students. If you are just interested in enlivening a particular area of the curriculum, consult the index to find many useful ideas to fit your needs.

Many of you will find our book helpful for specific supplementary uses in the classroom. You may choose activities for extra exercises for children who need special help or for children who finish their work early. If you have moments of extra time as you wait for the school bus or the lunch bell, select an activity from this book. Try it out with your class to make profitable use of extra minutes. If you, like most teachers today, are concerned with developing independent and creative learners, this book will be a useful resource for you. Above all, teachers of the gifted will find the entire book valuable in their classrooms.

Our Readings and Research in Divergent Thinking chapter (Chapter 3) provides background and overviews in the voluminous research that has been done in the area of divergent thinking. Those who want to deepen and expand their understanding of divergent thinking will want to study this chapter carefully. Those who want to explore divergent thinking in practical ways will skip the research chapter and turn directly to the curriculum chapters.

Special Features of Our Book Each curriculum chapter of our book includes several parts. Mind Stretchers and Building Your Mind Power are addressed directly to adults. The purpose of Mind Stretchers is to help you get started thinking divergently. Building Your Mind Power concludes each chapter and gives you the opportunity to apply your divergent thinking skills to the classroom setting.

Each curriculum chapter has a short introduction which is intended to give you an overview of some of the topics that will be included in that curricular area. The purpose of each introduction is to help you focus on the nature of the subject and to enlarge your perspective of the various facets of each area. The topics suggested are not all-inclusive. You will think of others besides those mentioned.

In each curriculum chapter you will find a series of large group activities for students. This is followed by a section of small-group student activities and a series of individual student activities. With large activities the entire class can be involved in divergent thinking exercises. Many large-group activities will lead naturally to small-group or individual explorations. Some small-group activities are addressed to teachers who will initiate the activities. Other student activities are written in a half-page format for student use. The directions for these student activities are simply written so that teachers can duplicate the instructions and give them to students to follow on their own. This procedure encourages groups of students to work without constant teacher supervision. The ideas in the individual

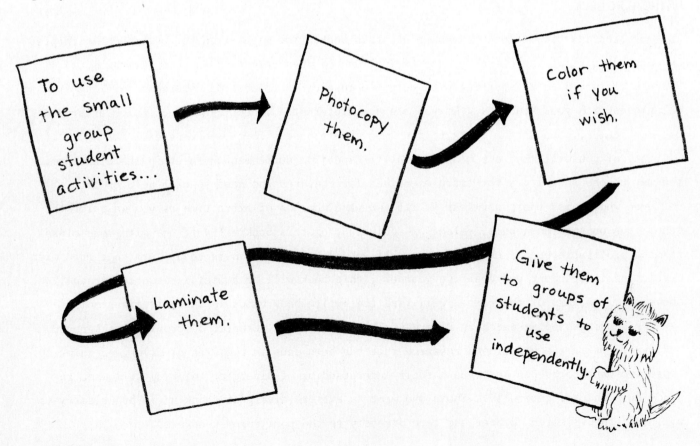

sections are intended for independent student work in the classroom or at home. Some individual activities are addressed to teachers who can initiate them with their students; others are presented in an attractive hand-drawn format to motivate children to work on their own. Individual activities are specially suited for fast learners or those who need extra stimulation. Remember that all of the hand-drawn activities can be duplicated and placed in learning centers.

Ways to Adapt Our Book to Your Classroom Our activities are arranged according to a suggested group size and within each group according to subject designation. These labels are intended to guide you, but feel free to adapt them to suit the needs of your own students and your particular teaching style. For instance, those activities suggested for large groups might suit your class better in a small-group setting. An idea that we suggest for multiplication may be changed slightly and used as you focus on another math skill. Perhaps a social studies idea could be more useful in language arts in your class. The index gives suggestions for appropriate grade level for each activity, but with some small changes, ideas marked "upper level" may suit the needs of your second graders beautifully. Often we suggest presentational forms such as discussions, pictures, writing activities, or making models. You should adapt these forms to suit your needs, the needs of your students, and your time schedule. Be flexible; make changes; adapt. This is the very essence of divergent thinking.

Preparing for Activities Before you use any activity in our book, check to see what kind of preparation you need to make. Most activities call for minimal preparation. A few activities will require you to introduce a subject one day and have the children bring something to class the next day. When activities require teaching aids, students can often make these materials themselves with a little supervision. For some research activities, your role may be providing books and other reading material. Check with your librarian for help in this area.

USING DIVERGENT THINKING IN THE CLASSROOM

Divergent thinking is new and different to children and adults. As with any skill, it will take some practice, some reinforcement, and constructive feedback before students begin to feel successful at thinking divergently. Teachers will need to be patient with the mistakes of children as they learn this new skill. Try not to become discouraged, and don't give up if you don't experience instant success. You can encourage students to persevere by making divergent thinking fun and building confidence with each new step.

As you begin practicing divergent thinking skills in the classroom, make it clear to the students that there are many possible answers, and that no one answer is correct or preferable in divergent thinking. How you word questions will make a difference in the way students respond. Phrases such as "How might . . . ?" "What could happen if . . . ?" "What are some . . . ?" are good starters for initiating divergent thinking.

You might want to ask provocative questions that cause students to think about things in ways they have never thought of before. Provocative questions usually have one or more of the following qualities: they confront students with ambiguities or uncertainties; they call for the exploration of puzzling situations; they require speculation or predictions based on limited information; they may juxtapose apparently irrelevant or unrelated elements. Provocative questions may involve fanciful thinking or may approach realistic problems (Torrance, 1970 and 1971).

When you begin to ask divergent thinking questions, your role as a teacher will change. Prepare yourself to be an open-minded <u>listener</u>. When you spend time listening, you show that you value students' answers. Encourage them to join in and build on each other's answers with a minimum of teacher direction. Learn to tolerate short periods of silence, and teach the children to live with silence. Students need time to think in order to be productive. When initiating divergent thinking in the classroom, remember every answer doesn't have to be useful or practical. You can accept "wayout" or fanciful answers.

Learn to be skillful in your response to students' answers. There are many ways to motivate student responses to divergent thinking questions. You might repeat students' answers or rephrase them. You may respond by praising the class with comments such as "We've had some good ideas" or "good thinking." It might be a good idea to express your approval of the answers in general rather than praise the specific answers of individual students. Approval of one particular child's answer might squash the courage of the less secure child. Constant, immediate evaluation of every student answer causes students to depend on teacher evaluation rather than their own divergent thinking powers (Hollander, 1977).

Another effective way to encourage divergent thinking is to build extending questions on student responses. For instance, when Mr. Wallace asked his fourth-grade science students to think of lots of ways to sort the rocks they had collected, Maria suggested size and Tom mentioned color. When Noi added texture, Mr. Wallace extended the children's divergent thinking by asking, "What are some ways we could sort by texture?" This question led the children into a discussion of the various qualities of texture.

To keep the divergent thinking going, you need to allow children to experiment with and extend the answers they give. One way to experiment is to take an answer given by a child and find many ways to vary that answer. Suppose you asked the students to think of all the words related to <u>brilliant</u>. They mention words such as smart, shiny, bright, and sparkling, and you record these words on the board. Then you select one of their answers, for example, the word <u>bright</u>, and ask them to change that word slightly using as many synonyms as they can. Then using <u>bright</u> as a stimulus, the children suggest words such as crystal, diamond, and star. After a few minutes of brainstorming, the board might look like the diagram on the next page.

The diagram shows how you can keep divergent answers flowing by taking a student's answer and encouraging the others to make slight changes based on that answer. Now let's use the

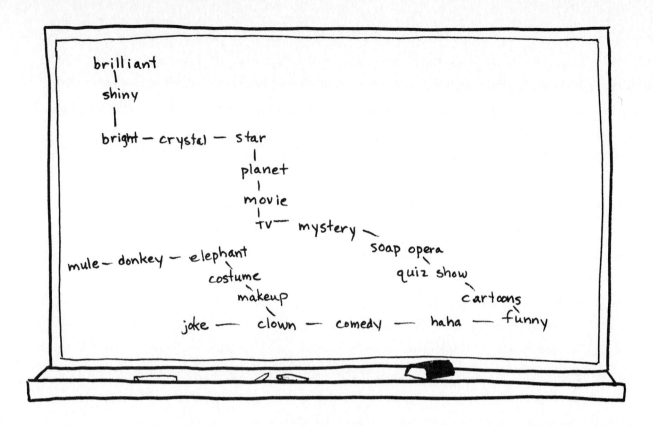

same example to see how we can take answers, juxtapose them, and come up with new answers. Look at the diagram. Find some of the words listed and combine them to make new phrases. We thought of mystery clown, elephant soap opera, and brilliant bum. To motivate your children toward divergent thinking, encourage them to change and juxtapose answers.

If you try some of these questioning techniques and students make no response or give you a blank look, think carefully about the level of the questions you have been asking. Perhaps the questions are based upon topics with which the students have had no experience. Be sure that you choose topics to which your students can relate.

Because children need varied experiences upon which to build, you might have to begin by providing the class with new experiences before they will be able to think divergently. When teachers present divergent thinking activities, they generally rely on a great deal of oral communication. Be sure that you vary your routines for sharing answers orally. Use both large and small groups. Sometimes children enjoy sharing ideas in pairs. Use divergent thinking exercises as an introduction to a lesson or to conclude a lesson and apply information learned. After a long, serious, difficult lesson, try divergent thinking exercises just for fun. Vary the length of time you devote to verbal answers for divergent thinking. It's challenging to come up with answers for only a minute. When pursuing questions related to the curricular area, extend divergent thinking time. Remember you can use a tape recorder in a learning center where children can listen to their answers.

Divergent thinking answers can be recorded in many written forms. Have children write their ideas in a scrapbook, diary, or journal. Students can jot down their ideas on a card and build a file for the class to use. Produce a newspaper to share divergent thinking ideas in writing. Let students post their divergent thinking ideas on a bulletin board. Your children can dictate their ideas for the teacher to record on an experience chart. Don't forget to take advantage of poetry as another form of expression in divergent thinking. If the class is writing answers on the board, have several students act as recorders.

For combining individuals' written answers, try this technique. Ask students to list their answers to a divergent thinking question individually. Now have each student work with a partner and cross out duplications from their lists. Partners combine into groups of four and again cross out duplications from their lists. Groups of four combine into groups of eight. Finally you are ready to combine the lists and cross out the duplications of the entire class. In a relatively short amount of time, you will have a list of the many different answers from the whole class.

There are various other ways for sharing divergent thinking answers. Songs, creative movement, and drama are a few potential ways of sharing divergent thoughts. Puppet shows, plays, or pantomimes allow children to express their ideas. Art forms such as murals, mobiles, paintings, drawings, collages, and three-dimensional constructions provide stimulating ways for children to share ideas with each other.

Encouraging and Maintaining High Quality Once your students are accustomed to using divergent thinking in the classroom, you are likely to be rewarded by the eagerness of the students and the level of motivation divergent thinking seems to generate. After they get started, you will need to concentrate on refining what they've produced. Torrance (1977, p. 6) establishes four basic aspects of creative thinking that might help you as you think about encouraging and maintaining high quality. These aspects are fluency, flexibility, elaboration, and original-ity. You can read more about the nature and testing of these aspects in Chapter 3.

Fluency, the ability to generate many ideas, is the first aspect of creative thinking that Dr. Torrance discusses. With divergent thinking the quantity of answers is a necessary part of quality. One way a teacher can encourage fluency is by the brainstorming technique. In brainstorming, the emphasis is on encouraging students to contribute as many ideas as possible in a short period of time. When a class is brainstorming, they don't stop to evaluate answers. Instead, they concentrate on the number of ideas they can produce.

Flexibility is another facet of high quality divergent thinking. Flexible divergent thinking involves suggesting ideas that fall into many different categories. For instance, in thinking of ways people use plants, students may name plants that we eat. When a student says, "We make clothes from cotton, another plant," that student has introduced a new category that others may pursue. If another student suggests the use of plants to make wallpaper, he has shown flexibility by introducing another category. Thus, flexibility is the ability to present many classes of ideas rather than just a lot of ideas in a single category. If students typically pursue only one or two categories in their divergent thinking, you might need to act as the leader, suggesting other categories for students to pursue. When students do suggest other categories, point out that they have shown flexibility in their thinking by introducing a new category. Making students aware that they have changed categories and encouraging them to do so will motivate others to seek flexibility in their responses.

Elaboration is extending ideas already mentioned and building on those ideas by supplying many details. One of the ways you can foster elaboration is by eliciting details based upon answers the students give. The following questions foster elaboration: "What do you mean by that?" "What are some ways we could do that?" "Why . . . ?" "What next?"

Originality comes into play in divergent thinking when people produce unusual, unique responses. Questions such as, "Try to think of something that no one else would think of," encourage originality. After each student has tried to be original in producing ideas, the class might gather and compare answers to see whether their ideas were really original or whether the same ideas occurred over and over again.

Fluency, flexibility, elaboration, and originality--all of these aspects are important to high quality divergent thinking. To get a better sense of how these elements work together, try picturing the building of a house. Fluency is analogous to the gathering of the many building materials. Flexibility is comparable to using the materials for many different functions throughout the house. The little details that add the finishing touches might be likened to elaboration. In building a house, people plan unique features to suit and express their personalities; these features add originality to their overall design. (See Chapter 3 for more details on fluency, flexibility, elaboration, and originality.)

Arranging the Room to Facilitate Divergent Thinking Room arrangement has a lot to do with the success of divergent thinking in the classroom. Students need to be relaxed and comfortable to be fluent in their thinking. The arrangement of the chairs in the room will affect the flow of conversation. When practicing divergent thinking, the teacher generally will not be the focal point. Rather, the students need to be seated so they can see each other.

For large groups of students, many different arrangements are possible. Arrange chairs in a circle around the room, or have students sit on the floor in a circle. Make two concentric circles with the students' chairs. In concentric circles students are closer to a larger number of people for a free flow of ideas. Form your group in clusters around a focal point. Your focal point might be a bulletin board, the chalkboard, an experience chart, or a real object. For an amphitheater-like effect, seat your class on stairs indoors or out-of-doors.

Small groups are easier to set up than large groups. Generally you will have several small groups working at the same time. Organize a group around a table or arrange four to six desks together to form a table-like surface. Invite one or two groups to pull their desks nearer to the chalkboard so they can use the board as a writing surface. Form desks in a circle. Plan a divergent thinking activity in a learning center. Utilize floor space or a rug for a small assembly area. Remember, there are other places to meet besides the classroom. Students can work in small groups in the hall, the library, or even out-of-doors.

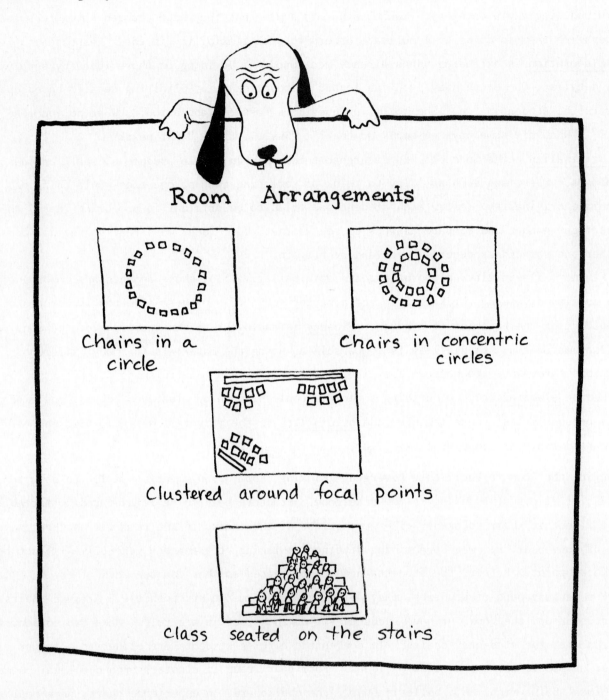

Room Arrangements

Chairs in a circle

Chairs in concentric circles

Clustered around focal points

Class seated on the stairs

   In planning the physical arrangement of the classroom, be sure that supplies are easily accessible. If simple art supplies are arranged on a shelf, students will be likely to use them. Blank bulletin boards invite student use. When butcher paper and a roll of adding machine tape are out, students can draw or write their thoughts on them. Maybe you would like to have an idea box in your room in which students can deposit divergent thinking ideas.

Getting Parents Involved Parent involvement is a vital part of any educational activity. You need to help parents understand what divergent thinking is and why it is important. Many parents today are concerned about getting back to the basics. Help parents understand that divergent thinking is a basic part of the higher levels of intellectual thought, such as problem solving, original thinking, discovering new ideas, and adapting to change. Without divergent thinking, many new inventions and great discoveries would never have been made. Once parents really understand the important role that divergent thinking plays in their children's education—that divergent thinking is truly a basic and not a "frill"—they will be supportive of divergent thinking in the classroom and at home.

You can talk with parents about divergent thinking both formally and informally. You can make divergent thinking a topic of your presentations for open houses and parent organization meetings. You can include divergent thinking tidbits in your newsletters to parents. In your informal conversations with parents, you can ask or answer questions related to the ways parents can use divergent thinking with their children.

A good way to bring divergent thinking into the home is to give nontraditional divergent thinking homework assignments. This type of assignment can tie in beautifully with whatever topic you are teaching. For instance, if the class is studying metric measurements of length, the teacher might ask students to find at home as many things as they can that are about a decimeter in length. To follow up on a lesson on nouns, assign the students the task of listening to a conversation around the dinner table and bringing back a list of all the nouns they heard. Both parents and children may appreciate the break that divergent thinking homework gives from traditional written assignments.

Divergent thinking assignments bring the home into the classroom and the classroom into the home. When students bring in objects, stories, and ideas from home, they share glimpses of their home lives with one another. In this sharing process children develop a better understanding of one another, broaden their perspectives, and find enrichment from learning about other people. Because divergent thinking assignments are so different and motivating, they bring the classroom into the home. Few parents can resist helping with and adding suggestions to these divergent thinking tasks. The whole family may want to join the fun. Divergent thinking assignments are good ways to bring family members together.

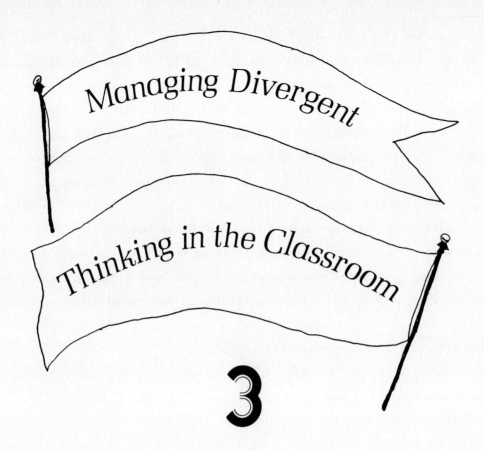

Managing Divergent Thinking in the Classroom

3

In our first chapter, we presented several of our own ideas that support the importance of divergent thinking. In this chapter, we will present and examine the opinions of experts who have addressed topics related to divergent thinking.

WHY STRESS DIVERGENT THINKING?

E. Paul Torrance (1971), perhaps the best known and most respected expert on creative thinking, pointed out that the knowledge explosion of the Space Age makes people realize that there is almost no end to knowledge and human potential. Machines and computers now do much routine, repetitive work and free people to behave productively and creatively. "Getting away from the main track, breaking out of the mold, letting one thing lead to another, recombining ideas or seeing new relationships . . . ," in fact, all divergent thinking tasks, are part of Torrance's definition of creativity (1977, p. 6).

Solving today's complex problems requires generating and evaluating many solutions. Adults should not lead children to believe that there is one simple "correct" solution to every problem (Williams, 1970). Divergent thinking is essential in generating new, unusual, or novel ideas (Wylle and Busse, 1974). Along with learning facts—things as they **are** or **were**—children must be taught how to think productively and critically (Raths, et al., 1967).

Williams (1970) described several benefits that accrue when teachers involve children in creative thinking. Children enjoy themselves because they produce ideas rather than passively "soaking up" facts from the teacher or text. Children have the opportunity to interact with things and people as they become actively involved in the process of inquiry. Teachers can promote both thinking and feeling within regular content areas without using expensive equipment. Finally, all levels of learners profit from divergent thinking activities as they become more creative, productive, and self-reliant.

HOW CAN DIVERGENT THINKING BE TAUGHT EFFECTIVELY?

General Suggestions for Promoting Divergent Thinking

Experts offer dozens of ideas on teaching techniques for promoting divergent thinking. Cole (1971) described an atmosphere conducive to divergent thinking when he related natural and enjoyable learning to a situation in which learners actively and aggressively seek knowledge and experiences. Many authorities seem to agree that such a setting promotes divergent thinking.

Meeker (1978) offered the following suggestions to teachers: allow children to work and experiment with materials to satisfy their curiosity; provide help when it is needed; and spend much time listening to children's ideas. Feldhusen and his colleagues (1975) stated that, in general, high quality activities for students should involve a small amount of direction, exposition, and didactic instruction. He advocated a high degree of student involvement, participation, and opportunity for practice of creative thinking skills. Torrance (1977) stressed providing opportunities for creative work, such as self-initiated projects, experiments, and other types of independent learning.

Authorities emphasize the importance of teacher attitude in promoting divergent thinking. Torrance (1977) wrote of respect for children's unusual questions, ideas, and solutions and valuing novel ideas and self-initiated learning. Davis (1971) and Williams (1970) described the need for an atmosphere of psychological safety and freedom if divergent thinking is to flourish. They emphasized acceptance of students' spontaneous, sometimes playful, thinking and suggested the use of humor used deliberately to foster a safe and open classroom climate. By the examples teachers set, students should learn to respect and value each others' original thinking and new approaches to problem solving. Teachers must value children's imaginings, unique expressions, and art forms.

Authorities suggest that teachers encourage divergent thinking in all curriculum areas and integrate divergent thinking as part of their regular studies. When divergent thinking is taught as an isolated skill, it is usually unsuccessful (Jones and Rich, 1973). Davis encouraged promoting sensory awareness and playfulness through questions such as, "Do you remember when you saw something strange and surprising?" Davis recommended leaving things incomplete and projecting into the future to stimulate divergent discussion. Questions such as, "What uses can be made of polar ice?" open the floor to all sorts of responses by students. Naumann

(1980) stressed questioning, manipulating, and associating reading material with other readings, as well as personal experiences.

Torrance (1971) reminded educators to allow for multimodal expression of divergent thoughts. Some children who have difficulty putting their ideas into words express them freely in creative movement, sounds and music, and drawings. Torrance emphasized the important of verbalizing thoughts and feelings before writing about them. A balance in modes of expression will sustain the children's interest in sharing their creative images with others.

Both direct and indirect techniques can help to promote divergent thinking. Williams (1971) outlined some direct teaching strategies, such as use of colorful "vocabulary stretching" teacher language, exposing children to a mixture of reality and fantasy and different moods in stories and conversations, and encouraging children to discuss solutions to problems that concern them. Williams encouraged teachers to provide a variety of opportunities for children to make contact with all sorts of people and cultures, places, and art forms.

Students also offered helpful advice regarding classroom atmosphere and teaching techniques related to divergent thinking. Fifth graders identified as highly creative in a study by Wright (1982) stated that they preferred teachers who encouraged independent thought and projects and who used discussion groups and encouraged students to ask questions. The fifth graders judged as most beneficial those teachers who were structured and yet child-centered. These creative children preferred teachers who were themselves creative.

Specific Suggestions for Promoting Divergent Thinking

Writers interested in promoting divergent thinking propose many specific strategies. Brainstorming is one technique that will help students produce a large number of interesting ideas on a topic. Brainstorming involves inviting participants to give as many solutions as possible to a problem. During the generation of ideas, no criticism is allowed; evaluation comes later. Proponents of this technique believe that the more ideas presented, the greater the chance that a good idea will be among them. Participants are encouraged to combine ideas and build on the ideas of others. A final step is the evaluation of the relative merits of the proposed ideas to select meaningful ideas worth pursuing (Gallagher, 1964).

Beaven (1975) described webbing as a technique for integrating ideas and forming new relationships between concepts. Taking a concept such as "fire," students generate many questions about the concept. In a divergent thinking session they might generate questions such as the following: How do people use fire? What descriptions of fire have you read? What does fire symbolize? As students research and share information to answer the questions, they fully explore the concept.

Knapp (1972) elaborated on pretending as a vehicle for divergent thinking. He encouraged students to imagine themselves a part of their environment. Students might pretend to be a utilities pole, for example. Then they analyze their characteristics and compare and contrast "themselves" to other things. They might suggest new uses or improvements for "themselves," describe the effects of environmental factors on "themselves," tell a "true" or fanciful story about "themselves," or use analogies, similes, or metaphors to tell about "themselves."

WHAT DO EXPERTS TELL US ABOUT THE NATURE AND MEASUREMENT OF DIVERGENT THINKING?

J.P. Guilford (1958) defined five areas of intellectual operations: cognition, memory, convergent thinking, divergent thinking, and evaluation. He described divergent thinking as a free and open operation resulting in large numbers of possible associations or problem solutions. Guilford (1950) wrote of creative thought, or divergent thinking, as something that almost all individuals could do to a certain degree. He stressed that creative thinking was based on knowledge of facts and experiences; no one creates in a vacuum. He also wrote of fluency (producing a large number of ideas), novelty (unusual responses), flexibility (ease of changing mind set or categories), and complexity (the intricacy of conceptual structures). To Guilford, fluency, flexibility, novelty, and complexity were all aspects of divergent, or creative, thought.

Williams (1970) described important affective factors that interrelate with the cognitive factors of fluency, flexibility, originality (Guilford's "novelty"), and elaboration (Guilford's "complexity"). The cognitive skills enable students to record, retain, generate, and process information. The affective traits challenge individuals to be curious, take risks, use complex ideas, and exercise their imaginations. A combination of cognitive and affective factors is necessary for full, effective creative functioning.

Torrance (1977, p. 6) defined creativity as "the process of sensing problems or gaps in information, forming ideas or hypotheses, and communicating the results." The process may lead to any one of several kinds of products—verbal or nonverbal, concrete or abstract. Torrance built on Guilford's four aspects of creativity, along with studies of creative historical figures, when he devised his widely used test of creative thinking (Torrance, 1969).

The Torrance Test of Creative Thinking (1969) includes an "Ask and Guess" section in which respondents, age five to adult, are asked to generate questions about a picture with the purposes of finding out about it, and guessing causes and consequences for what is happening in the picture. A "Product Improvement" task requires the examinee to suggest interesting or unusual ways to change a toy to make it more fun for a child to play with. "Unusual Uses" calls for interesting uses of common objects, such as tin cans or cardboard boxes. A final "Just Suppose" task asks the examinee to think of the results of an improbable situation.

The number of relevant responses given by subjects are tabulated and produce a fluency score. The number of shifts in thinking, or the number of different categories of responses, give a measure of flexibility. A measure of originality is calculated by judging the extent to which responses depart from usual answers from a large norm group. Elaboration is measured by the detail and specificity of responses.

Torrance's test also includes a figural, or nonverbal, section in which respondents perform three tasks. The first task is called "Picture Completion." Here examinees use a basic shape and complete a picture around it. They are encouraged to design something that "no one else will think of," to embellish the first idea to convey an "exciting story," and to entitle the picture (p. 33). The "Figure Completion" task consists of adding lines to ten incomplete figures to make unique pictures out of them. Finally, in the "Repeated Closed Figures" section, subjects use two pages of closed figures, such as circles or squares, and make pictures of them. They should make as many different and novel pictures as possible and add names or titles to them. The figural test, like the verbal test, is scored for fluency, flexibility, originality, and elaboration. Torrance purposely kept the test tasks free of technical or subject matter so that the test could be administered to people regardless of their educational backgrounds. However, researchers have found the test to be more reliable for adults and older children than for younger children (Torrance, 1967).

Is creative thinking ability related to other traits? Investigators have reported only slight relationships between intelligence and creative ability (Terman, 1967; Rosenbaum, 1973; Wallach and Kogan, 1967; Torrance, 1967 and 1968). Self-concept and interest seemed to show a positive correlation to creative ability (Sisk, 1966; Rookey and Reardon, 1972). Some researchers reported no differences between the sexes on tests of divergent thinking abilities (Daffron, 1971; Aldous, 1970), while another found girls superior to boys on many creative thinking tasks (Farless, 1974). Generally, socioeconomic status did not appear to influence children's divergent thinking abilities (Forman, 1979; Daffron, 1971; and Rosenbaum, 1973).

Besemer and Treffinger (1981) pointed out that valid assessment of creative persons and creative products are different but important matters. They proposed three main criteria for evaluating creative products: novelty, resolution, and elaboration and synthesis. Novelty refers to the originality and newness of the product and its applicability and effect on future creative products. Resolution addresses the degree to which a product meets the needs of a problematic situation. Products that resolve problems powerfully are logical, appropriate, adequate, useful, and valuable. Elaboration and synthesis describe the degree to which creative products involve considerations of style. This includes expressiveness, complexity, craftsmanship, completeness, elegance, and attractiveness as the six subcriteria. Besemer and Treffinger's criteria offer guidelines for teachers who want to evaluate the creative products of their students or who wish to involve students in evaluation of their own or each other's work.

What Do Empirical Studies Tell Us About Teaching and Learning Divergent Thinking?

The process of stimulating divergent thinking as part of the creative process has long fascinated and challenged educators. Hundreds of researchers have studied the results of various teaching and learning methods on many different groups of children. In general, researchers have found that training improves the divergent thinking skills of children. Formal techniques, such as guided problem solving and discussion of likeness and differences, have enhanced the divergent thinking skills of school children (Miller, 1974; Thomas and Berk, 1981). The effectiveness of commercially distributed programs, such as the Purdue Creative Thinking Program and New Directions in Creativity (Harper and Row, 1973), have been widely validated (Mansfield and Busse, 1974; Callahan and Renzulli, 1977). Informal techniques, such as play with games that allow for many possibilities or fanciful role playing, have also had beneficial effects on the divergent thinking abilities of children (Haddon, 1971; Pepler and Ross, 1981; Anderson, 1964; Berretta, 1971; Huntsberger, 1976; Goor and Rapoport, 1977).

All types of students, including those identified as gifted as well as retarded students, profited from instruction in divergent thinking (B. Cherry, 1972; Nickse and Ripple, 1971; Sharpe, 1976; Fults, 1980). Children as young as three years old dealt successfully with divergent thinking activities (Khatena, 1971; Turner and Durrett, 1975; Pepler and Ross, 1982).

Time spent on divergent thinking complemented acquisition of basic facts and traditional subject matter according to several researchers (Forseth, 1980; Scott and Siegel, 1965; Davis, 1976; Clague-Tweet, 1981; Johnson, 1974). Groups of students exposed to divergent thinking techniques in science, social studies, and math performed better than their untrained peers did on measures of divergent thinking. Most important, the students performed as well or better than control groups on tests of concept acquisition and academic skills. Training in divergent thinking also correlated positively with positive attitudes toward school and school subjects (Forseth, 1980). Interested readers will find numerous studies on using divergent thinking with students in educational periodicals, research journals, and dissertation abstracts.

HOW CAN WE SUMMARIZE THE MANY READINGS AND RESEARCH FINDINGS ON DIVERGENT THINKING?

The educational and psychological literature on creativity and divergent thinking abounds! Authorities such as Torrance and Williams provide a sound rationale for the encouragement of original thinking. Many experts and researchers suggest workable techniques for promoting divergent thinking in children, young people, and adults. Fairly reliable means for measuring aspects of creative thought exist. Now the task remains for teachers to actually provide opportunities for divergent thinking in their classrooms. The chapters that follow provide hundreds of original, practical ideas for promoting divergent thinking in schools and other educational settings. Hopefully, you will be motivated to start using them!

Language surrounds us. It permeates everything we see and do. Not only is language an intrinsic part of us, but it is also an extension of our thoughts and feelings. The more we know about language and the better we use it, the more precisely we express ourselves to others. Language helps us solve problems and guides us as we think and act.

Through language we receive ideas from others. By listening to others speak or reading what they have written, we can understand their opinions, attitudes, and values. Language helps us participate vicariously in other people's experiences. The expressions of others sometimes stimulate and inspire us to action. We express ourselves with spoken and written words as well as with drawings and actions. Receptive and expressive language are complementary and form an integrated whole.

In the schools, language arts typically encompasses the areas of listening, speaking, reading, and writing. Children spend a large part of the school day using and developing their language skills. Achievement in every area of the curriculum depends on language ability. A child with poor language skills is usually also deficient in social studies, science, and even math. Quite often strength in language correlates with a child's total development in its cognitive, physical, social, and emotional aspects. For example, children who express themselves adequately in a social situation tend to make friends easily and relate well to classmates.

Classroom activities involve many types of listening. Some types are simple and casual; others are more complex and require greater concentration. In marginal listening children are aware of sounds, but these sounds remain on the periphery of their attention; however, in attentive listening children eliminate distractions and focus on a message that is being given. Appreciative listening is of a slightly different nature in that children listen for pleasure. Analytical listening requires more of children. Not only must they hear the words that are spoken, but they must interpret or act upon them. For example, in analytical listening children might select and write about the main ideas of a message they have heard. Children must be taught how to listen. We cannot assume that children develop sophisticated listening skills on their own.

Speaking is another important element of language arts in the classroom. Teachers should include both cognitive and affective goals in their plans for oral language development. Cognitive goals include developing vocabulary, increasing language fluency, fostering syntactic growth, improving self-expression, and refining speech for everyday use. Affective goals might include developing confidence in speech and expressing feelings freely. Children need many opportunities to develop various speaking skills. Teachers should provide many settings for speech by having children talk formally and informally, in small groups, and in large groups.

Reading is the process of receiving information from written symbols. Beginning with recognition of sight words and simple phonics, reading progresses to comprehending and interpreting words, sentences, and paragraphs. Reading has many purposes such as gaining information, following directions, and finding pleasure. Children's ability to read skillfully opens a gateway to many rich and varied experiences.

Both practical and creative writing are important aspects of language arts. Practical writing might include lists and reminders, informative reports, social notes, and business letters. In practical writing, teachers typically emphasize correct forms, grammar, punctuation, spelling, and handwriting skills. Creative writing may be either poetry or prose. Creative writing is usually expressive and pursued for the pleasure of the writer or the audience. When working with creative writing, teachers encourage the development of imagery, interesting storylines, or logical flow of thought. The key to developing writing skills is practice with appropriate feedback. Children need to write, write, write!

What are some guides to facilitating language development in the classroom? Children need many rich experiences as a basis for ideas in speaking and writing. A relaxed atmosphere will encourage a free flow of expression. Teachers should show interest in and appreciation of each child. They need to identify those children who are having difficulties and find practical ways to help them solve their problems. Teachers must strive to be good role models. They should constantly polish and refine their speech. Children will do their best in language arts only if they are properly stimulated and motivated. Above all, teachers need to ask many divergent thinking questions to encourage creative expression.

The goal of language arts is effective communication. When children use language skillfully they can function more capably at home, with peers, in the classroom, and in society in general. This chapter includes many activities that stimulate effective communication through divergent thinking.

ENCOURAGING DIVERGENT THINKING WITH LARGE GROUP ACTIVITIES IN LANGUAGE ARTS

Language arts is an area that lends itself quite naturally to divergent thinking. In arranging our teaching activities we have chosen to use the traditional divisions of listening, speaking, reading, and writing. Because speaking and writing are expressive forms, they allow many outlets for divergent thinking. Since listening and reading are receptive, they are less divergent in nature; nevertheless, we have combined the two areas, listening and reading, to give you a variety of activities. In this section there are many questions on various topics that stimulate children to think divergently. Our large group activities are diverse. We suggest the use of some unique objects and several projects with a special twist to motivate students. You will find many activities that use newspapers as a resource. Our creative writing tasks range from kooky lists to writing poetry.

oral language

questions, questions, questions

Sometimes the period set aside for sharing becomes quite tedious. Students get bored with the same type of questions, yet students need an informal time to converse. They need opportunities to stretch their imaginations, to test their ideas, and to share their ideas with others. Try some of these questions to perk up sharing time and to stimulate divergent thinking.

• What was the most beautiful thing you saw this week?

• What is the funniest thing that has happened to you this week?

• What is the smallest thing you have seen today?

• How many ways can you use a stick?

• How many ways can you use your foot?

• What can you do when it rains?

getting to know you

Make a bulletin board display or use the side of a filing cabinet and some magnetic tape for this activity. If you make your display on the filing cabinet, have each child attach a small piece of magnetic tape on the back of his school picture. Encourage them all to record two likes, two dislikes, and what they would wish for if granted one wish. Attach magnetic tape to each of these answers. After everyone has recorded his answers, have each child stand by the display and talk about the things he likes and dis-

likes and what would happen if his one wish came true.

what would you do questions

Here are some more questions to get students involved in discussions that stimulate divergent thinking.

• What would you do if you were visiting a big city and got lost?

• Suppose you were on a camping trip and a bear ate all of your food. What are some different ways you could get food?

• What would you do if you found a raccoon in your bed one morning?

• If you found $100 on the sidewalk, what would you do?

• What could you do at the beach?

• It has begun to rain very hard, and you are out hiking in the woods. What can you do?

window peeking

Draw a picture of a big make-believe house. Cut out one of the windows. One at a time select different children to look in the window and tell what they see. Encourage other children to ask the child looking in the window questions about what she sees.

divergent chatter

Start a conversation about the president. Encourage your students to join the conversation mentioning everything they can about the president. Quickly change to another topic such as sports. See if the students can keep the conversation going, changing topics as you run out of things to say.

questions about pictures

People can learn a lot by asking questions. Learning to ask many different questions about something is a divergent thinking skill. Make a collection of interesting pictures. Choose one of the pictures and have students think of different questions to ask about the picture. Help them refine their questions by encouraging them to ask questions specifically related to the details in the picture. Carry out this activity often using different pictures.

telephone conversations

Cut out several different pictures each of which tells a story. Have a pair of telephones in the classroom. Ask two students from the group to volunteer to carry on an imaginary phone conversation based on their interpretation of the picture they choose.

junky conversations

Bring in a box of assorted junk items. Ask students to select an object from the box and tell what they could do with it. Solicit different suggestions of ways to use each object from the rest of the class. Then have the class select several objects from the box and think of ways they could combine the objects and use them.

a different kind of homework

Pick a T.V. show you would like the students to watch. Assign it for homework. Generate questions based on the program and suggest specific things to watch for. After the students have watched the program, have a class discussion based on the program. Ask questions such as "What was real or fanciful about it? Tell how you liked the outcome of the story." Have students add other endings and make up consequences. Encourage them to discuss the characters' motivations. Let the students suggest other topics for discussion.

unlikely matches

Let your students cut pictures of people, animals, and foods from magazines. Attach small pieces of magnetic tape on the backs of the pictures. Put the pictures of people and animals in one box and food pictures in another box. Have a student draw a picture from each box, display the magnetic pictures on the side of the filing cabinet and connect the two pictures by telling a brief story about them. For example, a student draws a picture of a little girl who has lost her front teeth from one box and a picture of jello from the other box. She connects the two pictures by saying, "This is Suzy. She picked jello because she has lost two of her teeth."

loving questions

Try these questions with your students and see the divergent ways in which they respond:

- Who loves you?

- Whom do you love?

- What is the difference between loving and liking?

- How would you define love?

- What are some ways we show love?

ole mo's dog

Do you need a quick, challenging vocabulary workout for your students? Try "Ole Mo's Dog" with your class. Seat the children in a circle. The leader begins by describing Ole Mo's Dog with an adjective that begins with the letter a. While the group claps, he

chants in rhythm. "Ole Mo's dog is an active dog." The next person in the circle describes Ole Mo's dog with an adjective that begins with the letter b. For example, he might chant "Ole Mo's dog is a bothersome dog." The next student takes the next letter of the alphabet and chants his description. The students continue describing Ole Mo's dog throughout the alphabet and around the circle until someone in the circle breaks the rhythm of the chant. That person is eliminated from the game. The next person in the circle begins the chant all over again starting with the letter a. Each time a person breaks the chant by not thinking of an adjective fast enough, she is eliminated from the game and the game starts over with the next person using the letter a. You may choose to play the game for only a short time, or you may let your students play until every student has been eliminated except the final winner.

listening and reading

poems we love

Share some of your favorite poems from time to time with your students. Bring a variety of poetry books into the classroom. Ask your students to select and share some of their favorite poems. Have students compile a classroom book of favorite poetry. Encourage them to illustrate their book.

talking about listening

Listening is a "lost art." So few people really know how to listen. Plan different strategies to help your students refine their listening skills. Encourage students to suggest bad listening habits that they might have picked up. Lead a discussion on ways we can improve listening skills in class.

tell the story's end

Read or tell an interesting story in class. Stop the story before you get to the end. Let the students discuss what they think is going to happen in the end.

inflections and interpretations

Take sentences such as "You ought to see the new girl in our class." Let different students make the statement using different inflections. Have other students interpret their meanings from the inflections. Record interpretations on the board. Encourage students to suggest other statements to try out.

name acrostics

Have each child put her name along the side of a piece of paper as shown. Use the newspaper or magazine to find nouns that name persons, places, and things that begin with each letter of the student's name. Share results by displaying the acrostic on a bulletin board for all to read.

	Persons	Places	Things
J	Jackson	Jonesville	jam
A	Andrew	Anchorage	apple
N	Nancy	Nome	name
S	Sally	Salem	snake
M	Mom	Montana	mouse
I	Irene	India	igloo
T	Tom	Trenton	town
H	Harris	Harrisburg	house

scavenge for nouns

After students are familiar with the idea that nouns can be either persons, places, or things, let them help you make up a noun scavenger hunt. Devise ten or more kinds of nouns to find in a newspaper scavenger hunt. You might propose some starters such as the list below. Then ask students to suggest more.

- Name of a thing with three syllables.
- Name of a person whose first and last name begins with the same letter.
- Name of a place in the eastern hemisphere.

Write the suggestions on the board, then let students work in pairs during this noun scavenger hunt.

compound words

Have students list all the compound words they can. Add to the list by skimming textbooks, magazines, dictionaries, or newspapers for more compound words. Post on a very long list made of shelf paper or adding machine tape. Have beginners underline the first root word of each compound word in red, and the second root word in blue. You might put the long list through the mouth of a cut-out character and place it in a learning center for the children to read.

cartoons convey meanings

To promote understanding of the concept that pictures convey ideas just as words do, study and interpret cartoons. For mature students, political cartoons are appropriate; for beginners any comic strip will have a lot of appeal. Have students study words in the cartoons as well as the poses of characters, facial expressions, and nonverbal symbols. Encourage students to describe and interpret what they see in the cartoons. As a conclusion have each student draw his own cartoon to display in a learning center.

new news

Encourage children to write little "news briefs" about things that are happening in their lives. Have your students write their news in column form as in the newspaper. Post these in a "New News" corner for everyone to read. Intermediate and upper grade students can be taught about the "5 W's and How" in newswriting—Who, What, When, Why, Where, and How. Ask them to incorporate these elements in their writing.

writing

rhyming race

Here's an activity that your class can do in just a few minutes, yet it stimulates thinking. Give the first person in each row a word on a piece of paper turned face down. At a given signal ask the leader of the row to turn the paper over and tell a word that rhymes with their given word. Each person in that row must in turn think of a differ-

ent word that rhymes with their word. The first row to finish without repetition wins.

comparing and contrasting with words

Have students think of a pair of opposite words like sad and happy, hot and cold, up and down. Write one word on a section of the chalkboard and its opposite word on another section. Let students take turns writing as many synonyms as they can for each word in the pair. After some examples ask students to write a paragraph incorporating several of the synonyms.

expanding kernel sentences

Let's use the newspaper again! Select some terse kernel sentences from the newspaper. Headlines provide many examples. Have students insert adjectives and adverbs to add color and meaning to the kernel sentences. Perhaps you will want to use a single headline and embellish it many different ways. For example, for the headline Burglars Sack Offices, some variations are Hooded Burglars Sack Bank Offices, Unsuccessful Burglars Sack Police Offices, Greedy Burglars Recklessly Sack Political Party Offices.

color walk

Give each child several different colored strips of construction paper. Take the children for a walk. Encourage each child to find at least one thing that is the same color as each strip of paper. When you return to the classroom, work together to make a large group chart. Paste each of the colored strips in a column and let the children dictate the names of things they found in each color.

Our Color Walk

blue	green	red	yellow
sky	bush	light	sign
house	grass	paper	door
feather	weed	bird	car
	leaf	berries	truck
	can		
	tree		
	car		
	door		

creative writing tasks

The best way to teach your students how to write is to let them write, write, and write some more. Here are a few creative writing ideas to get your pupils started.

Put each student's name on a separate sheet of paper and drop the names in a can. Ask them to write a biography of the person whose name they drew. They may "interview" that person to get some basic facts, or they may let their imaginations guide them. Encourage them to describe the person in the biography. They may wish to extend the biography through adulthood.

Get your students motivated for this writing assignment by telling a few funny things that have happened to you. Encourage your students to share some of their funny experiences. Now ask students to write about the funniest things that ever happened to them.

Have your students write about the most embarrassing or the scariest experience they have ever had.

mystery pictures

Select and mount several interesting pictures. Display them at the front of the class. Have each student select a picture and pretend to step into the picture. Have each one describe what she sees and to write about what it is like to be in the picture. Now ask those who wish to to read their description to the class. Their classmates should try to guess which picture they are describing.

relay with a beginning and an ending

Here's another relay to give your students a quick divergent break from routine school work. Have the first child in each row go to the board and write a word. The next student in line must take the last letter of that word and use that letter for the beginning of a new word and so on down the row. The first row to finish wins. Here is an example.

circle	leaf
egg	few
girl	wagon

As a variation of this idea try a relay with sentences instead of words. The first student makes a statement and the next person must start his sentence with the last word used in the previous sentence. For example

• Some sea shells are large, while others are small.

- Small people are often "smothered" in large crowds.

- Crowds of people came to see the president.

writing haiku

Haiku is one of the simplest forms of poetry writing. Even young children can learn to write haiku with a minimum of instruction. Haiku is a form of Japanese poetry generally centered around a nature theme. This type of poetry is unrhymed. The poem is composed of 17 syllables written in three lines. The first line has five syllables. The second line is composed of seven syllables, and the last line has five syllables.

____ ____ ____ ____ ____ (5 syllables)

__ __ __ __ __ __ __ (7 syllables)

____ ____ ____ ____ ____ (5 syllables)

Here's an example of haiku written by a class.

Deer are beautiful (5 syllables)

Gliding through woods and pastures (7 syllables)

Graceful as they run (5 syllables)

Teach your students how to write a haiku poem. Write several together with the entire class contributing and refining their ideas. After students have learned to write haikus as a group, encourage each student to write a haiku on his own.

more creative writing tasks

Here are some more open-ended creative writing tasks.

Ask your students to think back to different smells they remember in their early childhood. Encourage them to write about an experience related to one of those smells.

Have your students write about an interesting family story that they either remember or have heard a family member tell.

Encourage students to write suggesting ways to make school a better place.

writing lists

Making lists is appropriate for younger and older children. Younger children could dictate an experience chart to the teacher, while older students could record their ideas on long skinny pieces of scratch paper. Try some of the following lists for starters:

- Things that have legs

- Things that are slick

- Things that smell sweet

- Things that are soft

- Things that would be better if they lasted longer.

Compile some of the lists and talk about the different categories of answers. A discussion of this type encourages pupils to come up with more flexible answers.

braille writing

Divide your group into pairs. Ask the students to write their partners a pinprick message. Each student must try to read the "braille" message with eyes shut. Invite a blind person to visit your classroom. Let the group plan questions to ask that blind person.

ENCOURAGING DIVERGENT THINKING WITH SMALL GROUP ACTIVITIES IN LANGUAGE ARTS

When students work in small groups they have many chances to really get involved and spend less time waiting for their turns to participate. Another advantage of small group experiences is that they give students the opportunities to initiate projects of their own and the chance to assume responsibility for carrying out activities. Most of our small group activities call for minimal teacher supervision and provide maximum opportunity for children to think.

Some of the activities suggested in this section are very simple tasks. Others are larger, more time-consuming projects. The motivators range from a ball of string to peanuts to dice. Several projects call for the use of tape recorders. Since dramatics often flow more smoothly in small groups, we have included several ideas for drama in this section. You will find both teacher-directed activities and activities that the students should be able to initiate on their own.

oral language

string stories

Tie tiny bits of colored yarn at different intervals along a ball of string. Tell a story with a small group. Your story might begin something like this: "Once there was a little boy four inches tall." As you tell your story unravel the ball of string. When you come to the first piece of colored yarn, pass the ball of string to the next person, who must then continue the story where you left off. Each time the narrator reaches the next piece of colored yarn, he passes the ball of string on to the next student who then continues the story as he unwinds the string and so on around the group.

what happened before?

Give your students a group of pictures, such as a little boy sleeping, a burning house, an ice cream cone, or a child crying. Ask each person in the group to select a picture and to tell what happened before the picture was taken. Encourage each student in the group to add different ideas of what might have happened right before the picture was taken.

classy conversations

In large groups children have fewer chances to contribute to the conversation than in small groups. Split your class into groups of four or five to promote conversations. Devise several open-ended topics, such as, "What might you do if we had an unexpected holiday from school? Tell us about your favorite breakfast. Are you a morning person or a night person? How do you know?" Put several questions in an envelope for each group. Let students take turns reading the questions and discussing them. Circulate, listen in, and praise unique answers and self-motivated conversation. After a while, let each group share one or two interesting points with the entire group.

listening and reading

soft sounds

Since listening is a basic component not only of language arts but of all learning, we must create specific opportunities for children to listen. Encourage your students to stop and listen to "soft" sounds. (You might vary this activity with snappy sounds, flowing sounds, or busy sounds.) Let children compile a list of all the soft sounds that they actually hear. Let them add to that list soft sounds they _might_ hear. Ask a small group to go outside and tape record "soft" sounds. Let another group make a mural of soft sounds adding real objects to their mural wherever appropriate. Another group might orchestrate some music for soft sounds, while another group might write a haiku (see page 34) about soft sounds.

writing

a classroom newspaper

While studying the reporting styles of different newspapers, you may wish to help your students compile a classroom newspaper. Divide your class into small groups giving each group a different assignment. For instance, one group can report news about classroom activities. Another group may interview different students and write various feature articles for the sports section, the fashion section, and other appropriate areas. Some students may write up a weather report. Some might wish to draw pictures and write for the comic sec-

tion. Don't forget the advertisements. Let some of your students compose interesting ads.

goofy tales with odd adjectives

Urge a small group of students to write a story about their classmates. Tell them to leave out all adjectives in their story but to draw a blank line in the place where each adjective has been omitted. After they have written the story, they should ask their classmates to contribute interesting adjectives. Each adjective must be written on a separate card. Mix up the cards and turn them face down. Now is the time for the fun. Have a student read the class story. Every time he comes to a blank in the story where an adjective has been omitted, he draws a card and reads the adjective from the card to fill in the blank. You can shuffle the cards and read the story again. The story will always be different.

writing cinquains

Another form of poetry that lends itself to group composition is the cinquain. Cinquains are generally made up of five unrhymed lines. Line one contains one word, the title. Line two has two words to describe the title. In line three the writer uses three words to tell an action. Line four tells a feeling in four words. Line five uses one word to refer to the title. The following poem is an example of a cinquain.

- Horses (one word title)

- Flexed muscles (two word description)

- Streaking through wind (three words to tell an action)

- Energy full of force (four words describing a feeling)

- Majestic (one word which refers to the title)

Ask a small group of students to compose a cinquain about a rainy day.

elderly pen pals

Call a nursing home and ask for names of several people who would like to receive a letter. Have small groups of students select a person to whom to write a letter. You may want to begin by discussing different topics that might be included in their letters. Encourage them to "adopt" their friend and to write her often. Perhaps they would like to include a picture of their group.

writing myths

A study of myths can enrich a child's life immensely. Take time to read and discuss different myths. To contribute to students' understanding of myths, let them work in small groups and write their own myths. They might wish to write a myth about how the camel got its hump, why the sea is salty, why the moon-flower opens only at night, or they may wish to select a phenomenon to write about.

roll the dice and spin a tale

Students need a lot of practice in order to become skillful at writing. To provide variety in story writing, try this idea. Have a small group of students make three large dice out of cubes. Any size milk cartons can easily be converted into cubes. Cover each side of the cube with construction paper. Cover the finished cube with clear

contact paper. (For more detailed instructions see Junk Treasures by Cliatt and Shaw, page 197.) Let each of the three cubes represent a different element of a plot. One cube will be the "characters" cube. Another cube will designate the "time." The third cube will specify "places." On each face of the "character" cube have students write different characters. For instance, they might write words such as these on the faces of the character cube--girl, horse, soldier, bear, baby, and nurse. On each face of the cube which designates "time" have them write a different period of time. The third cube is the "place" cube. On each face of this cube students should write a different place. When the dice are made, have students roll them. Whatever the dice lands on specifies the plot of the story they must write; the character, the time, and the place. Each time the students roll they should get dif-

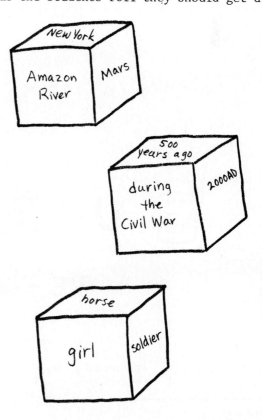

ferent combinations of plots about which to write.

drama

silent talk

We can say many things to people without speaking aloud. Have students work in groups of six and ask each pupil to choose a partner. Have a jar with directions written on different slips of paper. Here are some examples of directions you might give.

• Tell your partner hello.

• Give your partner a series of directions to follow.

• Ask for a drink of water.

• Tell your partner that you are very angry with her.

• Tell your friend you like him.

One student draws a slip of paper from the jar and tries to convey the message written on the paper without talking. As soon as the partner guesses the message, she draws a slip of paper from the jar and must express the idea written on the paper nonverbally.

prop box

Have a classroom "prop box" that contains a variety of props for use in creative drama. You may wish to include such props as a variety of hats, shoes, clothes, eyeglasses, canes, umbrellas, and scarves. Ask students to bring interesting props from home. Encourage children to work in small groups to put on a play for their classmates using the props from the box for costumes. Encourage them to brainstorm ideas from their own experiences, nursery rhymes, television, or favorite books.

REBUS MESSAGES

Make a rebus message for a friend.

* Answer below

* Answer: Our message says, "Can you make a rebus?"

Writing

mini STORIES

Word Bag...

Grab three and make a story!

gopher

running

Write lots of words on separate pieces of paper. Fold the papers and put them in a bag. Now draw three words from the bag. Make up a mini story to tell to your group using the three words.

Oral Language

PEANUT TALES

Write a sentence about something that happened last week. Now roll your sentence up and put it in an empty peanut shell. Each student in your group must select a peanut shell, read the sentence in it, and continue the story as if it happened to her. Compare the impromptu story to what really happened.

FROM ONE — NUT TO ANOTHER!

Oral Language

CREATIVE STORY TELLING

Prepare a creative way to share a book or a favorite story with a group of younger children.

- Act it out in an unusual way.
- Make a mural showing the order of events in the story.
- Show it on the overhead projector.
- Make a shadow show.
- What else can you think of?

Reading

PUPPET SHOW

Read the book, The Mitten by Alvin Tresselt. Make puppets of your own favorite animals. Tell your own version of the story to your classmates using your puppets.

Reading

CLASS INTERVIEWS

My Interview Questions

Your favorite snack food.

Where do you eat your favorite snack?

If you could go anywhere on a vacation, where would you go?

What do you enjoy doing with your mom or dad?

How do you help at home?

- Prepare a written questionnaire on something you would like to know.

- Use it to interview some of the students in your class.

Oral Language

Favorite NEWS Personalities

Check the news paper. Pick out your favorite personality.

DAILY NEWS

Tell your group why you picked that person and what you like best about him or her.

Reading

Small Group

SOAP OPERAS

"You have just had an argument with your best friend. You feel rotten."

"You come out of the school building just in time to see your school bus pulling away."

Show how you would solve the problem. Act it out. Write lists of other situations for your group to dramatize.

Drama

DRAMATIC Book Reports

Work up a fifteen minute play acting out one of the most exciting chapters in a book you have just read.

Drama

Cubs Win Over Phillies

Pretend you're a newspaper reporter who writes headlines for sporting events. Many are team sports where one team wins and one team loses. See how many different ways you can express the same message as these:

Cubs Beat Phillies

or

Phillies Lose To Cubs

Writing

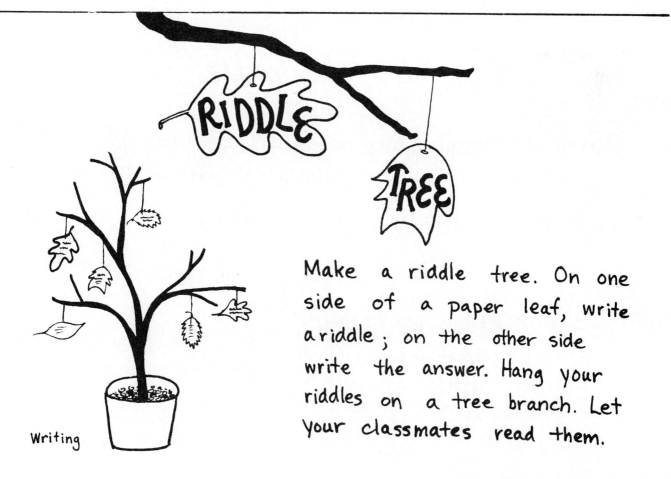

Make a riddle tree. On one side of a paper leaf, write a riddle; on the other side write the answer. Hang your riddles on a tree branch. Let your classmates read them.

Writing

FUNNY WORDS

Take a group of related adjectives such as funny words, noisy words, or big words. Use your group of words in a creative way.

For example:

☺ With a list of "funny" words, write a story about your group.

☺ Make a "tiny" collage using only tiny pictures and tiny words.

☺ You decide.

These Are A Few Of Our *Favorite Things*

Make a scrapbook by collecting pictures of your favorite things. Write a sentence explaining why you chose each item.

Baseball is my best sport. I can hit well.

We have fun eating pizza on Friday nights.

...WHIRR... ✦ROAR✦ ...BANG...BANG... sputter...sputter...⸻OOPS...

MACHINE SOUNDS INVENTORY

What are some different machine sounds that you hear? For the next three days, tune in to all the machine sounds around you --- machines at home, at school, in the yard, in stores, and on the street. As you listen, write down as many words as you can think of that describe all of the machine sounds you hear. Combine your list with the lists of those in your group. Create a big machine sounds inventory. Keep adding to your list.

...crackle... crunch...pop, pop, pop...Vrooooom. Listening

 # MACHINE SOUNDS PROJECT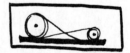

After you have done the "Machine Sounds Inventory", choose one the following projects:

1. Write a poem using some of the words from your machine sounds inventory.

2. Tape machine sounds. Improvise a dance to go with your "machine music."

3. Tape some of the sounds from machines. Compose a machine symphony by combining taped machine sounds with other sounds.

4. Create a machine by gluing together paper towel rolls, jar tops, and other discarded objects. Paint your machine. Tape interesting sounds. Place a tape recorder inside your "machine" and play it for sound effects.   Listening

TAPE RECORDER FUN

<u>Recorded Mysteries</u>   Tape interesting sounds and play them back for your friends. Let them try to guess what the sounds are.

<u>Wordless Story</u>   Make up a "story" without words. Tape background sounds to help you tell the story.

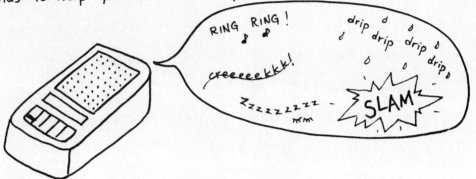

Listening

LISTENING WALK

Take a walk with your group. Make a list of all the things you hear on your walk. Then take the same walk alone. Make a list of all the sounds you hear while walking alone. Now compare your two walks. How were the two walks alike? How were they different? Write about your impressions.

Listening

Code 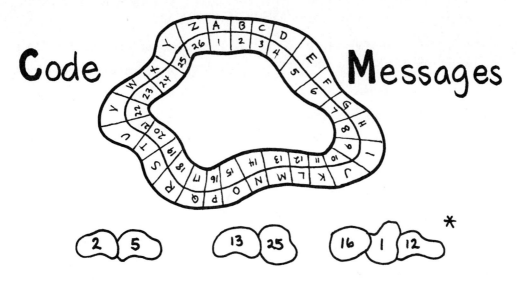 Messages

Can you figure out this message? Write a friend a message using this code. Ask him to write you back. Now make up your own code. Send a message using your code.

* Our message says, "Be my pal."   * Writing

ENCOURAGING DIVERGENT THINKING WITH INDIVIDUAL ACTIVITIES IN LANGUAGE ARTS

Now that children have had many opportunities to apply language arts divergently in both large and small group settings, it is time for them to test their skills at thinking divergently on their own. Some of the activities in this section are teacher-directed; others students can do by themselves. Many projects call for pensive times alone, but you will also find situations in which children work independently while mingling with the group. We have included in this section several activities used as follow-ups to reading specific books, many suggestions for creative writing tasks, and some unique homework assignments.

oral language

using stories that have no words

Children can be quite creative in making up stories for pictures and picture books that have no words. The two activities that follow are variations on this theme.

Show your students the picture book, The Good Bird, by Peter Wezel. The pictures tell the story of a bird who befriends a goldfish trapped in a bowl. Have a student "read" the book and then take it to a group of young children and tell his own story as he shows the pictures in the book.

Do you save interesting pictures from magazines for teaching purposes in your classroom? Put a big stack of pictures on the table for students to look through. Ask a student to select a number of pictures from the stack, rearrange them in an order that might suggest a story sequence, and tell her story to a friend using the pictures.

pretending pillow

Put a pocket on a big overstuffed pillow. In the pocket place small, illustrated cards that have captions such as "I am a computer programmer," "I am a salesperson," "I am a truck driver," or "I am a T.V. star." Place the pillow beside a tape recorder in a quiet section of the room. Have students select a card from the pillow pocket, sit on the pillow, and pretend to be the person suggested in the card. She describes her job telling where she goes, what she does, and who she meets in her job. Each student records her experience on the tape recorder.

reading

descriptive adjectives and adverbs

For a week have your students collect descriptive adjectives and adverbs from magazines and newspapers. Each student should work until he has accumulated many words. Place a big stack of pictures on a table. Let a student select a few pictures and see which of his descriptive adjectives and adverbs apply to the pictures. He may wish to trade descriptive words with his classmates, or he may write other descriptive words on his own.

word blurbs

Let students select interesting pictures from newspapers or magazines and write words to go with them. Each student should cut out her pictures, then add a paper "blurb" beside it.

Choose a category, such as nouns, verbs, adjectives, or feeling words, and have each child write all the words she can think of that are applicable to the picture on the blurb shape. Have students add their pictures and word blurbs to a bulletin board so others can read them.

takeoffs on good books

There are so many good books in children's literature today. Learn to utilize some of these books in creative teaching assignments.

• Alexander and the Terrible, Horrible, No Good, Very Bad Day by Judith Viorst tells the experience of a young boy on one of those terrible days when nothing goes right. Place the book in the reading center. After students have read the book, then have them write their own story of a very bad day. Ask them to read their story to a younger brother or sister at home or to a younger child in the neighborhood.

- **Fast-Slow High-Low: A Book of Opposites** by Peter Spier is a simple book to get children started thinking about opposites. After they have read this book, ask them to make their own book of opposites by cutting and labeling pictures from a magazine. They may carry out this assignment at home or at school. Encourage them to share their books of opposites with younger friends.

writing

letters to write

Children need many opportunities to write letters in order to improve their letter writing skills. Provide many occasions for children to write and give them many choices. Here are some suggestions of people who children might write to.

parents	the mayor
friends	the principal
neighbors	T.V. stars
the mail carrier	another teacher

a letter of appreciation to someone who has been a big influence in their lives

things to write about

Keep a list of stimulating topics for students to write about. Use that list for major classwork, for brief breaks from usual classroom activities, or for homework assignments. Here is a list for starters. Write about

fears	wishes
goals	pets

best friends	sports
homework	your suggestions
feelings	students' suggestions
favorite free time activity	

shades of meaning

To stretch children's vocabularies, try brainteasers such as these. Post sheets of paper with one word on each sheet. You may choose words from different categories such as foods, colors, people, animals, places, things, or feelings. At the bottom of each paper tape a long strip of masking tape sticky side up. Ask children to think of words that have the same meaning as the posted word. Have them write their words on small cards and stick them on the masking tape below the paper. Each child can add to the list on his own time throughout the day.

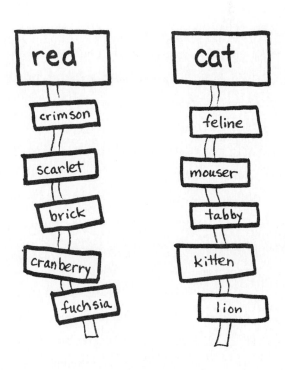

the problem jar

On a slip of paper write a problem. Tape the problem on the outside of a big jar. Ask students to come by; read the problem, write a solution on a slip of paper and drop it in the jar. Once many students have contributed answers, read them all to the class. You might choose practical problems or "way out" problems such as these:

We need to make a big hole to build a swimming pool on the playground. How can we do it?

Our school building has burned down. How can we continue to hold class?

A goat has just walked into our room. What can we do?

a special gift

Some of our nicest presents are gifts where we give of ourselves. Help children learn to value such gifts and to become aware of useful gifts they have to offer others. Ask them to suggest ways they could help at home. They might suggest jobs such as doing something special with a younger sibling, setting the table and washing the dishes every night for a week, mowing the lawn, or cooking supper for the family. Then have the children work individually and design a gift card. It might be a Christmas card, a birthday card, or a Mother's or Father's Day card. Encourage them to think of some gifts they could give that would be most helpful. Suggest that they design the inside of the card like a clip-out coupon in an advertisement section with offers of different tasks that they will perform. They may wish to write up the jobs they will give as gifts in a unique way--on a calendar, in a coupon book, or on a checklist.

creative writing assignments from old calendars

Do you use your calendar to record important appointments, tasks to be done, birthdays, or special parties? Don't throw those old calendars away. Use them for creative writing experiences. Ask each student to thumb through the calendar and find an activity recorded on the calendar that intrigues him. Then ask him to write about that activity as if he actually did it, describing the details of what happened.

idea box of similes and metaphors

Place ideas for similes and metaphors on cards in a file box. When students have extra time, ask them to pull a card from the box. They should write as many metaphors or similes for each task as they can think of. Here are some starters for your file box.

A rainbow is like _____.

The sun is a _____.

Raindrops are like _____.

Ice cream tastes like _____.

Happiness is _____.

Mud feels like _____.

Doughnuts are _____.

Ask students to compose new metaphors and similes for their classmates to work with.

hidden treasure

Bring a small chest to school. Any size or type of chest will do. Tell your students that you found this chest in a very unusual place but that you would rather not tell them where. Ask them to write about what might be hidden in the treasure chest, where it might have come from, and who put it there. Ask students to read their stories to each other.

sticky homework

Ask your kids to make a list of all the sticky things they can find at home. The next day have them work together and combine their lists (see page 14, Management chapter). After they have made one big list of sticky things, help them generate descriptive words for their sticky things. Now ask each child to write a "sticky paragraph" using some words from the two lists. You might want to let your students look for squashy things, crumply things, or smooth things.

observing nonverbal language

Discuss with your class the nonverbal language that people use. Talk about ways we silently say "I like you," "I'm tired of you," "I don't want to listen anymore," or "I'm embarrassed." Talk about little nonverbal communications that you see students demonstrate every day. Then ask each student to take a notebook sometime within the next week and to watch their classmates' nonverbal actions. Have them record their nonverbal actions on one side of each page, and interpret, to the best of their ability, these nonverbal actions on the opposite side of the page. You might have the children label the two parts like this: "What I Saw," "What I Think It Meant."

how do people see you?

Begin a class discussion by saying, "The way other people see us is not always the way we see ourselves." Let students tell about different ways their family members and friends view them, and how these views compare to the way they see themselves. Then ask students to work individually and record the way they think three different individuals see them. They might choose parents, teachers, friends, neighbors, or others. Ask them to write about the way they see themselves. Encourage them to tell which person sees them most nearly the way they see themselves.

tombstone rubbings

Take your students to the cemetery for a field trip. Let each student select a tombstone and make a rubbing. Ask each one to write a story about that person's life, telling how he might have lived and how he might have died. Let them write their stories while they are still in the atmosphere of the cemetery. When you return to class, let each child staple her tombstone rubbing and her story together for a classroom display. (See page   .)

Recycled Newspaper

Suppose you are a newspaper that has been read and is ready to be recycled. How would you want to be recycled? Why? Write about it.

Writing

Divergent LANGUAGE ARTS Activities

for individual students to do on their own

Dreamscapes

Have you had any weird dreams lately? Why not draw a scene from your dream? Discuss your dream as you show your "dreamscape" to a friend.

Oral Language

YOU KNOW ANDY, I'M REALLY INTO THIS DIVERGENT THINKING NOW. JUST LISTEN TO ALL THESE NEAT IDEAS!

Interesting Noise

When a door creaks, it makes a noise. What does it say to you? Write about it. Find other interesting noises and interpret them.

Writing

Guess Who I Am

Tell all about yourself by making a tape recording, but don't tell your name. See if your friends can guess who you are.

Oral Language, Listening

Class Notes

Go visit another class for 20 minutes. Observe all the things that happen in that class. Take notes on what you observe.

Writing

Unique Book Reports

Have you read a really good book lately? Pick one of these followup assignments:

- Draw a picture of one of the characters as you see him. Add little unique features to show how you picture the character.

- Draw a picture of the funniest, scariest, or most inspiring scene in the book.

- Compare yourself to one of the characters. How are you alike? Different?

- Write a letter to one of the characters.

- Create an ad for the book or author. Try to make others want to read the book or other books by the author. Display your ad beside the book.

Reading

Learning Through Interviews

There are so many interesting people around us with fascinating areas of interest to share. Do you know someone with a unique hobby, someone born in a foreign land, a person over 65? Interview that person to find out more about her areas of interest. Plan your questions ahead of time. Take notes during the interview. Share what you learn with your classmates.

Oral Language

My Diary

Keep a diary for at least a week. Every day be sure to record the most important events of each day. Describe how those events made you feel.

Writing

yup...

The Listening Game

Choose your favorite spot to play the listening game. Sit very still for two minutes. Tune in to all of the sounds around you. After your time is up, make a list of all the sounds you heard while you were listening. Then write about one of those sounds.

Listening, Writing

In our "Mind Power" section you will find many exercises for you, the teacher. Use some or all of them to practice divergent thinking and to create and individualize activities for students in your classes.

1. Try your skill at generating divergent thinking in your classroom. Suppose one of your students is moving to a new school, or perhaps you have a pupil entering the hospital. Choose a problem situation similar to one of these. How could you capitalize on the interest of your other students to teach one of the areas of language arts utilizing divergent thinking techniques?

2. Brainstorm ways to let children talk informally without chaos. Think of ways to encourage specific language behaviors, such as talking in complete sentences, communicating clearly, or refining listening skills. Carry out and test your ideas in class.

3. Writing is a very important language arts skill. Discuss with your class all the times and places people write and the reasons they write. Then set up a writing center for students to practice different writing forms creatively. For instance, people write messages, so make a message board on which pupils can write contributions. People write letters; let your students write and mail a letter. People write checks; let them practice writing checks. With each writing form your students suggest, give them an outlet for practicing that form.

4. Practicing handwriting skills can become very dull if you use the same old drill techniques every day. How many different ways can you think of to help

young children practice their handwriting skills? Plan at least three new handwriting exercises. Try them with your students.

5. What's a different way to read a story to your students besides reading it word-for-word from the book? You might think of a variety of techniques, from puppets, to shadow stories, to dressing as one of the characters as you tell the story. What's a unique follow-up for a good story? Have you thought of reading a book that could lead naturally into a cooking experience with your class? Plan an unusual way to read a story. Think of a different follow-up for a story. Carry it out in class.

6. Because cinquains involve learning to write titles, action words, and descriptive words, they can be introduced in connection with a study of grammar. Teach your students how to write a cinquain (see page 36). Lead your class in writing a different cinquain every day for a week. During this week use your classroom cinquains as a basis for studying the different parts of speech and their functions.

7. Think of some language arts skills that your students need work on. Create a new folder game for them to use in class. In the folder game, the complete game with parts and instructions are inside a manila folder. The game can be folded up and filed away for the next use.

8. Make a list of conversation starters to use with your class. Here are some starters.

Chocolate reminds me of. . . .
If I were school principal. . . .
The person I would most like to spend this Saturday with. . . .

Add to this list.

MIND STRETCHERS

for math

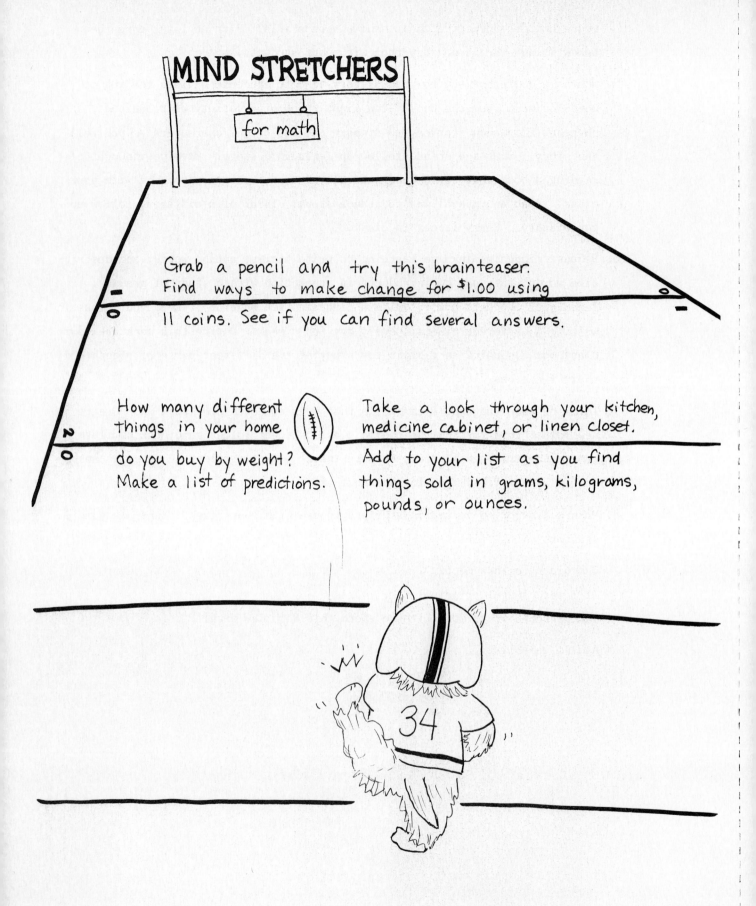

Grab a pencil and try this brainteaser.
Find ways to make change for $1.00 using

11 coins. See if you can find several answers.

How many different things in your home do you buy by weight? Make a list of predictions.

Take a look through your kitchen, medicine cabinet, or linen closet.
Add to your list as you find things sold in grams, kilograms, pounds, or ounces.

34

Chapter 5 MATH

YEAH! YOU GOT IT, ANDY

Think of a simple question you could take a poll on. You might use something like this:

"Do you like to drink something hot or something cold first thing in the morning?" Try to predict your results, then take your poll. Compare the results to your prediction.

Remember how hard you worked to master percentage problems in elementary school and junior high? Think of all the places you use them in everyday life. Make a list. Can you top 10 uses? 20 uses?

When you think of mathematics, what is the first thing that comes to your mind? Most people think of numbers. However, many other elements are important in math. The National Council of Teachers of Mathematics recommends ten basic skill topics in school mathematics. This large professional organization stresses: computer literacy, using mathematics to predict, estimation and approximation, dealing with graphs and tables, measurement, and problem solving as well as the more traditional topics, such as applying mathematics concepts, alertness to reasonableness of results, geometry, and computational skills.

Three kinds of learning are necessary and appropriate in school mathematics. One kind of learning is the acquisition of knowledge. Students must develop knowledge of number concepts, geometric ideas, and the meanings of operations. They need to acquire an understanding of the basic principles that govern the structures of number systems. They must recognize the usefulness and power of such modern mechanical devices as calculators and computers. Students need a basic knowledge of mathematical symbols, terms, and measures.

Another type of learning is acquisition of skills. Performing computations with ease and reasonable speed is a basic requirement. Problem solving is another skill area that has attracted much current attention. Students must be able to apply mathematical skills to solve problems in textbook and real life situations. Problem solving is greatly facilitated when students know of and can apply many types of strategies. To have a sense of direction in problem solving, students should be able to estimate answers and appraise the reasonableness of their results. Another skill area concerns geometry. Students need to be able to draw and construct geometric figures and models. They must be able to handle and use measuring tools. They should also be able to read, interpret, and construct graphs, tables, and charts. Another skill is using manipulative and technical devices with ease and confidence. These devices might be as simple as counting sticks or as complex as microcomputers.

The development of attitudes is the third kind of learning in school mathematics. A student's attitude toward math makes a tremendous difference in the way he performs. A student with a positive attitude toward math will see a need for learning about math. She will find places to apply it. Such a student has confidence in her ability. She tackles problems with pleasure and enthusiasm. Because she is intrigued with math, she is willing to persist until problems are solved. Knowledge, skills, and attitudes are complementary types of learning. They are inseparable and interdependent.

Besides these three types of learning, Whitman and Braun suggest three interrelated levels especially appropriate for each type of mathematical learning. These levels are physical, verbal, and symbolic. The physical

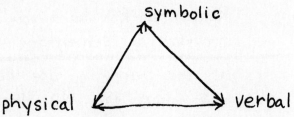

level involves dealing with objects in performing mathematical tasks, while the verbal level consists of talking about what is being done. On the symbolic level, students use abstract symbols as they interpret, record, and work with mathematical problems. All three levels should be used in planning mathematical experiences. Without all three levels, mathematical experiences remain muddled and fragmented in children's minds. Many traditional textbooks and teaching techniques emphasize the symbolic, and to a lesser degree, the physical levels. You will find that many of the activities in this chapter focus on verbalization and the sharing of ideas, and therefore complement traditional approaches.

Often people think that math is a convergent subject. Many times this opinion is appropriate because we generally want just one correct answer to a problem. Nevertheless, we wish to show some of the ways that math can be approached divergently. To make math discussions more divergent, try using questions such as: "Is there another way to do that?" "Can you explain that in some other ways?" "How can you make that idea make sense to someone else?" Rising and Harkin suggest other ways to stimulate divergent thinking in math lessons. They suggest questions such as "Can you make up another example?" "Can you find any exceptions to that?" "Where do you think you could use that idea?" To encourage nonverbal thinking, teachers might ask, "Can you show me what you mean?"

Most traditional math programs also utilize large group work and individual work almost exclusively. This chapter includes many small group activities. Some are intended to be teacher-directed; others may be done independently by small groups of students. Our small group activities may add a needed dimension to math instruction because they encourage children to work together cooperatively and exchange ideas.

In this chapter you will find many types of activities that promote divergent thinking in the mathematics classroom. Some involve manipulative procedures while others are based on experiments and laboratory work. Many activities in this chapter focus on problem solving. These problem-solving activities call for many different answers to given problems or a variety of approaches to one problem. You will find some activities in which students devise math games, use calculators and computers, and practice relating math to everyday life. Finally, our chapter includes some unique ideas for nontraditional math homework.

ENCOURAGING DIVERGENT THINKING WITH LARGE GROUP ACTIVITIES IN MATHEMATICS

Large group divergent thinking activities in mathematics give students many opportunities to exchange ideas. In some of the activities in this section, the teacher can ask for many answers to just one problem. With other activities students discover many different ways to work out a single problem. Still other activities use a single stimulus to generate many problems. Some of the activities in this section are oral; others involve the sharing of written results. As you use this section you will find both typical arithmetic problems and situations in which students can apply math to everyday life.

relationships

patterning

Provide children with several objects of two or three types. You might use paper clips and tongue depressors, leaves, sticks, and acorns, counters and crayons, or plastic spoons, forks, and knives. Arrange the objects in patterns. You might start out with knife, knife, fork, spoon, knife, knife, fork, spoon, or leaf, acorn, acorn, twig. Ask children to continue each pattern and then discuss it. Now split into groups and let the children start, continue, and discuss each others' patterns.

the category zoo

Ask primary school students to bring a stuffed animal or two to school. Use large boxes as cages. Categorize the animals as many ways as you can think of. You might begin with categories such as pets and wild animals, noisy and quiet animals, or carnivores, herbivores, and omnivores. Arrange and rearrange the animals in their cages as you categorize them. Help the children to think of as many different ways to categorize them as possible.

numbers
and operations

count it off

It's fun to count by 2's, 5's, or even 7's. When children are involved in the act of determining how to count, they're motivated to participate. Have a first child suggest a way to count--by 2's, 10's 8's, for example. Ask a second child to suggest where to start--at 0, 100, or elsewhere. Finally, ask a third child to decide whether to count forward or backward. Begin to count as the children have suggested and continue for several numbers. Now ask three more children to start the group in another "Count It Off" exercise. Perhaps you will want to record numbers on the board as the children count. Often it's easier for children to count when they see a pattern as well as hear it.

patterns and functions

Show some patterns and functions such as the following:

2 → 5
17 → 20
30 → 33
(adding threes)

7, 11, 9, 13, 11, 15, 13, . . .
(add 4, subtract 2)

10, 30, 32, 96, 98, 294, 296, . . .
(multiply by 3, add 2)

20 → 4
60 → 14
100 → 24
(divide by 4, subtract 1)

Let students write other patterns on the board and challenge their classmates. Patterns can usually be explained in more than one way. Once the group has caught on to a pattern, encourage them to verbalize and explain it in several different ways. After working many patterns, have each student write up a pattern or two to post in the puzzle corner.

always smaller

For any given number, you can always find a smaller number! Work with whole numbers first. Name a large number and let children suggest a smaller number, and a still smaller number, and so forth. If your students are studying fractions and decimals, choose a value close to 1, such as 7/8 or .9. Let children take turns naming numbers smaller and smaller than the original. You might have students take turns recording values on the chalkboard or showing where they would appear on a number line.

brainstorming about numbers

Try some math brainstorming on such topics as

• What would happen if you had no numbers or numerals to use?

• Where do we use negative numbers? You might start with games, checking accounts, and temperatures, and ask the students to name places they use negative numbers.

• Where do people use numbers in everyday life?

• If people had three fingers and a thumb what might be different about our number system?

budgeting

In our Social Studies chapter, we suggest an activity on budgeting an allowance (page   ). Have the children suppose that their allowance is doubled and decide what they will do with their new found wealth. Now have children pretend their allowances must be cut by one third. Have them figure out what spending they would have to curtail.

spinner math

Make a spinner game with two or more dials as shown.

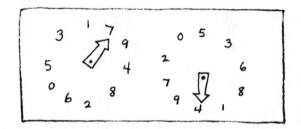

Show your students how to make up a task, spin the dials, and perform the task. You might use tasks such as these:

• Make a number sentence use, =, >, or <.

• Multiply the first number by 10, then divide by the second number.

Encourage students to make and try many variations.

number families

Number families (groups of related facts) have many members. For example the "6 Family" might include 3 + 3, 2 + 4, 5 + 1, 6 + 0 as well as 13 − 7, 3 x 2, 36 ÷ 6 and 50% of 12. You might work with groups of related facts in several different ways.

NUMBER APARTMENTS

Build an "apartment building" of several shoe boxes, and tape together two pieces of cardboard for the roof. Make window openings. Write family names on the doors. Let children write lots of family members' names on scraps of paper, and place them within the correct apartment. Later take the papers out and see all the facts that belong to each family.

SUBTRACTION SIBLINGS

Let children use cutouts of body parts to put together subtraction family members.

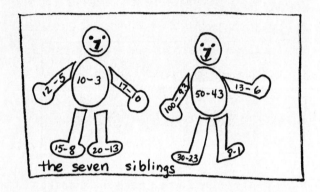

the seven siblings

TOSS IT

Use a shoe box lid, a piece of plastic wrap for a cover, and two or more little pieces of sponge to make a versatile math game. Write various numerals inside the box, add the sponges, then fasten the cover with a big rubber band. Show your students how to shake the box, see where the sponges land, and then use the indicated numbers somehow. You might use tasks as simple as adding the numbers or as complex as using the numbers to form a three-digit number then dividing it by 17. Let the children make up many different tasks to perform with the numbers.

fraction family flowers

Similar to "Subtraction Siblings," children write equivalent fractions on leaves, petals, and centers of flowers. Challenge children to make as many parts of each flower as possible.

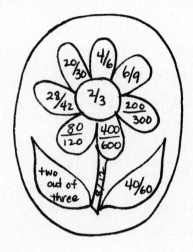

productive practice

Fill in that extra five minutes of class time with some productive practices on basic facts and some divergent thinking, too. Pose some simple problems, such as "What number is 6 more than 4?" "What number is twice 3/4?" "What's the next prime number after 61?" "Six plus 8, minus 2 equals?" "What are some numbers greater than 100 <u>and</u> divisible by 7?" Now let students take turns asking questions of each other. Keep this exercise moving quickly. You might want students to get 5 to 10 answers on scratch paper, then pause to check them.

palindrome play

Numbers that read the same forward or backward are called palindromes. Some examples are 787, 15251, and 4664. Show your students a neat trick about palindromes. Select any whole number. Add it to the number you get when you reverse its digits. Keep adding until you make a palindrome.

Here are some examples:

```
  145
 +541
  686   (686 is a palindrome)
```

```
   48      132
  +84     +231
  132      363   (363 is a palindrome)
```

The next example takes several steps but eventually produces the palindrome 43034.

```
   79      176      847
  +97     +671     +748
  176      847     1595
```

```
  1595     7546     13003
 +5951    +6457    +30031
  7546    13003     43034
```

Discuss with the class all the patterns that can be noted. Try palindrome play with other numbers. Motivated students can use large numbers and get a lot of addition practice as they work with palindromes.

problem solving

problem formats

Many problems have certain formats such as "get then spend money" or "have an amount and split it up" or "how many more are needed". Present one or two formats and have students suggest many word problems in that same format. Next ask the students to propose some formats and give many examples of word problems for each.

miniproblems

Many experts suggest miniproblems as a way of conveying problem situations in short, terse language without becoming bogged down in long narrations. Have students make up

miniproblems for each other. A sample might be "Have 48 pieces of candy. Split among 7 people. How many each?" Put the problems in a file box or in a problem-solving corner for individual use.

a kilometer walk

Walking and jogging for exercise have become popular activities. Capitalize on the students' interest by posing the questions, "How many kilometers per hour can you walk on the average?" or "About how far can you jog in 15 minutes?" Figure out different ways each question might be answered. Your students will have to cope with measuring time and distance as well as figuring rates of speed. Now a unique and challenging homework assignment--within the next week actually answer one of the questions by trying it out. Reporting the results is certain to generate much discussion!

graphing, probability, and statistics

sampling techniques

Challenge your class to discuss this practical problem. Suppose you want to know the opinions of people in a town of 10,000 on a certain political issue, but you can only ask 100 people for their views. Who will you pick? Why? What would be the results of choosing the proposed sampling techniques?

graphing gadgets

Students have probably seen bar graphs, line graphs, circle graphs, and even pictographs. Instead of usual graph symbols, let

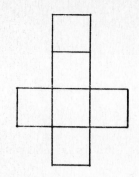

your students propose some unusual symbols to graph with. They might suggest such things as pictures to represent themselves, jar lids, old gloves to represent a single person or vote, or even lip prints to indicate favorite choices. See what other graphing gadgets your class can generate.

groovy graphs

Students often become very interested in making graphs when they can propose the topics. They could invent topics and then use some of their graphing gadgets to make the graphs.

Have students brainstorm a long list of graphing topics. The list might begin with "favorites" and range from "Favorite Toothpaste" to "Favorite Video Game" to "Least Favorite Vegetable." Other graph topics might concern the material of which each student's home is built, the average number of soft drinks consumed each week, or the number of pencils each student has in his desk. Let students work with a partner, choose a graphing topic from your long list, then collect their data and actually make a graph.

geometry and measurement

cubic centimeters

Examine a little centimeter cube. If you don't have a plastic one, make a paper model from our little pattern. Have students name all the things they can think of that are smaller than the little cube.

hot 'n' cold

On a bulletin board, draw a big thermometer shape. Mark the following temperatures on it: 0°C for freezing of water; 20-25°C for room temperatures; 37°C for body temperature; and 100°C for boiling of water. Have the children draw pictures of all the different things they do or see at various temperatures. Add pictures clipped from newspapers and magazines.

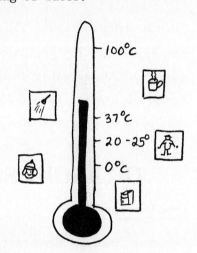

model students

How much does your average student weigh? What is the height, shoe size, and clothing size of the average youngster in your classroom? Challenge your students to find out and have a lot of fun in the process. Predict what the vital statistics of an average student in your room might be. Appoint committees to collect vital statistics from their classmates and find averages. Then let your class create a model student! Stuff clothes of an average size, provide the figure with average-sized shoes, and add a head and hands. Make your figures as close to average height as you can. Your model student probably won't weigh too much, so label its "weight" in a conspicuous place. Invite another class to review the results of your creative research.

brainstorming about measurement

Try some of the following topics to promote discussion of many possible answers.

What would life be like if all the clocks stopped running? What would life be like without clocks? What kinds of things come in standard-sized packages in units such as 1 pound, 500 grams, 1 liter, 350 milliliters? Note the students' suggestions, then give several days for research or investigation and add more items that come in standard-sized packages.

Grams are a small measure of mass. A raisin weighs about 1 gram. Kilograms are a thousand times larger. A fresh pineapple's mass is about 1 kilogram. What are some things that weigh about 1 gram? Close to a kilogram?

geoboards for tots

Almost any age child can learn from using a geoboard. Middle and upper grade students will also profit from using geoboards to teach younger children. Have your class brainstorm many different ways to use geoboards to teach younger children something about math. Split the class into groups and let students practice teaching and asking questions about the geoboards. Then arrange

for them to teach younger children using geoboards.

look around you--geometry style!

Let students browse through magazines to find examples of geometric shapes such as those suggested below. Ask students to describe examples they see around them.

Display and discuss examples of cubes, spirals, ellipses, hexagons, cylinders, or spheres.

Examine examples of symmetry. Perhaps you should start the class thinking about animals' or people's bodies and then move to architecture and nature. You might want to try our small group activity "Axes of Symmetry" to follow up.

Draw a picture using only straight lines.

How many things can you name that are circular in shape? Ask this question one day, and list some answers. Come back to it again two or three times and watch your list grow as the students' awareness of circles increases.

calculators and computers

calculator usage

Propose the question, "Where do people use calculators?" Have students give some answers, then look around them and think about the question. After several days, add to your list of answers.

What can calculators do? How can we find out?

Brainstorm some ways to find out about the many functions and capabilities of calculators. Students might suggest interviewing people who use calculators, watching others work with calculators, reading books about calculator usage, or perusing catalogs. Appoint groups or individuals to gather information about things calculators can do and share it with the class.

input, output

Any sort of computer has input and output devices that serve complementary functions. Input devices are for feeding information into the computer. People tell the computer what they want it to "know" through an input device. Cards, magnetic tape, or typed in messages are examples of input devices. Output devices such as printers, plotters, speakers, or monitor displays, allow computers to share their results with people.

Discuss different kinds of input and output devices on various types of computers. Magazine pictures will be a good source of information. Input and output are appropriate terms for noncomputer situations also. Discuss input and output in many situations of everyday life.

ideas for flow charts

Flow charts show a logical order of activities. They show where a series of steps starts and ends, where the consequences of various decisions are, and what processes or actions are done. Flow charts use arrows and different symbols to convey meanings.

Show your class a flow chart or two. You might want to start with the example of getting a glass of milk.

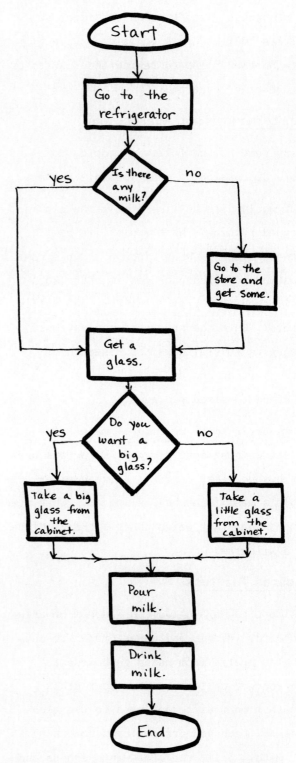

This chart might continue on to show the sequence a person would use to wash, dry, and put away the glass.

In the chart ovals represent the starting and stopping points, diamonds represent decisions, and rectangles stand for actions or processes. Arrows indicate the order in the flow chart.

Have your students suggest some topics for flow charts. It is best to start with something fairly simple. You might use topics such as

Catch a fish.

Clean, cook, and eat your fish.

Shovel the snowy sidewalk.

Eat a grapefruit.

Have groups of students choose a topic they really like from your list and create a flow chart to explain and display. Use the small group variation on flow charts that appears on page 72.

ENCOURAGING DIVERGENT THINKING WITH SMALL GROUP ACTIVITIES IN MATHEMATICS

Group thinking and interactions are important skills in problem solving. Studies have shown that groups of students solve more problems than individual students do. Our small group math section features dozens of situations in which students can put their heads together and use divergent thinking to solve problems. The problems involve computation, relationships, geometry, measurements, and use of calculators and computers. Using these small group activities, students have the opportunity to contribute to a final <u>product</u> as well as participating in the <u>process</u> of problem solving.

relationships

relationships galore!

Talk to children about the many different ways collections of objects or pictures might be sorted. Try some activities such as

If we want to sort things by <u>touch</u> or <u>feel</u>, how could we do it? Start with categories such as wet and dry, hard and soft, or rough and smooth.

What can we find outdoors to sort? A natural follow-up to a discussion of this question is a quick trip outside to gather some materials and sort them.

How could we sort Bobbie's rock collection

in many different ways? Any kind of collection is a prime candidate for a sorting exercise.

Have the students collect pictures of different kinds of clothing and decide how to sort them. You might sort by color texture, style, or season.

Ask the children to find something "sortable" at home, to sort it, and then to show or tell the class what they did.

numbers and operations

comparing texts

This activity uses readily available material in an unusual way! Have groups of youngsters compare two different texts in one or more ways. They might investigate the following topics:

- number of pages
- numbers and kinds of illustrations
- numbers of charts, graphs, or maps
- number of colors used
- average number of pages per chapter.

After allowing plenty of time for perusal of texts, let groups discuss all the similarities and differences they found.

ancient numerals

When students research ancient number systems they often begin to appreciate our simple decimal system and learn a lot about history as well. Challenge groups to find out some facts about number systems from different periods of history, and share their results with the class in a unique way. For example, students who investigate the Babylonian system of counting might show some symbols on clay "tablets." The group that presents Egyptian numerals might draw their symbols on a scroll. After groups have reported to your class, display the results in the hall for other classes to see.

prime and composite patterns

Use bean counters or grid paper to make representations of prime and composite numbers. Have children work in groups and create different arrays for numbers. The number 18 could be represented as shown here.

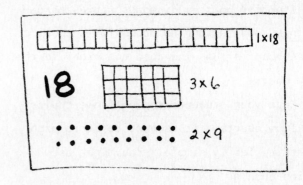

Prime numbers, such as 5, can be arranged in only one way.

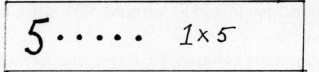

Groups of children could fill notebooks with their results or put rectangles cut from grid paper on a bulletin board.

ratios from the yellow pages

Use the yellow pages of the phone book to reinforce counting skills and ideas about ratios. Let groups decide on several ratios they could make from information found in the yellow pages. They should then gather their data and report the results to the class. They might use yellow paper to post their results on a bulletin board.

piggy banks

Make lots of little piggy banks from milk cartons or baby food jars. Label banks with different amounts of money, such as 78 , $1.25, $.50 or 32 . Give several banks and a handful of change (real or play money) to a small group of children. Let them see how to make each amount of money several different ways. For example 78 might be made with 3 quarters and three pennies, 7 dimes and eight pennies, a 50 cent piece plus 5 nickels and 3 pennies or several other ways.

problem solving

picture problems

Appoint a group to look through magazines and select some interesting pictures that have potential for writing word problems. Ask the group to write several problems based on each picture. Have them display their pictures and problems. As part of a math assignment, let each class member choose five or more of the picture problems to solve. The next week let a different group write picture problems and display them. For example, with a picture of a smiling fisherman with a string of fish children might write

- Mr. Grey caught 18 fish yesterday. The picture shows how many he caught today. How many fish did he catch altogether?

- Mr. Robinson caught 4 fish. He had another 8 fish on his line, but they got away. How many fish bit the line in all?

math adventure stories

This activity combines math, writing, art, and lots of imagination! People in adventure stories solve problems all the time. Set up groups of four or five students to write adventure stories where the characters encounter all different sorts of math problems. Have each group write and work the problems so they can provide the answers. Next let groups exchange stories, then work and check each other's problems.

fit the problem to the equation

Give groups of students several equations or inequalities, for example, $a < b$, $c + 4 = 13$ or $49 - 7 = y$. Have them write several different word problems to fit each equation or inequality.

graphing, probability, and statistics

graph-a-car

Send small groups of pupils to the parking lot and see what graphing topics they can devise. Each group should examine the cars in the lot, make categories, and gather data for a graph. When they return to the classroom each group should finish and display their graph. Some fourth graders we worked with used the following graph titles:

Two-Door, Four-Door, and Five-Door Cars

Cars versus Trucks

Colors of Cars in the Parking Lot

Station Wagons and Sedans

Brand Names of Cars

probability bag

Spray paint about 100 beans red and leave about 100 beans their natural color. Have a small group of students prepare a probability bag by putting a number of red and a number of natural beans into an opaque bag. Let them invite class members to draw out samples of beans--perhaps 10 beans--count their colors, then return the sample to the bag. On the basis of several samples, have the class draw conclusions about the numbers of red and natural beans in the bag. Let the group confirm or deny the conclusions of the class. Next have another group prepare another probability bag for the class to sample and discuss.

geometry and measurement

balancing act

Have groups take turns working with a balance scale and different kinds of materials to find many answers to the open-ended statement "_____ balances _____." For example, a group might find that 3 peanuts balance 7 raisins, that 14 paper clips balance a pencil, or that it takes 60 milk carton tops to balance a heavy rock. Let groups add several statements to a long list of items that balance each other.

same volumes, different masses

Do objects with the same volume always have the same mass? Of course they don't! A liter of feathers has a lesser mass than a liter of sand; a garbage bag full of styro-foam bits weighs considerably less than a garbage bag full of trash. Have groups of children make problems for the class using equal volumes that might have different masses. One group might fix 35 mm film cans filled with different ingredients and ask the class to put them in order from the smallest to the largest mass. Another group might fill lunch bags with air (!), Easter grass, shredded paper, and rocks, and ask the class to determine the mass of each. As groups devise problems for others, they gain experience measuring and dealing with the concept of different masses for different objects.

calculators and computers

largest answer

Groups of students can use the calculator profitably to check large answers to problems. Challenge groups to use only the digits 5, 6, 7, 8, and 9 to write different problems. The groups may use each digit only once and may use any operation signs. Each group should write several problems, predict which will have the largest answer, then check answers with a calculator. One group may end up checking the answers to problems such as these to see which answer is the largest:

567 x 89

98 x 765

$98^5 + 6^7$

9876^5

When the students encounter the problem of calculator "overflow"--answers so large they cannot be displayed on the calculator--show them how to estimate the answers or figure them by hand. Let groups put some of their results on the board and try to determine the largest possible answer.

to calculate or not to calculate-- that is the question

Challenge a small group to investigate the following question: Can your classmates write answers to the basic facts faster than they can key in values and get the answers on a calculator? In other words, can Billy write the answer to 8 x 7 faster than he can find the answer on his calculator?

Have the group figure out a way to test their classmates' abilities to get answers with and without the calculator. Encourage them to devise a way to convey their results to the class. Once an answer to the question about basic facts has been found, see how classmates do on the problems that follow.

- two- or three-digit numbers times 10. (Example: 78 x 10 or 235 x 10)

- problems that involve a two digit times a two-digit number. (Example: 23 x 19 or 87 x 54)

- long division problems.

calculatin' pairs

Here's a calculator challenge for pairs of students. The first student suggests a beginning number and an ending number. The second student's challenge is to use the calculator and get from the first number to the second in 3 different steps and at least 2 different operations. For example, to get from 100 to 10, a student might use:

$$100 - 99 = \boxed{1} \times 5 = \boxed{5} + 5 = \boxed{10}$$

1st step 2nd step 3rd step

or

$$100 + (-100) = \boxed{0} \times 16 = \boxed{0} - (-10) = \boxed{10}$$

1st step 2nd step 3rd step

After the second student has solved the problem in at least one way, he can give the calculator back to the first student who must solve the problem in a different way. Next the second student names a starting and ending number for the first student to use. As you can see, this calculator game involves strategy and thinking as well as correct entry of values and operation signs.

computer responses

If you have PILOT or another microcomputer authoring system, let your kids get together in small groups and help to generate words and phrases to be parts of teaching programs. The kids should make up some responses for correct answers. "Right on!," "You got it!," and "Congratulations!" are some starters. They should also write some responses to incorrect answers. They could use phrases like "Try again," "No, the answer should be . . .," or "One more time!" Incorporate the group's suggestions the next time you use your authoring system to create a classroom computer lesson.

programming play

Children catch on to varying steps in microcomputer programs easily. Let a group of two or three start with a program such as

```
]NEW

]10 CLS

]20 PRINT "TYPE IN YOUR AGE."

]30 INPUT A

]40 PRINT "YOUR AGE IS "

]50 PRINT A

]60 END
```

For Apple II BASIC add two program lines
between NEW and line 20

```
]10 TEXT

]15 HOME
```

Ask students to vary the PRINT statements and see what kinds of information they
can have the computer print. If they input
words rather than numbers, they should use
A$ instead of A for the variable name.

flow chart comparison

After large group work on flow charts,
divide your class into groups of three or
four. Assign them to do a flow chart on
one topic--perhaps a topic the class has
suggested. When the charts are finished,
compare them, noting similarities and
differences in the groups' interpretations
of the problem.

the smiley face and other
simple pictures

Microcomputers can be programmed to
"draw" pictures in many different ways. One
of the simplest is to tell the computer to
print a series of "x's" or other symbols in
appropriate places. Show a small group of
students the preceding program; then encourage them to vary it making their own original
pictures.

```
]NEW

]10 CLS

]20 PRINT "XXXXXXXXXX"

]30 PRINT "X          X"

]40 PRINT "X XX    XX X"

]50 PRINT "X          X"

]60 PRINT "X     O     X"

]70 PRINT "X  X    X  X"

]80 PRINT "X  XXXXX   X"

]90 PRINT "X          X"

]100PRINT "XXXXXXXXXX"

]110 END
```

For Apple II BASIC use these two lines
instead of line 10.

```
]10 TEXT

]15 HOME
```

Here is how "Smiley" will appear on the
monitor screen. If you have a printer,
of course the picture could be printed
out.
```
        XXXXXXXXXX
        X        X
        X XX  XX X
        X        X
        X   O    X
        X  X  X  X
        X  XXXXX X
        X        X
        XXXXXXXXXX
```

Use a die or number cube. Toss it 3 times. Record your scores and add them up. How many different scores did you get?

How many different ways can you get a score of 12 with 4 rolls? What are some ways you could score 20 with 5 rolls?

Operations

Mathematics

Card Games

Use an old deck of cards or make a special set of cards with fractions or decimals on them. Make up a card game. Show another group how to play your game.

Numbers, Operations

Problem Solving With
DIAGRAMS

PROBLEM
CHALLANGE

Make up some problems that can
be solved with the help of diagrams.
Make up the diagrams too. Now
test others in your class. Ask your
teacher if you can put your problems
in a special "Problem Challange" envelope
for others to use.

Problem Solving

Find a diagonal with 4 numbers to make the largest possible sum.

Use some old
calendars to make games
for number practice. What
games could you make?
Work hard to make your
game instructions clear.

Choose a row or column of numbers. Find a quick way to add them up.

Numbers, Operation

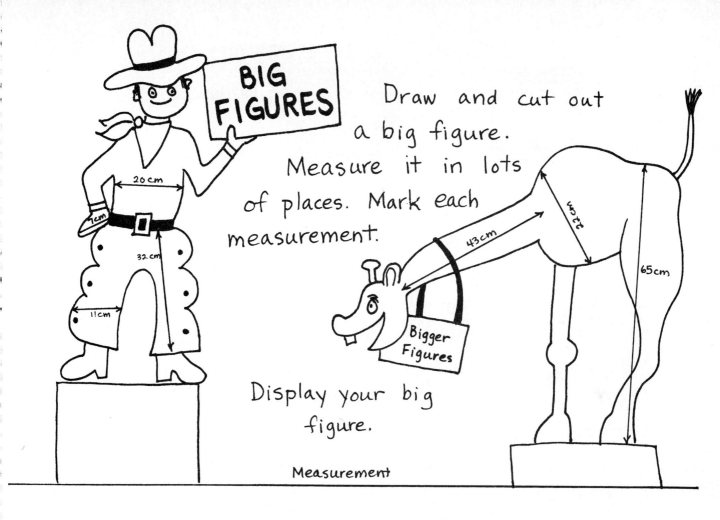

BIG FIGURES

Draw and cut out a big figure. Measure it in lots of places. Mark each measurement.

20 cm

7cm

32 cm

11cm

43cm

22cm

65cm

Bigger Figures

Display your big figure.

Measurement

TOOTHPICK

GEOMETRY

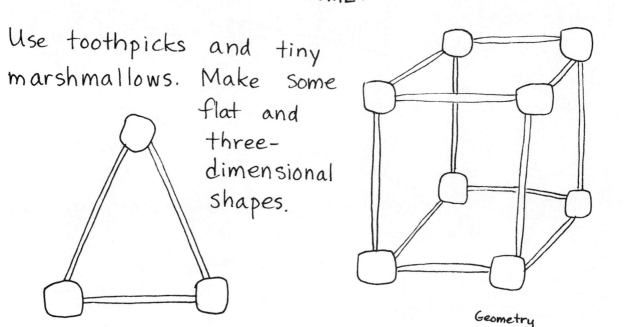

Use toothpicks and tiny marshmallows. Make some flat and three-dimensional shapes.

Geometry

How can you turn dominoes into a learning game for math? Here are 2 suggestions:

6 x 7 — Multiply the total numbers shown

52 + 41 — Use 2 dominoes. Make a 2 digit number from each. Add the numbers.

Create some good games using dominoes. Teach one of them to another group.

Numbers, Operations

HOLEY MATH!

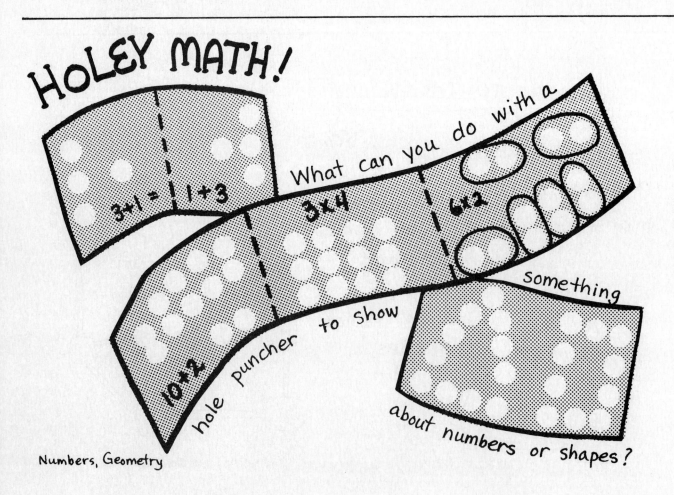

What can you do with a hole puncher to show something about numbers or shapes?

3+1 = 1+3   3×4   6×2   10×2

Numbers, Geometry

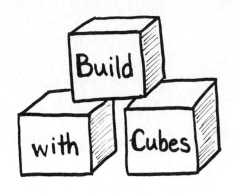

Build with Cubes

Here's a three dimensional challenge! Use 10 cubes for this activity. You could use building blocks, sugar cubes, or little centimeter cubes. Use the cubes to build as many different structures as you can think of.

Geometry

TANGRAMS

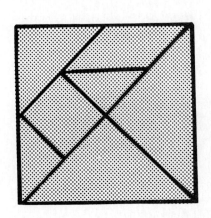

Here's a tangram puzzle. It was originally invented by the Chinese thousands of years ago. Carefully make a larger tangram. Cut the 7 pieces apart and arrange them lots of different ways to make many shapes. Draw the outlines of some of the shapes. Get some friends to see if they can fit the 7 pieces onto the outlines.

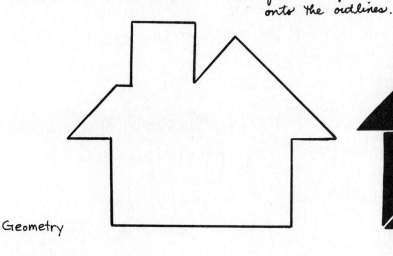

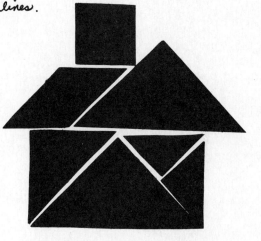

Geometry

Lay a small object flat on the table. Hold a mirror up to the object. See if both sides of the object are the same. If they are, the object is <u>symmetrical</u>.

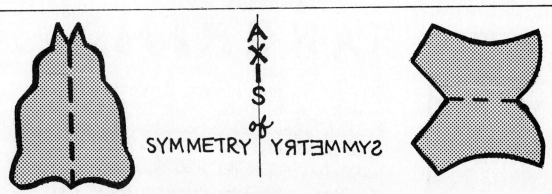

Cut out figures from paper that is folded over once.
Mark the fold line. It is the <u>axis</u> <u>of</u> <u>symmetry</u>.
Now fold the paper twice, and cut some shapes. Mark <u>two</u> <u>axes</u> <u>of</u> <u>symmetry</u>.

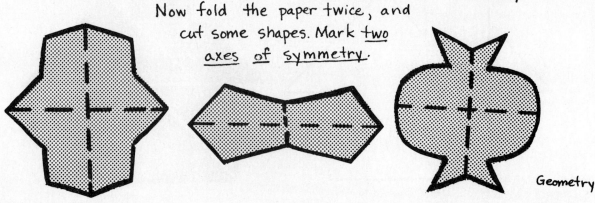

ABOUT AS LONG AS........

- How many paper clips will fit along the top of a 30 cm ruler?

- How many peanuts will fit along the edge of a floor tile?

- Investigate some statements like these using common objects.

- Write some conclusions.'

———— is about as long as ————.

———— is about as long as ————.

Measurement

CALCULATOR CHALLENGE

Make up some problems to solve on the calculator. You might try things such as:

- Find the sum of the first 25 odd numbers.
- Double 1¢ until you get to $100.00 or more.
- Find the number of seconds in a week.

Calculator

As a complement to large and small group divergent thinking activities in math, be sure to use many individual activities. You might assign some activities for individuals to do as homework, display activities in the math corner for children to use in their free time, or set up one day every few weeks when each child is free to choose and complete one or more divergent thinking math activities. Be sure to consider different ways to display individual math projects. You might use a hall display, math table, bulletin board, or scrapboard. You could ask students to attach projects to their desks for others to see, or have students add their original problems to your math puzzle corner.

numbers and operations

cataloging

Almost everyone likes to browse through catalogs. You can combine some math and categorizing skills with the pleasure of examining different kinds of catalogs in using this activity. Ask children to bring in lots of different catalogs. They might bring in sporting goods, automobile, fashion, toy, jewelry, and household catalogs. Let children browse through the catalogs and fill out an order form for five or more things they would like to buy. Have each student figure her total, including applicable taxes and shipping charges. Have students categorize their purchases two or more different ways.

folding paper

Give children ten minutes to use folded paper to show something about the numbers they're studying. You could use either squared or plain paper. Children might show fractions, operations, place value, or number properties using folded paper.

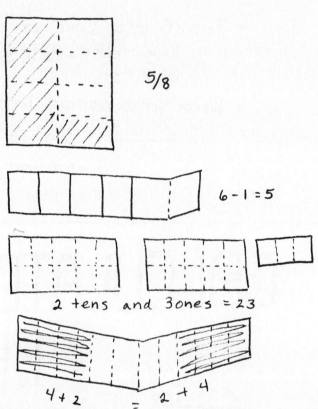

puzzle corner

Add these problems to your puzzle corner. Each has several solutions, so it encourages divergent thinking. Challenge individual students to work the problems. As they try the problems, they get a lot of practice in computation and checking answers.

Find change for $1.00 using 13 coins.

Find change for $1.00 using 21 coins.

Find change for $1.00 using 50 coins.

Use the digits 2, 3, 4 and 5 plus any symbols you wish to express as many numbers as you can. For instance

(2 + 5) − (3 + 4) expresses 1
(3 x 4) − (2 x 5) expresses 2
[5 x (4 − 2)] x 3 equals 30
3^2 + (4 + 5) expresses 18

Arrange nine 9's using any symbols to equal 1000.

Insert addition and subtraction signs to make a true statement
1 2 3 4 5 6 7 8 9 = 100

Make cards with the even numbers as shown. Arrange the cards in pairs so that all pairs will have the same total. Can you invent more tasks to do with the even number cards?

Play number solitaire. Take a two-digit number and add the squares of its digits. Now add the squares of the digits in the sum. Now add the squares of the digits in the second sum. Continue the process until you see a pattern. Here's an example. Choose 57.

$5^2 + 7^2 = 25 + 49 = 74$
$7^2 + 4^2 = 49 + 16 = 65$
$6^2 + 5^2 = 36 + 25 = 61$

Continue until you see a pattern.

Then play number solitaire with three-digit numbers too. You might want to use a calculator as you work.

number collage

Have students make number collages from the types of numbers they're studying. They might use prime numbers, multiples of 7, or

fractions in lowest terms to create an original picture.

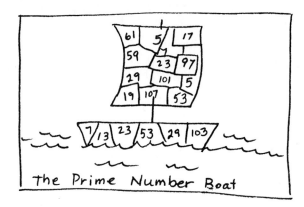

the Prime Number Boat

number diary

For a period of about two weeks, have students record something they notice in a number diary. They might record the number of minutes they spend watching TV each day, prime numbers they notice, or a new arithmetic fact learned each day. When the diaries are finished, display them in your math center.

problem solving

road map math

Decision making and budgeting are practical aspects of problem solving. Have each student bring in a road map. Ask him to choose two places at least 250 km apart. Let him plan various routes he might travel to get from one place to another. He could describe features he might see going by the most direct route and other things he might observe if he traveled by the scenic route. Have him figure travel costs using current prices for gasoline and food.

You might vary this activity by posting a big map on a bulletin board and having each child contribute at least one question and answer about the map. If you use a map of

Canada, your students might pose questions such as

- Which is longer, the land route from Fort George to Fort Severn or the water route? By how much?

- About how many kilometers is it from Quebec City to Ottawa?

- What is the northernmost town in Saskatchewan with an airport?

- Suppose you can travel about 600 km each day by car. How long would it take to get from Vancouver to Winnipeg?

geometry and measurement

even split

Show students that they can split an area into equal halves in many different ways. For example, an area of 12 cm^2 could be split

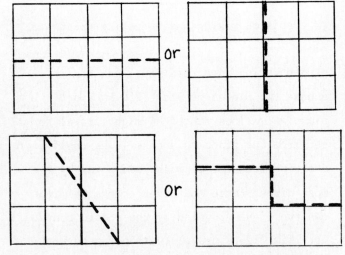

as well as many other ways. Have students use grid paper to cut out rectangles of certain areas. Ask them to split each area in half several different ways. Students place one paper half on top of the other or count

squares to verify that their two halves are equal.

wallpaper patterns

Place several different wallpaper samples inside clear acetate report covers. Have students pick out patterns they see and trace around them with crayon in each place they occur. When a student has finished with one sample, she should erase her crayon marks with a tissue to leave the acetate clean for the next student.

plotting practice

Students need a lot of practice plotting points with coordinates. Show them how a series of points, connected in order, might form a picture. You could start with this.

Connect these points in order.

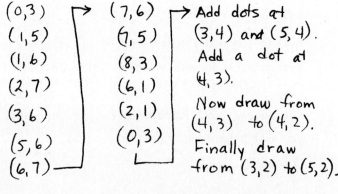

(0,3) → (7,6) → Add dots at (3,4) and (5,4). Add a dot at (4,3). Now draw from (4,3) to (4,2). Finally draw from (3,2) to (5,2).

(1,5)   (7,5)
(1,6)   (8,3)
(2,7)   (6,1)
(3,6)   (2,1)
(5,6)   (0,3)
(6,7)

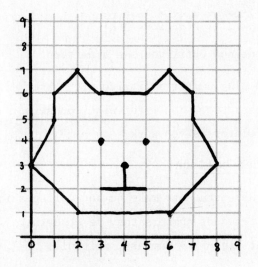

Now have students create their own pictures and share the coordinates with the class.

same area, many shapes

An area such as 12 cm^2 can be shown many different ways. It might appear as a 12 x 1 cm rectangle, a 3 x 4 cm rectangle or an odd-shaped polygon like this

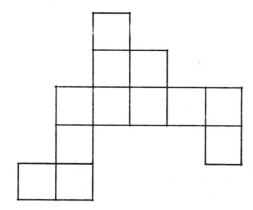

Challenge students to use centimeter grid paper and show areas such as 18 cm^2, 24 cm^2, 36 cm^2, or 50 cm^2 as many different ways as they can think of. Little areas that show up will be mounted on colored construction paper. After students have dealt with areas using whole square centimeters, let them tackle the problems of showing given areas in circular, triangular, or parallelogram shapes.

same perimeter, different areas

Have your students check the perimeters of the figures they have constructed in "same area, many shapes." The perimeters will vary even though the areas are the same.

Now tackle the problem of making geometric figures with the same perimeter but different areas. Using a perimeter of 20 cm, students might use grid paper and cut out a square with 5 cm sides, a 9 by 1 cm rectangle or a shape like the one that follows.

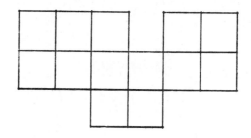

The areas of the shapes vary considerably! The square has an area of 25 cm^2, the rectangle has an area of only 9 cm^2, while the odd shape has an area of 13 cm^2. Have students suggest different perimeters and make many different areas for each. Check and record each area by counting squares.

the "metric me" book

This activity appeals to almost any age student. Everyone is a different size and shape, and it's fun to measure and record unusual things about oneself. Have students brainstorm some things that could be included in a "Metric Me" booklet.

Now turn students loose to make "Metric Me" booklets. They should include some of the measurements the class has suggested and several of their own. In Kelley's "Metric Me" booklet, she recorded her height, weight, neck measurement, foot measurements (bare and with her shoe on), waist measurement, and arm span. Kelley also drew and labeled a picture of herself smiling and included the width of her happiest smile!

"Metric Me" booklets are fun to display at a Parents' Night or Open House. Students may want to include data about their families or homes in their "Metric Me" booklets.

Divergent Thinking Activities

1 Really Big and Small

Make a long list of some of the biggest and smallest things you have ever seen or heard about.

Relationships

for individual children to do on their own

2 Dart Boards

Decide how many "darts" to use and see how you could get certain scores. For example, on the dart board below with 3 darts, how could you get scores of 50? 68? 100? Make up similar problems for your classmates.

Operations

3 Percent Collage

Percents are all around us. Find lots of examples of percents in ads and other newspaper sections. Make a collage of them. Make up some percent problems for others.

Operations

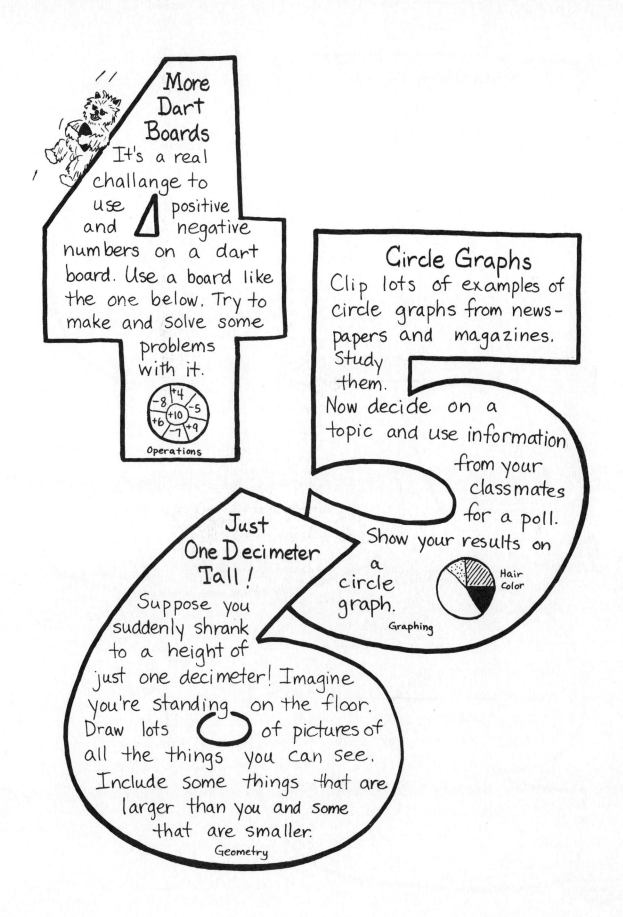

More Dart Boards

It's a real challange to use positive and negative numbers on a dart board. Use a board like the one below. Try to make and solve some problems with it.

-8 | +4
+10 | -5
+6 | -7 | +9

Operations

Circle Graphs

Clip lots of examples of circle graphs from newspapers and magazines. Study them. Now decide on a topic and use information from your classmates for a poll. Show your results on a circle graph.

Hair Color

Graphing

Just One Decimeter Tall!

Suppose you suddenly shrank to a height of just one decimeter! Imagine you're standing on the floor. Draw lots of pictures of all the things you can see. Include some things that are larger than you and some that are smaller.

Geometry

As Long As A Meter...

Find many objects that are about 1 meter long. Display the items on a bulletin board or table. Use a title such as "As Long As A Meter." Also look for objects that are about 1 cm or 1 dm long. Display these too. Use a title for each display.

Measurement

More Divergent Math Activities

Geometry Rubbings

Cut out some small geometric shapes from heavy paper or lightweight cardboard. Arrange them in a pleasing design. Place a piece of thin paper on top of the geometric shapes. Rub over the shapes with crayon. Now rearrange the shapes and make a different geometry rubbing.

Geometry

Stair Studies

Stairways are all around us but often people don't think too much about them. Take a careful look at some stairs and try to answer some questions such as these: How does the distance up and down compare to the slope? Do all stairs have the same slope?

Measurement

Individual Students
for

Depends on How You Look

Find some solid objects at home that look different from different angles. For example a piece of bread looks like this from the top ⌂ and this from the side ▯. A pencil looks like this from the side ✎ but very different from the top: o Trace around 2 or 3 objects from at least 2 different views. See if your classmates O can tell what the objects are. Now see if you can find any objects that look the same from <u>all</u> views.

Geometry

BIG Volumes

Besides your bathtub at home, what objects will hold the most water? What different ways can you measure or calculate the approximate volume of large objects? Bring your data and methods of figuring volume to school. Share your results with your classmates.

Measurement

BUILDING YOUR MIND POWER

Now it's time for <u>you</u> to think about and carry out some divergent thinking activities on your own. Choose several of the following suggestions and carry them out with your class.

1. Always introduce a math concept or skill in the context of a meaningful situation. This good advice is offered by almost every expert in the teaching of mathematics. It applies to virtually every situation and grade level. Apply it by choosing a skill or concept you will be teaching in the near future. Brainstorm ways to make the skill or concept real and meaningful. Choose what you think is the best way and carry it out with your students.

2. Fractions are often taught with circle or "pie" illustrations. Devise some other ways to present fractions to your class. You might have children work with such materials as accordian-folded paper, felt rectangles, materials on a magnet board, or Cuisinere rods. Perhaps you can think of some materials where each child can make and use her own set of materials for work with fractions.

3. Study an old or unique technique for doing multiplication or division. You might find literature on techniques such as the following: Chisanbop, Russian Peasant Multiplication, Lattice Multiplication, division with the abacus, Napier's "Bones," or division as repeated subtraction. Present the technique to your class as a reinforcement or reteaching device, or simply as a curious and workable method.

4. You've probably known a child or young person who has special needs in mathematics. Perhaps the child is a slow learner, has math anxiety, or is extremely bright and interested in mathematics. Brainstorm several ideas to

help or challenge the child. Discuss some workable ideas with him. Choose two or three ideas to carry out in the next month.

5. Review is essential if students are to maintain their math skills, but time is at a premium in most classrooms. What review strategies could you use three or four days a week for just five minutes to keep your students' math skills alive? You might have partners use flashcards, dictate brief problems for mental arithmetic and have the kids write the answers, or you might use the overhead projector to briefly show numbers to be written or facts to be computed. What else can you think of? Carry out an idea regularly over the next six weeks.

6. Make a reusable calendar to teach or reinforce a math topic. For example, you might construct a large calendar with hooks to arrange tags for each month's dates. Instead of conventionally written dates, you could use Roman numerals, basic facts, numbers, or numbers expressed in place value.

7. What are some ways you could use recycled resources, such as samples from wallpaper books, to teach mathematics? Explore some uses for the recycleables, such as counting, patterning, or finding geometric shapes.

8. Spice up your math class with a walk! Think of a theme that would fit in with your current unit. Take your class outdoors or simply work around your school building. Look for items that relate to your theme. You might concentrate on geometric shapes, numerals, or things people have measured. You could have your group post labels on the items they find. Such a math walk increases awareness of mathematics in the world around us.

If you could design a robot to help you with your work, what would it do for you? Would it talk? How? What would it look like?

Recent space probes have taken pictures of Saturn and Jupiter. What information could you learn from studying these photos? What would you do with the information?

PAR4

Think of a phenomenon that has always puzzled you. For example:

- What direction does water move as it goes down the drain? Why?
- Where do spiders seem to prefer to make their webs?
- Why is there more frost in the upper part of the freezer than the lower?

Choose some questions of your own. Observe and experiment to find the answers.

PAR5

Before we proceed to the next fairway, here's one more mind stretcher. What are some problems that have been solved by scientists? What problems are left to solve?

Science is important because it complements all areas of the curriculum. Science and math are so intertwined that it is often hard to discern where science ends and math begins. Graph making, counting, and measuring are skills that are used constantly in both math and science. Reading is also a vital part of science. Students would have a hard time advancing in science without having first achieved competence in reading. In addition, some of the most motivating and interesting reading material concerns science. From reading, children can learn about subjects as diverse as butterflies, sea shells, molecules, and minerals. Language arts is also important in the study of science. Without the ability to communicate through writing, speaking, and listening, people would know little about science. With a little thought, we could find many ways other areas, such as music, art, and social studies, blend with science.

The nature of science is such that it influences not just the school curriculum but many facets of life. Science develops reasoning processes that serve us every day. A scientific attitude makes us curious to know more about the world. Thus, we become eager students of life. Through the study of science we develop an appreciation for the aesthetic qualities of life. This appreciation fills us with wonder and joy which adds zest to our very existence.

Why should we study science? In order to understand the way things around us work and grow, we need to know some basic facts and generalizations. Knowledge of basic science concepts are necessary for simple problem solving. To remove a tight lid from a jar, most of us know that running hot water on the lid will be effective. We apply the science concept that states that metals expand when heated. To grow healthy plants, we routinely apply our knowledge of their needs of water, light, and nutrients. Without sufficient knowledge of science, our lives would be a constant struggle of trial and error.

Most of us will agree that knowledge is important in science, but the processes of science are equally important because through these processes scientific knowledge is accumulated. What are the processes? They're the way scientists "do" things. Scientists tune into the world around them and make meticulous observations. Scientists go through life with keen sensitivity. They know how to organize data that they have collected and communicate it to others through words, pictures, and graphs. From this data, they are able to make meaningful inferences and predictions. As they generate and test hypotheses through careful experimentation, scientists expand and extend the horizons of scientific knowledge. Scientists operate on a very sophisticated level, but any child or adult can become increasingly skillful at scientific inquiry.

Knowledge of science and its processes is very important, but one other ingredient is necessary for effective work with science. This ingredient adds spark, motivation, and staying power to the study of science. The more we know about science and the more we learn to use its processes, the more this ingredient unfolds and matures. This mysterious ingredient is a scientific attitude.

A scientific attitude is an eagerness and a curiosity about the world around us. It makes us sensitive to the wonders of nature and gives us an appreciation of the simplicity of scientific principles and the intricacy of their interrelationships. A positive scientific attitude adds interest and color to all of life.

Knowledge, processes, and attitudes--these three things are important objectives in this study of science. They take us from a selfish orientation to a concern for others. These objectives help us refine our competence in rational thought and action. Knowledge, processes, and attitudes of science give us a sense of responsibility for making wise decisions to improve the world around us.

Adults must be aware of the broad range of topics covered in elementary school science. Textbook authors divide scientific topics in various ways, but generally they include the same basic areas. These areas are life sciences, physical sciences, and environmental sciences. Typically, these areas are treated through a spiral approach in which children study the areas at increasing levels of sophistication as they progress through the grades.

Life sciences include the study of plants, animals, and humans. In studying life sciences, children learn about the many species of living things, their needs, variations, and unique characteristics. As children study the interrelationships of living things, they also develop a knowledge of ecology.

In the physical sciences, children explore the nature and properties of nonliving matter and energy. Physical sciences include topics such as air, water, light, sound, magnetism, electricity, machines, and matter and energy. The diversity of physical science offers teachers and children a variety of opportunities for divergent thinking.

Environmental sciences encompass studies in geology, weather, and astronomy. Logically, study of environmental science might start with exploration of more familiar phenomena, such as dirt, rocks, and weather, and progress to the less familiar environments--the sun, moon, planets, and stars. Careful observation of the environment promotes readiness for study of the origins of the universe and conditions that cause change in the environment.

ENCOURAGING DIVERGENT THINKING WITH LARGE GROUP ACTIVITIES IN SCIENCE

From x-rays to magnets, insects to rust, there are many ways to incorporate divergent thinking into science activities for large groups. Some of the ideas in this section will help you introduce science units. Some can be integral parts of courses of study. Still others will provide creative follow-ups of science concepts. Whatever level you teach and whatever science concepts you deal with, you will find many motivating activities in the following section.

biology activities

tree gazing

Children can learn a lot about trees from observing. Generate interest in trees through an informal group discussion. Have children brainstorm some things they would like to find out about trees. Let each child volunteer to answer a specific question that especially interests her. Let each one go outside, investigate by observing trees, and report to the class.

Have the children make a "Tree Gazing" bulletin board to display their questions and answers.

facts about food

Food is a motivating topic. Discussions about food provide many opportunities for divergent thinking. Ask children questions such as: What foods are salty? How many foods can you think of that have protein in them? What foods are crisp? Mushy? Let kids think of other questions to ask the class about foods. Follow up your discussion by asking students to bring in and share foods from the groups you have discussed.

testing variables for plant growth

Here's an activity that not only lets children practice divergent thinking but also lets them practice science process skills, such as separating variables, designing ex-periments, and testing hypotheses. Begin a discussion on the different variables that affect plant growth. Make a list of the answers the children give and encourage them to extend the list. Let the children choose a variable that especially intrigues them and ask them to design an experiment to test selected aspects of that variable. Children may need help in learning how to separate variables and in designing appropriate tests.

A group that chooses light as their variable might want to explore the ways that different colored lights affect plant growth. They will gather and set up the necessary equipment to grow plants in red, blue, yellow, and ordinary light. They might also want to see if plants can be grown with no light at all. After plants are grown, have each group display and discuss their results with the class.

original ice cream recipes

Classroom cooking is an activity that not only intrigues most youngsters but can also provide opportunities for divergent thinking. After making ice cream in class, ask your students, What could we have used in the ice cream to make it sweet if we had no sugar? When they run out of answers, extend their thinking by asking, What things are sweet? This type of questioning need not always follow a cooking activity, but it will probably be more meaningful to children if it is related to an actual cooking experience.

inquiries about animal products

Display a collection of animal products, such as shoe leather, a can of tuna fish, a camel hair paint brush, fur, and a natural bristle hairbrush. Ask the class open-ended questions such as the following:

What do you know about the animal products here? What features can you notice? What are some questions you could ask about these products? What are some other animal products?

Follow the discussion by making an experience chart on animal products. Suggest that each child bring an animal product to share the next day.

creatures of the sea

Children's imaginations can be whetted with visions of sea creatures. During a study of oceanography, ask your students such questions as these: What creature would you want to be if you lived in the ocean? Where would you live? What would some of your adventures be? Who would your enemies be? How would you escape from your enemies? What would you eat? Urge your students to base their imaginings on facts. If the kids are interested in the topic, you might encourage them to follow up with pictures of their imaginary sea creatures.

creative bird watching

Why do birds tilt their heads before they dig up worms? Do birds have teeth or tongues? Where is a bird's ear? Children can discover a lot about birds and their habits by reading interesting material and following a routine of bird watching. Encourage children to generate some questions they might be able to answer after watching birds. Provide opportunities for bird watching, research on birds, discussion of answers, and creating and refining more questions. Remember that it's only through the generation of good questions and answering them that scientific knowledge grows.

sensory handicaps

Thinking about the loss of a sense is serious business, but it may encourage new understanding and respect for persons who are blind, deaf, or have lost a limb. It also offers many chances for divergent thinking. Ask children to describe how they might feel if they lost a sense. Have them tell how they might try to compensate for the loss and what they think they'd miss most. Now have children simulate a sensory loss for an hour or so by wearing blindfolds or earplugs, tying or bandaging a hand, or carefully closing their noses with loose spring clothespins. Come back to the discussion topics again after the sensory loss experience. Ask them to expound on their frustrations. Have children write about how they might be empathetic and helpful to persons with sensory losses. Have children design and draw helpful equipment or features that might be added to a classroom to assist people with sensory handicaps.

the foot bone's related to the ankle bone . . .

In the human body many body parts work together. One part complements the functioning of another. Give some examples and have your students discuss them. For instance, teeth and fingernails have many similarities and differences. The stomach and liver are in close proximity in the abdominal cavity and work in concert to aid in the digestion of food, yet these organs have many differences. Compare and contrast pairs of body parts, such as the heart and lungs, the elbow and knee, or the esophagus and trachea. Let children suggest more pairs and talk about their likenesses and differences.

x-ray exam

Bring some x-rays to class. Display them by taping them to a window. Let children discuss divergent thinking questions such as: What can you learn from x-rays? How would you find out about medical problems without x-rays? Besides people, what else would be interesting to x-ray? Children might also draw and display their own "x-ray" pictures.

environmental science activities

life chain

Even small changes in one part of the environment create "ripple effects" that influence other parts of the environment. Have children originate some suppositions and discuss their results. If Kevin supposed that all insects have suddenly grown to twice their former size, Rachel might say that they would take over the world. Jody might add that they'd cause more diseases. Mary Lou might add a touch of humor—birds that ate them would get too fat! When one supposition

has been discussed thoroughly, ask another child to suggest a different supposition related to the life chain. Whether answers are factual or fanciful, this exercise will show children the interrelationships among different aspects of the environment.

interrelationships

Have children brainstorm three lists. The first list should contain animals; the second list should include plants; the third list should encompass minerals. Now let children take turns choosing an animal, plant, and mineral and talking about the interrelationships, or possible interrelationships, between them. How might the three affect or depend on each other?

the great iceberg melt

Present this hypothetical problem during a group discussion. "Suppose all the icebergs on earth melted." Provide the information that there would be 10 percent more water when the icebergs melted. Now ask the class, How would all the icebergs melting affect life on earth? How would it affect you personally? How would you try to solve some of the problems that resulted? What might be some beneficial outcomes of the great iceberg melt?

rock recipes

Near the end of a unit on rocks, children will be interested in making their own rocks. Make several kinds of "rocks" in class. Here are some recipes you might want to start with.
CEMENT BLOCKS
Mix 60 ml (1/4 cup) of dry cement and 125 ml (1/2 cup) of sand. Put several small pebbles

into the cement-sand mixture. Slowly add water until a thick mush is formed. Pour the mixture into a cardboard box mold to harden. Wet the top of the concrete each day. Allow the block to harden several days. Then remove it from the box.

PUDDING STONE

Mix 125 ml (1/2 cup) of plaster of paris, 125 ml (1/2 cup) of pebbles and sand mixed, a few twigs and leaves, and 60 ml (1/4 cup) of water. Stir all the ingredients together. Pour mixture into styrofoam container and let it set. Provide materials such as sand, plaster of paris, gravel, clay, different types of dirt, or flour. Let children experiment with some of these ingredients and make their own unique types of rocks. Test the rocks to see which are hardest, softest, roughest, or smoothest. Ask them how they might vary their "rock recipes" to improve them.

rocks and more rocks

Most kids have a collection of rocks and can share their ideas about rocks with others. Let your students bring any rocks they have to class and tell about them. Have the kids talk about questions they might ask and answer as they work with the rocks. Hopefully, by now your class is good at proposing questions, but if they still need some starters, you might use some questions such as, "Do rocks look different wet or dry? How? Do rocks feel and look different when they're rubbed with salad oil? How? How can you find out more about rocks? How can you find out the names of rocks? What rocks will scratch other rocks? Will rocks make marks on sidewalks or bricks?

rain walks

Rainy days need not bring restlessness and boredom. When the temperature is high enough, you might have your children don raincoats and grab umbrellas for a walk in the rain. Before your walk, ask the children questions such as, What are some interesting things we could do in the rain? What could you do with the rain? How could we make a picture using the rain? Are there any ways we could collect rain splashes? Have them carry out some of these suggestions.

making weather instruments

When studying a unit on the weather, lead children into a discussion about different phenomena related to the weather, such as temperature changes, wind directions, rainfall, and rainbows. Investigate various instruments that are used for measuring these phenomena. Then have children invent their own instruments for observing weather. They might design an instrument for measuring rainfall, create a device for making a rainbow for observation purposes, or make a wind gauge.

sun fun

Ask your pupils to name as many facts as they can about the ways the sun changes from day to day, season to season, or year to year. Let pupils choose topics and discuss ways that changes could be recorded or measured. For instance, ordinarily the temperature increases from dawn until noon. Pupils might record changes in temperature by making measurements at hour intervals. Shadow lengths change throughout the day. Pupils might record this phenomenon by tracing shadow patterns with chalk on the sidewalk. After such a discussion, small group work for the next day might be planned. Pupils could record changes and phenomenon and report their findings to the class.

mini moon craters

After studying photos of the moon's surface, students will be intrigued with the opportunity to create their own minicraters. Set up several flat boxes or trays of "soft" ingredients, such as flour, cornmeal, sand, or plaster. Let students take turns dropping marbles, golf balls, jack balls, or other small "Meteors" into the ingredients. See what kinds of "craters" result. Encourage students to vary the height, angle, and force with which the "meteors" are dropped. Discuss the results.

solar system

Let's develop a new meaning for the phrase "solar system." Have your group brainstorm the advantages and disadvantages of the sun. Someone is sure to mention harnessing solar power to help people. Ask your students to think of ways they might heat a house with sunlight. Encourage them to design a system that will operate even in cloudy or rainy weather and at night.

spacey sortie

The ultimate trip for most adventuresome students would be a trip to outer space.

Imagining such a trip provides many opportunities for divergent thinking. You might have students generate answers to questions such as, How would you get to another planet? What safety or comfort features would you incorporate if you could design a space suit? How would you amuse yourself on a long space flight? To keep in shape on a space trip, what exercises could you design that could be done in close quarters? How could you make the interior of your space ship cozy or home-like? What would you like to eat on a space voyage? What special names could you give to foods designed for use in space? As you can see, these questions generate a lot of discussion. There's also the possibility of following them up with writing stories, drawing pictures, or designing menus.

reducing energy consumption

We're all interested in it, but it really takes some creative thinking to figure out acceptable ways of accomplishing it! To establish the need for reducing energy consumption, have youngsters work together to compile a long list of ways that they use energy in a typical week. Provide some simple background research on energy conservation for the children to study. Now the challenge—figure out ways to cut energy consumption by 10 percent. Let youngsters "buzz" with others who sit near them for a minute or two, then list possible solutions to the problem of cutting down on energy. After many solutions have been proposed, critique them for practicality and appeal. Urge youngsters to try the best proposals for a week and report the results to the class.

life on another planet

Suppose your space trip has ended. Basing answers on what the children know about the planets, ask them to describe what they'd encounter when they reached another planet. They might like to deal with the following questions: What problems will you have to solve on the planet Venus? How will you solve them? What will you miss most about Earth? What resources can you utilize from the planet and what must you bring from Earth? What science specimens and souvenirs will you bring home? After an initial discussion, have groups of students choose planets to investigate. Let each group further expand on the previous questions and others they might generate. Have groups present their findings in a dramatization.

physical science activities

a close look at physical properties

Here's another idea for using a collection to teach or review science principles. Your students can deal with physical properties of substances in the following way. Have each student bring several objects to class. Put the objects in a central spot, then discuss various characteristics some of the objects have in common. Most of the characteristics the children name will be physical properties—color, texture, shape, size, odor, for example. Encourage children to think of more physical properties. They might use conduction of electricity, magnetism, hardness, brittleness, heaviness, or solubility. Now have the children take turns

choosing three seemingly unrelated objects and telling about the physical properties that make them alike. For example, Vicki might choose a plastic spoon, a hairbrush, and a TV guide. She might report that they're alike because none conduct electricity, none are soluble, and all have a smooth area on them. After selecting a penny, a marble, and a clay flower pot, Billy might explain that they all have a circular part, they have no distinctive smell, and they all would sink in water. Extend the discussion of physical properties by having students choose one object each and describing as many of its physical properties as possible.

soap bubbles

Soap bubbles are fascinating to almost any age child. Let children make up and test hypotheses related to soap bubbles. For instance, they might suppose that bigger bubbles last longer than smaller bubbles, that bubbles will freeze in freezing weather, or that a square bubble wand will produce square bubbles. Give the children a few suggestions and encourage them to think of other hypotheses. Have equipment ready so that children can test out their ideas. Be sure to follow through by asking children to report on their findings.

Have the children invent a unique device for making bubbles. Let them demonstrate their new bubble blowers.

Present a problem such as this to the children. What can you do to change the bubbles in some way? Children might suggest ways to change the shape, size, color, or number of bubbles. Be sure not to settle for just one answer. Quality divergent thinking depends upon many ideas. Give children time and equipment to test their ideas on changing bubbles.

candles, whale oil, and peanuts

What does this unlikely trio have in common? You guessed it—they all burn. Let students make as long a list as possible of things that burn and things that don't burn. You might introduce the words "flammable" and "nonflammable." Under supervision you might allow students to burn some unusual objects, such as nuts, salad oil, or wool cloth. You can easily improvise a little stand to burn a nut by bending a paper clip and inserting one end into the nut. Sneak in a mini-lesson on fire safety. Let students brainstorm a long list of precautions and safety procedures for dealing with fire and hot materials.

dissolving test

Bring at least three items to class and let children see whether or not they will dissolve in water. Ask the children to suggest other things that might dissolve. Have each student bring in at least two things to test to see if they will dissolve.

marble capers

Marbles can provide a variety of opportunities for motivating kids to think creatively. Encourage children to talk about the properties of marbles. Then ask, What are some different things you could do with marbles? Kids might present ideas, such as rolling them, dropping them, putting them in boxes and shaking them. Pick up from some of their suggestions and extend their thoughts by saying, "I know we can roll marbles on the floor. What are some other things through which we might roll marbles?" Suggestions might include carpets, sand, grass, flour, gravel. Now move on and pick up on their next suggestion. Ask them to name different substances in which they might drop marbles. They might mention substances such as water, syrup, and oil.

Have your students dip marbles in various colors of tempera paint and roll the marbles on a long sheet of white paper. Encourage them to describe what they observe, to discuss the different designs, and to give their "marble painting" an appropriate name. After several discussions and activities using marbles, ask the children to plan at least one other experiment using marbles.

transparent, translucent, and opaque

In a unit on light, the words "transparent," "translucent," and "opaque" are generally discussed. Children can react capably to questions such as these: What are all the things you can think of that are transparent? What things are translucent? What's something really unusual that's opaque? How can you determine if something is transparent, translucent, or opaque? Bring in some samples of different materials. Let children hold these materials in front of their eyes, look at a book or picture, and describe what they see. Follow up this discussion and experimentation with our "Overhead Art" in the small group section of the chapter on art.

mystery machine box

Place a "machine," such as a can opener, a pair of scissors, or a hammer in a box. Divide your class into two groups. One group should know what the mystery machine is. Let the other group try to find out what the machine is by asking questions. Allow them only fifteen questions to solve the mystery. Encourage the group to plan their questions carefully so as not to waste them.

machine collage

In a study of six simple machines, have your youngsters look through magazines and newspapers for machine pictures. Identify which of the simple machine categories their pictures fall into. Group the pictures. Divide into small groups to design a machine collage, such as a ramp collage, a wheel and axle collage, or a lever collage.

gravity gabble

Let students find pictures or cartoons where gravity is at work within the picture. Have them exchange pictures and then explain whatever gravity phenomena they find in their pictures.

repellattract

Often students have experience with only a limited number of materials that are attracted to and repelled by magnets. Challenge students to help collect a wide variety of unusual materials for use with magnets. One day you might ask each student to bring five materials that attract magnets and five materials that are repelled by magnets. Encourage them to bring materials

that no one else would think of. The next day let them display and test the materials. The students might also group the objects by other categories that they generate. For instance, they might use objects that can be lifted by a magnet, objects that repel a magnet, or objects that are red and attract a magnet.

sounding boards

Students are often fascinated with the study of the properties of sound and realize that many factors affect the pitch, quality, and intensity of sound. Encourage them to create demonstrations on sound properties. Provide scraps of board, nails of various sizes, rubber bands, strings, wires, and hammers. Have students work in pairs to create "instruments" that illustrate principles of sound. When the instruments are finished, let students show how they work and discuss the principles that are involved. Some of our students came up with these ideas:

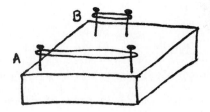

"String A is higher because it's stretched tighter than B"

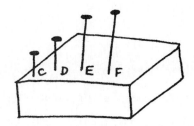

"When you pluck on F, it's the lowest because it's the longest"

rusty research

What will happen when a nail is buried in wet sand for a few days? If the children don't know, suggest they experiment to find out. Encourage them to discover some ways to put a nail in wet sand and keep it from rusting. Gather enough materials for them to set up the experiment and find out what happens.

Children have seen that water contributes to the rust formation on iron nails. Can rust or corrosion form on other materials?

Pick some small objects of easily obtainable materials, such as aluminum pop tops, copper pennies, or steel paper clips. Have children devise a list of liquids, such as milk, ammonia, salt water, soft drinks, lemonade, lemon juice, baking soda water, or vinegar. Choose some of these liquids and let the children immerse the metal objects in them for several days. Encourage them to predict what might happen and to record their findings.

ENCOURAGING DIVERGENT THINKING WITH SMALL GROUP ACTIVITIES IN SCIENCE

In small groups children really get a chance to be active in delving into science. Whether directions are given orally or groups are handed cards with directions on them, small groups can work independently and creatively with activities such as the ones suggested in this section. You will find two types of activities: those addressed to adults and those that can be handed directly to children for small group work.

activities emphasizing science processes

buttons 'n' bones

How many different ways could kids sort a button collection? Given a pile of cleaned dried bones, how many arrangements could your students make? Ask students to bring objects from home to make several collections of small articles such as

buttons	small toys
bones	office supplies

Divide your students into groups. Give each a collection and ask them to sort the collection as many ways as possible. Encourage them to discuss and confirm the basis for sorting.

alike and different

Scientists compare and contrast phenomena constantly. Pupils need practice to develop this important skill. For this easy yet challenging activity, you'll need a set of attribute blocks or a collection of small toys and household articles. Show the children how to play the alike and different game. They must choose two objects, lay them side by side, then tell one way they're alike and one way they are different. Then they choose a third object, place it in line, and compare and contrast it to the second object. Then the game continues with more objects. Put the collections in your science center and provide groups of children with time to play the alike and different game.

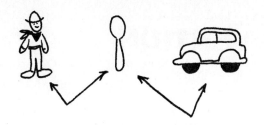

Alike because they both have rounded tops. Different because the spoon has one handle and the doll has two legs.

Alike because they're both plastic. Different because you eat with one and play with one.

the eclectic mystery boxes

Collect several small boxes. In each box put a number of one type of item. In one box you might place five buttons. In one box you might place three marbles. Another box might contain several dried peas. Tape the boxes shut so that they can't be opened.

Have small groups of children work with the mystery boxes to try to guess the contents of each box. Encourage them to devise appropriate questions and to test their questions by making keen observations about the contents of each box.

physical science activities

sun and shadows

The sun is a source of heat and light. Shadow lengths vary at different times of the day and during different seasons. Only when the sun shines do shadows appear outdoors. Present these concepts to your students. Have groups of students choose a concept and demonstrate it to the class.

shadow shows

Presenting a shadow show is a good way to help children assimilate newly learned concepts related to light and shadows. You'll need various supplies such as

boxes	heavy paper
yarn	coat hangers
lightweight fabric	
various light sources (flashlights, candles, small lamps)	

Shadow shows basically involve using a light source behind small cut-out figures to create shadows on a screen. Suspend the figures from a coat hanger "stick" or a piece of yarn to prevent your hands from casting shadows.

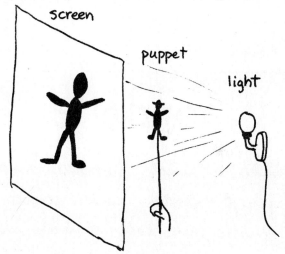

After presenting the basic concept of shadow shows to your class, suggest that groups of children plan little shadow shows. Let them experiment with different materials placed in various positions. Encourage them to find out how to make their shadows larger, smaller, or clearer. They might discover different ways to hold their props up or unique ways of making props. Suggest that they experiment with different light sources. When the groups are ready, dim the lights and watch each group present their shadow shows.

BIRD FEEDER INVENTION

Various birds like different things
to eat and will come to different
kinds of bird feeders.

Work with your group.
Choose a kind of bird
that lives in your area.
Find out about its habits.

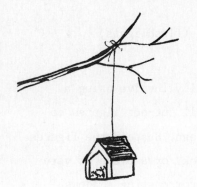

Get some materials and make a
bird feeder. Fill it with the food
your bird likes. Place it outdoors.
See what birds will come to your
feeder.

Biological Science

Sandpile Greenhouse

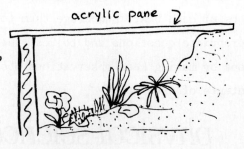

acrylic pane

Take a walk outside with your
group. Gather small plants, seedlings,
flowers, and lots of green moss. Dig
up these plants, being very careful to
include the roots. Now let's make
a pretty little woodland scene. In the schoolyard
sandpile dig a cavity about 30 cm square. Arrange and
plant your tiny seedlings in the cavity, lining the cavity
with moss. Spray your woodland scene with water.
Cover the top with an acrylic window pane. Whenever it
needs it, add water to your sandpile greenhouse.

Biological Science

S E E D Sort

👁 Form a group and go for a nature walk.

👂 Collect as many interesting seeds as you can. Get a good variety.

✋ Sort your seeds into the sections of an egg carton.

❄ Now dump out the seeds and start again. Try sorting them in a different way. Can you find at least three ways to sort the seeds?

🌱 When you have finished sorting, work with your group and make a collage of your seeds.

Biological Science

Delectable Dinners

Work with some classmates. Cut out _lots_ of pictures of foods. Remember the four food groups --- meats, dairy, fruits and vegetables, breads and cereals. Put each picture in the correct group. Now think of other ways to sort the pictures. Group them at least three _other_ ways.

Each person in your group should now choose one picture. Decide on a way to make the food in the picture _more_ delicious.

Biological Science

Animal Information

Select an animal picture for
    your group to talk about.
Each person takes a turn and tells
    one thing about the picture.
Now go around the group again.
    See how many new bits of
    information you can add.
Did you get a lot of information? What did you learn
    from your classmates? Select a new picture and
    try this exercise again.

Biological Science

DESIGN - A - BETTER - BUG - TRAP

Work in a group. Spend at least 20 minutes
observing the habits of one kind of insect. How
does it move? How big is its territory? What is it
attracted to? What seems to scare it away?

Now gather some materials and see if you can
make a trap to capture the kind of insect you
picked. Test out your trap and see if you can catch
one of these insects. Be sure to free it after observation.

Biological Science

Foot Feelings I

Can your feet feel things as well as your hands? Let's find out. Find at least 3 objects that might be interesting to touch with your feet. Put one object at a time in a sack or box. Be sure your classmates can't see. Let your classmates take turns putting their feet in the box or sack and describing what they feel. Now let them choose some things for you to test with your feet.

Biological Science

Foot Feelings II

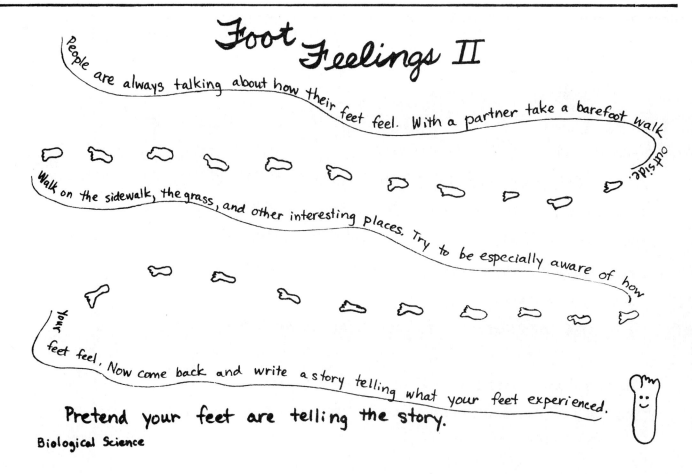

People are always talking about how their feet feel. With a partner take a barefoot walk outside. Walk on the sidewalk, the grass, and other interesting places. Try to be especially aware of how your feet feel. Now come back and write a story telling what your feet experienced.

Pretend your feet are telling the story.

Biological Science

STOMACH CEREALS

In the ads you read a lot about stomach problems. Collect many of those advertisements. Work with your group to make a list of all the things you think people could do to prevent stomach problems. To make your information accurate, you might want to check in your science book, in reference books, or in encyclopedias. Decide a unique way to share the information you have gathered with your class.

Biological Science

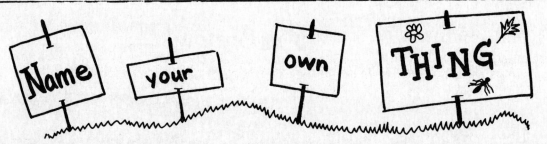

Name your own THING

People name nature specimens with descriptive names that tell something about the item's characteristics. For instance bloodroot has a red sap in the root that looks like blood. Fleabane was probably once used to repel fleas. A rhinoceros beetle has a big horn on its head.

Find a flower, leaf, insect, or some other interesting object you can't identify. Make up a unique name for that object. Be sure the name includes a description of the object. Show the object to your group and explain why you gave it that name.

Biological Science

HOUSE DETECTIVES

Detectives and scientists use clues to find out about things. Gather many pictures of houses. Look at them carefully to see what you can find out. By looking, see if you can answer questions such as:

- What might tell you if many people or just a few live there?
- What clues might indicate that pets live in the house?
- How could you estimate the age of the house?
- How could you figure out some of the hobbies of the residents?
- What might tell you that a handicapped person lives there?

The next time you go through town, play house detective. Look at houses. See how many clues you can find that tell about people who live in the houses.

Environmental Science

 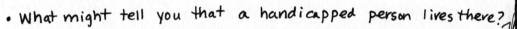 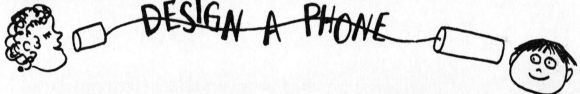

DESIGN A PHONE

You've probably made a "phone" using a string and some paper cups. You know how you can talk to a friend using the homemade phone.

Work with your group and design a kind of phone using different materials. Try some of these:

- different sizes of wire
- plastic food containers
- nylon cord
- coffee cans
- styrofoam cups
- rope

Test out various designs and see how they work.

Physical Science

the GREAT WATER TRANSFER

Besides pouring it, how can you transfer water from one container to another?

List as many ways as you can.
Now gather some materials and test out some of your ideas.
Can you think of other ways to transfer water? Try them out?

Physical Science

SPARKS 'n' SHOCKS

Gather some equipment to make static electricity.
You might use things like these:

- nylon scarf
- plastic comb
- wool fabric
- dry rice
- styrofoam bits
- piece of fur
- bits of tissue paper
- inflated balloon

Rub the nylon scarf on the comb. Bring the comb near the balloon. What happens? Now hold the comb near the dry rice or your hair. What do you notice? Try rubbing the balloon with the wool, then bring it near the tissue paper. Go around the room and find other combinations to charge with static electricity.

Physical Science

FANTASTIC ⫿⫿⫿ FLASHLIGHTS 1

Discover what light patterns you can see if you shine your flashlights <u>onto</u> various colors and textures of materials. Notice how the light reflects when you shine the flashlights onto materials like these:

- mirrors
- flat foil
- crumpled foil
- white cloth
- black velvet
- red paper

What kinds of mirrors or materials reflect light best?

mirror

crumpled foil

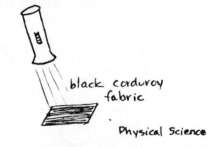
black corduroy fabric

Physical Science

FANTASTIC ⫿⫿⫿ FLASHLIGHTS 2

How can you shine a flashlight <u>down</u> and see a light pattern on the <u>ceiling</u>?

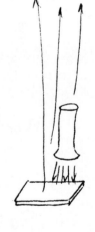

How can you point your flashlight toward <u>one corner</u> of the room and see a reflection on the <u>floor</u>?

Experiment with mirrors and flashlights to find out.

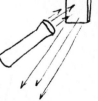

Physical Science

DRAMAS

about
Discoveries

Choose a famous invention or discovery with your group. Find out all you can about the invention or discovery.

Now plan a play. Act it out before the rest of your class.

Science Processes

SOLAR COOKER

Work with your group to figure out a unique way to use the sun to cook some thing.

Gather the materials you'll need.

Make your solar cooker. Use it to cook things such as hot dogs, apple slices, or marshmallows

styrofoam cup lined with foil

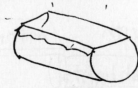
foil-lined oatmeal box

can with lid on top

Physical Science

TESTING ADS

Some detergents claim to get clothes brighter than other detergents. Several advertisers of cereals say that their products stay crisp even in milk. According to ads, some candies won't melt in your hands.

Think of an ad that makes a claim. Design your own test and experiment to see whether or not that claim is true.

Science Processes

ENCOURAGING DIVERGENT THINKING WITH INDIVIDUAL ACTIVITIES IN SCIENCE

Now that students have practiced divergent thinking in large groups and small groups, they should be ready to work alone. Individual work gives students the opportunity to test their abilities in divergent thinking and to pursue their ideas in greater depth. In this section you will find activities for you, the teacher, to assign to individual students and activities that students can use without your assistance.

biology activities

natural dyes

Experimenting with different natural dyes can be an interesting experience for young people. After using natural dyes in a large or small group activity in class, give your students several small swatches of unbleached muslin and encourage them to experiment using an unusual natural dye at home. They might try boiling the following things in water: onion skins, leaves, flowers, vegetables, or bark from trees. A few tablespoons of alum added to the boiling water will make the dye more vivid. Have your pupils bring the results to class and share them.

design a pot

It's fun to observe roots as plants grow. Challenge each student to design or construct a container that lets her observe root growth. Our students invented containers such as these

Lift the flap and see the roots. Plastic wrap holds dirt inside.

Just plant in a plastic bag with seeds near sides.

Plastic glass with damp paper toweling holds seeds near sides.

See what your kids can come up with.

pudding creations

Ask your students to help bring in the ingredients for a pudding, including instant pudding, milk, paper cups, and plastic spoons. Have each child bring at least one interesting, tasty ingredient to add to the pudding. They might make such choices as raisins, nuts, vanilla, sprinkles, coconut, marshmallows, or various fruits. Let kids make individual servings of instant pudding in paper cups. Have each child add at least one new ingredient to make his pudding special and unusual.

add-on bulletin board

There's no need for you to make every bulletin board. Children can learn a lot from becoming involved. Let children make an "add-on" bulletin board. Have them illustrate their facts in a unique way that helps to convey the idea. For example, they might write plant facts on leaves, facts about the human body on cutouts of bones, or mechanical facts on a picture of a machine.

environmental science activities

crystal pictures

Let your students make pretty, sparkly crystal pictures. Have them draw with heavy crayon strokes onto dark-colored construction paper. Then dissolve as much table salt, alum, or epsom salt as they can in hot water. Have students generously dab or "paint" the solution all over the drawings. The crayon marks will "resist" the solution. Let the pictures dry. Crystals will form as the water evaporates.

draft meter

In winter time, try some individual research with draft meters. They're easy to make with a 20 x 20 cm (8 inch) square of plastic wrap taped to a straw.

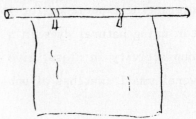

Have children take home their draft meters and list all the places they detected drafts. Children might predict where they will find the strongest drafts and why.

more add-ons

After a general "add-on" bulletin board for science, try a more specific theme. You might have children research and add on facts about such topics as "How Animals Adapt to Their Surroundings," "The Solar System," or "Dinosaurs."

physical science activities

power boats

We know that we can make simple boats that move on their own power by applying various science concepts. For example, one can make "air" boats by applying the concept that air exerts force. When one applies the concept that stored energy can be released, he can make a paddle boat move by winding the paddle with a rubber band. By placing soap on the end of a flat styrofoam boat, one can break the surface tension of the water and make the boat move through the water. Make these three different types of boats in class with your children. Then encourage each child to design his own boat by applying a specific science concept.

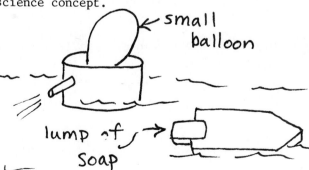

small balloon

lump of soap

machines help us

You can provide children with a vivid example of the advantages of machines. Have them take turns transferring sand from a sand box to a small wading pool. After they've gone back and forth with several loads, ask each child to make a list of ways to move the sand more easily. Discuss the items on the list and categorize them. Some categories will probably involve hand machines; others will include mechanical devices; still others may use cooperative procedures, such as assembly lines or bucket brigades.

shell boats

When children make shell boats, they can learn a lot about floating and sinking, balance, and propulsion devices. Provide a variety of empty nut shell halves, small bits of cloth, wire toothpicks, straws, pieces of modeling clay, and paper clips. Have children design little boats, test them for seaworthiness, and make them move in the water.

A small lump of modeling clay holds oars or sail in place.

Divergent SCIENCE Activities

for individual students to do on their own

Nature's Symmetry

Find at least three objects in nature that have the quality of balance or symmetry. You might find things such as leaves, pine cones, or nests. Share your findings.

Biological Science

Fingerprint Designs

Make some fingerprints on a piece of paper. Draw little lines and features to turn them into neat original designs. Try to make designs that no one else would think of.

Biological Science

Pet Poems

Observe a classroom pet for several days. Instead of writing a report, write a poem about what all you saw. Draw a picture to go with your poem.

Biological Science

Careful Look

Carefully observe your face in the mirror. Find 3 things about your face you never noticed before. What is one feature about your face that pleases you? Name some things you would change. How would you change them?

Biological Science

Scent Test

People's noses have about 5 million cells that sense smell. Dogs' noses have 125-300 million cells! Plan an experiment to test a dog's sensitive nose and compare it to your own.

Biological Science

An Insect's Point of View

"Adopt" an insect such as an ant, a beetle, or a fly. Observe the insect for fifteen minutes. Try to find answers to questions such as these: Where does it live? How far does it travel during the time you observed it? How does it handle obstacles such as bushes, rocks, and trees? Does it seem sensitive to light or sound?

Tell a story from your insect's point of view. In your story include details about some of the interesting things you observed. Add some pictures.

Biological Science

Animal Senses

Choose a creature such as a bird, cat, earthworm, or fish. Plan a few tests for your creature to try to find out which of its senses are more highly organized.

Biological Science

If I Were A Worm....

Imagine that you are a creature or a plant. Write a story that begins "If I were a worm ..." or "If I were a cornstalk... "

Biological Science

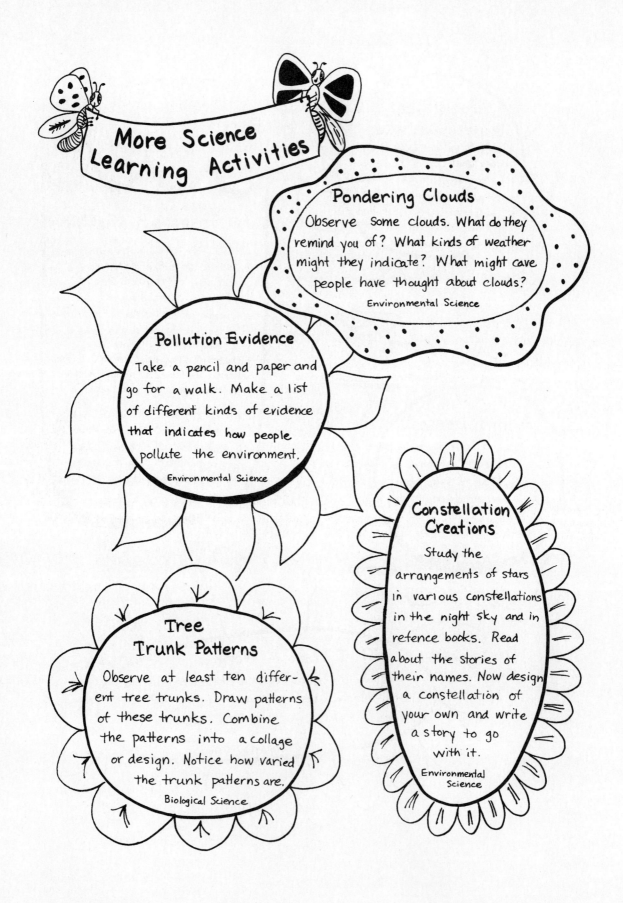

More Science Learning Activities

Pondering Clouds

Observe some clouds. What do they remind you of? What kinds of weather might they indicate? What might cave people have thought about clouds?

Environmental Science

Pollution Evidence

Take a pencil and paper and go for a walk. Make a list of different kinds of evidence that indicates how people pollute the environment.

Environmental Science

Constellation Creations

Study the arrangements of stars in various constellations in the night sky and in refence books. Read about the stories of their names. Now design a constellation of your own and write a story to go with it.

Environmental Science

Tree Trunk Patterns

Observe at least ten different tree trunks. Draw patterns of these trunks. Combine the patterns into a collage or design. Notice how varied the trunk patterns are.

Biological Science

Planets Beyond Pluto

Is there a planet beyond Pluto? How might scientists find out about another planet in our solar system? What would a planet beyond Pluto be like? Draw or write some answers to these questions.

Enviromental Science

Parachute Designs

Design at least two kinds of parachutes. You might use cloth or paper, yarn or string, and different kinds of weights on the bottom. Predict how they will fall. See how their design affects their fall.

Physical Science

Noisy Pictures

Collect newspaper and magazine pictures that show things that make sounds. Show the pictures to your class and imitate their sounds. For variety, add some pictures of silent things.

Physical Science

Paper Clip Perusals

How many different ways could you use a paper clip? Take just 60 seconds and write down all the uses you can think of. Now, in just one minute, write down all the uses you can for a piece of string or a cardboard box.

Science Processes

Building Your MIND POWER

Now that you've examined and tried some divergent thinking activities with large and small groups and with individual children, test your own expertise. Build your divergent thinking power by designing science activities based on the following suggestions. Decide on a schedule for carrying out the activities you have designed. You may choose to do one each day for the next week with your students, or you may want to do one each week for the next six weeks.

1. Create your own kitchen chemistry. Think of some science lessons you could teach using ingredients or equipment from the kitchen.

2. Handicapped children need to be included in your science classes. Create a hypothetical handicapped child--one with any problem you choose. Take one science unit and plan a way to actively involve the child in your unit. Plan at least five direct steps you might take to help your handicapped child receive the greatest benefit from the unit. Be specific in your plans. Don't forget to take advantage of the child's peers as helpers.

3. Do you remember a science topic that you particularly enjoyed as a child in elementary school? Since you liked it so much, you could probably make it interesting to your students. Think of some ways to modify this topic to inspire divergent thinking in your pupils.

4. Find a unique way to help children become better acquainted with concepts related to water.

5. Design a shoebox science kit to add to your science center. Decide on a concept you need to teach or reinforce. Place all the equipment that will be needed in the shoebox. Add appropriate directions and you're all ready to go!

6. Brainstorm a list of resource persons to enrich your health class. Besides the doctor, nurse, or dental hygienist, you might include a high school athlete to talk about body conditioning or your cafeteria manager to expound on meal planning. What other unusual resource persons can you add to your

list? This semester, invite one person from your list to your health class.
Next semester, get out your list and draw on the expertise of another
resource person.

7. Decide on something new, different, and divergent to do on your next nature
   walk.

8. Children use their senses of sight and hearing almost constantly in school.
   In this chapter we have suggested several cooking experiences in which
   children use their sense of taste. Now here's your next challenge. Plan and
   carry out something unusual to encourage children to use their sense of touch
   or smell.

9. What science concepts could you teach around a mud puddle? Plan some specific
   observations or investigations to use the next time a puddle is available.

10. You have planned a nature walk, but alas, it is raining! Not many of your
    students have the proper rain gear to use outdoors. What can you do inside
    for the next 45 minutes? Plan some new and exciting science-related activi-
    ties. Use them at the next available opportunity.

Social Studies

Culture Study

Think of another culture that has intrigued you. Plan and pursue ways to learn more about that culture. For example, you might interview someone, read a book, or try a new recipe.

Bartering

Bartering has recently become popular. If bartering seems like a good idea to you, decide what you could barter. What are some things you would want in return?

TRY YOUR LUCK GETTING
AROUND THE BASES
WITH DIVERGENT THINKING!

Influences on Art

Study an artist who lived during another period of history. How do you think the way of life influenced his or her art? How might the art be different if the artist lived today?

Public Works Jobs

Public works jobs may be one substitute for the welfare system. What are some useful public works jobs that could be created?

7 SOCIAL STUDIES

In the social sciences we study people and the ways they interact with each other and the environment. We live the social sciences every day. As we come together in a classroom, meet with our friends at a party, gather as a family, or worship in church, we are involved in the social sciences. When we dress to fit the weather and the occasion, plan a budget, listen to the news, or relate current experiences to historical events, we live the social sciences.

Why should we teach the social sciences to children? The reasons are many. We need to help children develop an understanding of cooperative group living. This understanding involves helping children learn to appreciate and respect the rights and property of others, to develop feelings of honesty and courtesy, to practice effective group work, and to cultivate a sense of responsibility. Once learned, these skills help children live harmoniously with others throughout life.

The social studies broaden a child's horizons. These studies provide opportunities for children to work and play with others from different backgrounds, religions, and races. The social sciences open children's eyes to ways of life in other countries, other periods of history, and cultures different from their own. Work in the social studies helps to provide children with flexible attitudes that will help them adjust to the world of the future.

Young children learn the first lessons of social studies in their homes. Social studies learnings broaden in the school, blossom in the neighborhood, and spread in the community. These learnings further expand into understandings of the state, region, nation, and world. Social studies can help children to learn to deal effectively with life's problems whether they involve situations in the classroom, in the nation's capitol, or across the world.

The social sciences encompass many areas. Sociology and anthropology, for example, interrelate. In sociology we explore human relationships in different settings, while in anthropology we study people's customs and their cultures. Art, music, and literature in the humanities are also a part of social studies because each of these areas depicts people and their relationships with others and the environment.

History, political science, and geography are also important facets of the social sciences. History is the study of life and relationships of people in the past, while political science is the examination of governing bodies and their structures. Geography provides a setting in which to explore history and political science because geography relates to the study of land, weather, resources, and the ways these elements influence people and society in general.

Economics and career education complete the spectrum of the social sciences. Both deal with production and exchange of goods and services. In economics, the emphasis is on the goods and services themselves, while in career education, we focus on the jobs that produce the goods and services.

We have just explored some aspects of the social sciences. Now let's examine several of the skills that are involved as we acquire an understanding of the social sciences. These skills fall into two broad areas: academic skills and social skills.

One of the first tasks that a student faces is that of learning how to acquire knowledge and information. Students need to learn how to refine their study skills. Social studies provides a context in which students can practice essential study skills. As they deal with social studies content, students develop inquiry skills. They learn to deal with information by categorizing and interpreting what they have read or heard. By picking out the main points and learning to list relevant details in their order of importance, students learn to outline and organize. The ultimate goal of these study skills is for students to learn to apply and evaluate information they have learned.

A variety of references are available to help students acquire social studies information. Traditional resources include books, magazines, encyclopedias, maps, globes, and charts. Students can also learn a great deal from pictures, filmstrips, films, television, and computers. Teachers should not forget to make use of relics, the immediate environment, and people in that environment as resources.

After students have utilized available resources to acquire information, they must learn to relate their findings and conclusions to others. Children should practice using many presentational forms. They might share the results of their study by using spoken or written words, pictures, models, dramatic presentations, and many other divergent forms of expression.

Another important area in the social sciences is the development of social skills. Basically, all social skills complement the broad aim of learning to live and work effectively with others. Students must learn to be good leaders and good followers and to move with flexibility from one role to the other. They need to learn to work harmoniously in groups and to resolve differences agreeably. This skill involves learning how and when to subjugate one's own desires for those of the group.

Communication skills are necessary social skills. Children need opportunities to practice and refine speaking with clarity. Many people do not know how to listen. Adults need to actively focus on training children to be good listeners. Interviewing is a skill especially pertinent in the social sciences because children can learn so much when they interview others. Students practice both speaking and listening skills when they conduct interviews.

As they work together and communicate, children develop respect and appreciation for the rights and property of others. Cooperative activity should foster concern for the feelings of other people. In a social setting, children should develop an appreciation and understanding for rules, and ultimately for the system of government under which they live.

The social sciences provide many opportunities for divergent thinking. The activities in the following section encompass a wide range of areas. They will help you broaden your view of the social sciences from a mere study of history and geography to topics such as career education, anthropology, and economics. Some of these activities will add spice to your classroom discussions; others will involve your students in hands-on project work. Through involvement in these activities, students can learn valuable lessons related to the social sciences. Students can practice and refine research skills, develop valuable social skills, and gain insight into cultures and customs different from their own.

sociology and anthropology

rules, rules, rules

Rules help us keep order in societal units such as the family, classroom, or nation. Conduct a discussion about rules and work in some divergent thinking situations. You might ask your students what they like and do not like about rules. These thoughts might generate a lively discussion. Make up some classroom rules. Evaluate these rules after a trial period of several weeks. Complement your discussion of current rules with a study of rules and laws in the past. Have groups of students research topics such as conduct and punishment in the colonial classroom, laws in prerevolutionary France, or justice in ancient Egypt. Discuss divergently such topics as the strengths and weaknesses of rules and laws of the past, changes in thinking about the roles of rule enforcers, and rules that modern life necessitates. Culminate the discussion with speculation about rules and laws that will be necessary in the future.

working together

A productive discussion at almost any level can be held about the ways in which people cooperate. Have your class generate a list of appropriate cooperative behaviors for the family, classroom, community, or other social settings. Discuss specific ways these behaviors might be carried out. Have students suppose that each of them is seeking a partner for class (or for a business enterprise). Discuss qualities one would value in an effective partnership. Explore the students' perceptions of good leaders and good followers. If you make notes of the main points of the discussion, you can use these later to plan and evaluate effective classwork by partners.

arty artifacts

Examine artifacts such as coins, articles of clothing, pieces of art, or other souvenirs from different countries or cultures. Make a list of words to describe each artifact. Create a poem--possibly a haiku--about each article.

secret buddies

Because of its mysterious atmosphere, working with secret buddies in a classroom can become quite motivating. This activity is full of social value, and it can be very useful for developing divergent thinking skills. Let each student draw a name of a child to be her secret buddy for the week. Encourage class members to discuss different thoughtful things they could do to help or surprise their secret buddies. Make a long list from their suggestions and add to it from time to time. Now each child must plan covert ways to be helpful to her secret buddy without revealing her identity. At the end of the week, encourage the children to guess who they think their secret buddy is and to thank their secret buddy. Ask your class questions such as, What are some of the different things you found to do for your secret buddy? How did it make you feel? Did you think that someone else was your secret buddy when she was not? What happened to make you think so?

more consequences

Discuss all the possible consequences of events such as the following: Students no longer attend schools. The United States turns communist. There is a twenty-year drought. The apple crop completely fails this year. Draw conclusions and discuss implications.

"roots"

On a large map, mark all the countries that represent the ancestral backgrounds of students. Talk about customs associated with different families. Draw inferences. Perhaps the class is really a "melting pot" of different cultures. Perhaps a Latin American or northern European culture predominates.

blindfold walk

Trusting others and being a trustworthy person are attributes that make us better people. Lead your class in a discussion on trusting others and being a person worthy of trust. Follow your discussion with a blindfold walk. Divide your children into pairs with one child in each pair blindfolded and the other child acting as guide. The guide must lead the blindfolded partner on a walk twice. The first time the guide directs the partner without a word, using only touch for guidance. On the second trip the guide directs verbally, avoiding leading the partner by touch. Now each pair reverses roles and follows the same procedure.

After the blindfold walk, gather your students and ask questions such as these. On which walk did you feel most secure? Why? What techniques did your partner use that you found very helpful? At what point on your walk did you feel afraid? As a leader, what problems did you encounter? How did this walk require a great amount of trust on your part? In what specific incidences did you have to be diligent to be trustworthy? What are some feelings a blind person might have if he had to spend the rest of his life depending on others for locomotion? What particular problems might he encounter? How might he compensate for a lack of sight?

consequences

Choose a social system, such as the school, family, or community. List or picture its interdependent parts. Fourth graders might produce a diagram like this.

Now have children suggest situations and speculate about their effects on the social system. They might deal with situations such as: What if a family member was too sick to do the usual jobs for six months? What if the family budget was cut in half? What if the house burned down? Discuss consequences and possible solutions to problem situations.

hot springs cooking and bathing

Near the town of Rotorua on North Island in New Zealand, the Maoris use the hot springs for outdoor cooking. They put their food in pans which are placed in small vats of steaming hot water. Encourage your students to discuss how this method of cooking is different from the way we cook. Ask them to think of ways this type of cooking is similar to their own. The Maoris of Rotorua also take their baths in outdoor tubs of water fed by hot springs. The tubs are located in "outhouses" for a certain degree of privacy. Elicit questions from your students related to hot springs bathing. Remember children can refine their divergent thinking skills by asking good questions.

conserve, conserve, conserve

Choose a topic such as conservation of gasoline, electricity, or dealing with noise pollution. Brainstorm ideas for solving the problem. Have students study the topic using resources such as books, pamphlets from conservation groups, or the Environmental Protection Agency, or materials from businesses or service agencies. Add to the ideas from the initial brainstorming session. Finally, challenge each student to choose at least one "solution" and try to carry it out for a week. Encourage them to report on results, feelings about the effectiveness of each solution, and ideas for future conservation.

life in a different environment

Our daily activities would change slightly or drastically if we were transported to another setting or a different period of history. Choose a setting or time you are studying in geography or history. Let children discuss all the things that might be different if they lived in a setting such as London, England, a space satellite, a rural village in the Andes, or in Cairo, Egypt. After the discussion, have each child write and illustrate a story about life in the different environment.

family mementos

Ask a few children at a time to bring in one small object that reminds them of home. They may bring things such as a used birthday card, a grocery list, a picture of their dog, a swatch of cloth, or a package of seeds. After they have shared their objects and discussed why these objects remind them of home, have them make a group collage by pinning or gluing their family mementos to a large piece of paper.

the great time machine

Cast your students in a scene such as the one that follows: Choose three people to play the roles of peasants who lived in the Middle Ages. The rest of the class will be characters who live in current times. A great time machine has lifted the peasants out of the Middle Ages and has thrust them right into the twentieth century. Get your "characters" started in a dialogue that would be interesting and enlightening to both groups. Encourage them to find out as much as possible about each other and the period in which they live. When the conversation lags, you might need to contribute an idea or two to extend it. This particular activity would be fun to use as a review for a unit in history or geography. Adapt your characters to fit your unit.

travel memories

Children can learn many interesting bits of information from hearing about their friends' travel experiences. Encourage students to choose the most interesting place they have visited. Have them point out this location on the map. Ask them to tell what they saw that could not be found at home. Encourage them to relate what they liked best about the locale and what they liked least. Your students will suggest other topics for discussion.

living style of eskimos

Eskimos have adapted their life styles to fit the extremely cold climate in which they live. They used to live in ice homes—igloos made of ice and canvas and covered with ice to keep out the wind. Ask your class how they think the extremely cold climate in which the Eskimos live might affect their life style. Encourage them to ponder questions such as the ones that follow. What could you do if you lived in this cold climate that you could not do at home? What do you do at home that you might be unable to do if you lived with the Eskimos? How would you keep warm? Where would you get your food? How might daily routines, such as bathing, be different?

a city under the sea

We are living in a period of rapid change. Even now, scientists and city planners are developing innovative ideas for the cities of the future. Present this situation to your class: Suppose in the future you lived in an underwater city. Tell all of the ways that life would be different from life on land. What might some of your problems be? How would you solve them?

wood carriers in Ethiopia

Here's another anthropological topic that might evoke some divergent thinking. In Ethiopia women carry wood on their backs; goats carry wood on their sides; men never carry wood. How might these customs have developed? Do we have any customs in our country that are similar? How else might people carry wood?

history, geography, and political science

now and then

After study of a different historical period, challenge your students to focus on one aspect of life in that period. Make a chart similar to the ones below and record as many comparisons as possible.

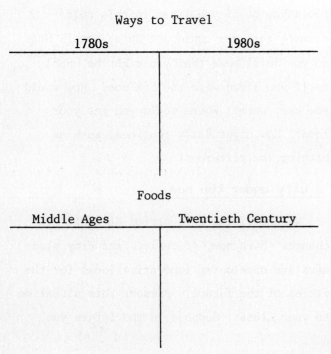

Ways to Travel

1780s	1980s

Foods

Middle Ages	Twentieth Century

solving mysteries from the cemetery

The cemetery can become a very unique and divergent resource for helping children learn to make inferences. Take your class to the cemetery. Divide them into pairs. Have the class research the entire cemetery, each pair being responsible for the collection of information from the tombstones in a small area of the cemetery. Help the group fit their information together to see what they can find out about the history of the town.

Some of the information that kids discover from their research might be family names that are prominent in the town, family relations and sizes, nationalities, and occupations. In some cemeteries you might find certain years in which many people died or periods when there was a high infant mortality rate. These irregular clues will call for further research to help solve the mystery behind the deaths.

history of my name

Ask students to share the history of their names. Some may know what their names mean and who or what they were named after. Others may need to research the history of their names by consulting family members or reference books. Ask students to suppose they must give themselves a new surname or given name. The new name must relate to their family heritage in some way. Let students tell what name they might choose and why they would choose it.

changes

In a classroom discussion ask children, How do things change? How can you tell? Encourage your pupils to pursue ideas related to change in many areas, such as people, buildings, places, and policies.

Take a walk with your students. Ask them to observe and record changes they notice during their walk. On another day, lead students in a discussion of changes that have taken place in the class during the last year. They may wish to follow this discussion by recording changes that have taken place in each of their families during the last year.

A classroom study on change should make clear that some changes are good and some are not so good, and that all changes demand a degree of flexibility on our part. Children might wish to discuss problems that they have encountered with certain changes and ways they have had to be flexible. Other students might contribute suggestions to problems yet unsolved.

who am I?

Have individuals or pairs of students research facts about famous persons you are studying. They might find out about the lives and accomplishments of famous inven-

tors, explorers, or politicians. Let the class play "Twenty Questions," asking the "researchers" questions and trying to guess the famous person based on the answers to the twenty questions.

economics and career education

family economy

Adults should plan many opportunities to cultivate children's understanding of economics. Even young children can contribute good ideas for family economy. Ask your class questions such as, What are some ways you could earn money to supplement your family economy? What changes could you make to help you save more money from your allowance? Suggest three realistic ways your family could save money. Encourage each child to plan and carry out a money earning project for one month. Ask them to report on their project at the end of the month answering questions such as the following: How much time did you spend working during the month? How much money did you earn? How much did you save? Did you use any of your earnings for your family? If so, how?

label search

Intelligent consumers are usually good readers of labels. Make a list of the kinds of information that students think might be found on labels and boxes of different products. They might suggest nutritional value, caloric information, and recipes on food containers. For clothes labels, students might expect to find information about fiber content and care instructions. Have each student bring in a product or two. Examine the labels, adding information to the list. Categorize the kinds of information found on labels and boxes.

truck collage

Trucks come in many sizes and shapes, and they serve a wide variety of purposes. Have children cut pictures of trucks from magazines, and ask them to draw as many different types of trucks as they can think of. Encourage them to "stretch their minds" and to think of unique types of trucks. They might consider such trucks as cement mixers, mail trucks, book mobiles, milk trucks, moving vans, and florist trucks. Have kids label their trucks and glue them on a big sheet of paper to make a large group truck collage. Lead the group into a discussion of the trucks in their collage and the services performed by the people who drive those trucks. Ask questions such as the following: How would our lives be different if we didn't have the services provided by this truck? What type of things would you do if you drove that truck? Which truck would you prefer to drive? Why?

bartering

To dramatically illustrate both concepts of interdependence and bartering, try this activity. Divide the class into five groups. Set up samples of or instructions for the following five projects: making popcorn and putting it in bags, wrapping trinkets brought in by students for exchange, dramatizing a story using simple props and wigs, making a classroom "post office" from a large box with dividers, and making fancy gift tags for the trinkets. Pass out materials to each group, but give each set of materials to the wrong group. For example, give out the following:

Group 1 (the popcorn group)—trinkets, pens, yarn, dramatic props

Group 2 (the gift wrap group)—popcorn, construction paper, story for dramatization

Group 3 (the drama group)—corn popper, funny papers for gift wrap, tape, crayons

Group 4 (the post office group)—small paper bags, pens, salad oil, glue

Group 5 (the tags group)—large box and dividers, wigs, yarn

Now the challenge! Each group must barter for the materials they need to complete their project without oral communication. After the bartering period have children carry out their projects and share the results. Discuss and analyze the bartering process. Talk about problems children encountered in bartering without speaking and different ways they found to communicate. Extend the discussion by talking about ways that bartering is valuable in everyday life.

old and new jobs

Many jobs from the past have become obsolete or involve far fewer people than they once did. For example, we now have few linotype operators, shepherds, or valets. With your students, extend the list of "old" jobs. Now speculate about some modern jobs that may become obsolete and some of the reasons why. For example, bus drivers may eventually be replaced by computerized space vehicles driven without human help. Dentists may no longer be needed when all tooth decay is prevented. Farmers may decline in number as food production becomes more automated and as synthetic foods are invented. Work with your young futurists to deliberate about occupations in the years to come.

search the classified ads

Use the classified ads from the newspaper and the yellow pages of the telephone book for an informative look at jobs and services. Have your students work on activities such as the following: classify the ads different ways; pose questions such as, where can one buy new tires? Find the answers to problems such as the following: figure out which jobs seem to be most in demand; find out about jobs you weren't aware of; see which jobs require experience and which ones will provide on-the-job training.

ENCOURAGING DIVERGENT THINKING WITH SMALL GROUP ACTIVITIES IN THE SOCIAL SCIENCES

Working together in small groups is especially important in the social sciences. Students build valuable social skills as they work together. Small group work helps children learn to plan as a group and carry out projects. In the giving and taking process, they learn to accept and appreciate others' thoughts and ways of doing things. As students work in small groups, they develop skills for becoming effective leaders and good followers. Teachers should encourage pupils to evaluate how well they have worked together.

In this section you will find both teacher-directed activities and activities addressed specifically to children. Remember to be flexible, and adjust the activities to fit your classroom needs.

history, geography, and political science

local folklore

Help your students work in small groups and plan projects in which they research local folklore or history. Some of the projects may include endeavors such as tracing the changes in a certain city block over a hundred-year period, finding out about local home remedies, discussing with "old timers" what life was like at the beginning of the century, or tracing the roots of families who have lived in the area for a long time. Encourage your pupils to pursue a variety of resources, such as the library, public records, and interviews. Have each group culminate its project by presenting its findings in an interesting way.

classroom calendar

Compiling a classroom calendar has several learning values. Not only does this activity help children develop a sense of time and its relationships, but it also teaches children to synthesize and to extract the important events from the whole.

Divide your class into small groups, with each group keeping a classroom calendar for a month. Give each group a large sheet of paper and let them make and decorate a calendar for the month, leaving big blocks for each day of the month. At the end of the day, remind the groups to record the important events of the day on their calendars. At the end of the month, your class might enjoy seeing each of the calendars and comparing the events that each group considered important. Students might then choose the most important events of the whole month.

imaginary trips

Encourage small groups of students to schedule imaginary trips, plotting on a map their courses of travel and specifying how many miles they will travel, and at what locations they will stop each day. Have them determine their means of transportation and their expenses for their trips. The students should plan the places of interest they will see, research each particular point of interest, and decide how long they will stay in each place. Suggest that your children probe into the special foods that are

unique to those particular areas. They might wish to plan appropriate gifts from the region to bring back to friends. Supply a variety of maps, travel brochures, and books to help them formulate plans for their trips.

antique fantasy

Bring an antique or relic to class. Discuss the period to which this relic belonged and display several books related to that period in history. Be sure to include a good antique encyclopedia. Now encourage small groups of children to compose stories in which they tell about the family to which that particular relic belonged, the family's customs during that time, and the ways the family used that relic. Urge them to be imaginative and fanciful in their story but to base their fantasy story on true facts about the period.

passports

Have a group of students find out information about passports. They can research how to get a passport, when and where a passport is needed, and what a passport looks like. Have another group make passports for the class. All students can fill in the blanks and add pictures and signatures. In your next unit on another country, let students "enter" the country by showing their passports.

maps, maps, maps

Extend students' map skills by having them make maps or scale models of familiar but unusual places. Perhaps they could recreate their rooms at home, their dresser tops, or the hallway at school.

more mapping and modeling

Have a group of students make a table top map or model of an ideal setting. It would be interesting to challenge them to create the perfect classroom, an ideal shopping or entertainment center, or their idea of a utopian future space colony. They might also create an undersea world or planetary surface, and add human and animal figures. This exercise encourages students to use critical and creative thinking as well as map and math skills.

sociology
and anthropology

holidays in foreign countries

Christmas is a holiday celebrated in a variety of ways in many countries all over the world. The United States celebrates the unique holiday of the Fourth of July when fireworks are set off. In England on May Day children collect flowers still heavy with dew then they dance around a maypole. Have small groups of children select and research an unusual holiday in a foreign country. Let them plan a celebration for their classmates based on this holiday.

comparative family studies

Select two children in your class and let your students do a comparative study on the families of these two pupils. Encourage your students to ask questions to find out ways the two families are alike and customs and practices that make the two families different. Record findings on a chart.

Likenesses		Differences	
Family Members	2 brothers, mom, dad	Recreation	Joe's camping / Luke's movies, TV
Discipline	Dad in charge	Favorite Meal	tacos / hamburgers
Allowance	$2.50	Family Jobs	mom-secretary dad-electrician brother-bus boy / mom-parttime programmer dad-surveyor
Work	dishes, sweeping make beds		

After children have made a comparative family study as a large group project, divide the class into pairs and have each pair make a comparative family study with a partner. Have each pair record their findings on a chart. Display the charts for the other class members to observe.

helping the handicapped

Social skills can be put into action in dealing with handicapped persons. Ask groups of students to plan how they might help a specific handicapped person and make that person feel welcome and accepted. This exercise might be especially valuable just before a handicapped student is to be mainstreamed into the class. Have groups share and critique others' ideas.

games around the world

Have groups of students find out more about different games that are played around the world. Have each group follow up by making up a new game, using equipment or rules that they have read about. Let each group have time—perhaps each on a different day—to explain their games, then to involve everyone in playing the game.

information bank

Let groups of students use sources such as a community calendar, almanac, newspaper, city map, or telephone book to find out more about their communities. Have the class devise questions such as

- What is the average temperature in our city in January?

- How far is the corner of West 7th and Green from our school?

- What's playing at the movies?

- Will we be able to see the moon on the night of November 18?

- Who delivers pizza?

Now have groups of students use the sources to answer the questions.

economics
and career education

improving community operations

A visit to the fire department, police station, or the mayor's office can become an inspiration for some responsible community planning. After a field trip of this sort, have your class work in small groups and plan a unique way to improve the operations of the place they visited.

ways public servants protect us

Have your class work in small groups to research and enumerate various ways they are protected by public servants. Each group should choose a different public servant to investigate. They may choose sanitation workers, health workers, police officers, firefighters, or any others they can think

of. Encourage each group to present its information in a unique way, such as discussions, written reports, chalk board presentations, or murals.

assembly line

Help students understand an assembly line by having them work on one. You might make party favors, little model cars, or tray decorations for an old people's home. Let groups of five or six students plan different jobs, appoint a boss or quality control person, and go to work! When the jobs are finished, discuss the advantages and disadvantages of working on an assembly line.

more "ads"

Students can study the ways the news media influences people to vote. Have different groups choose different advertising techniques, such as snob appeal, "plain folks" approach, or appeal to "rational" thinking. Study the media at an election time and find instances where the advertising techniques are used. Extend the use of the techniques further by designing campaign buttons, slogans, banners, TV ads, and other political paraphernalia for a chosen candidate.

yellow pages

The Yellow Pages of the phone book offer a wealth of information to consumers. Obtain Yellow Pages from phone books of two communities of different sizes. Let groups of students study the Yellow Pages and make many comparisons about the number and kinds of goods and services that are available. Follow up with our Yellow Pages math activity on page 68.

TIME CAPSULE

1500 1550 1600 1650 1700 1750 1800 1850 1900 1950 2000 2050 3000

Suppose you dug up a box that had all sorts of interesting objects that dated back to the early 1800's. This box or time capsule could tell you a lot about the way life was at that time. Make a time capsule for someone in the future to find. Put objects that represent the present time in a bottle, shoebox, or plastic bag. You might wish to add things such as a favorite toy, a popular phonograph record, pictures of the way you look and the way you travel. Write a message and put it inside. Add the date. Dig a hole and bury your time capsule in the ground.

After studying a particular state or country, design a new flag for it. Each part of the pattern must be based upon the country's history or some other information about the country. For instance, you might choose to represent the country's products, its famous people or its interesting places in the design.

JOB RESEARCH

Choose two people who work at two different jobs or professions.

With a partner, list all the ways you can think of that the people's jobs are alike and different.

Find out more about the people's jobs. Maybe you could interview them.

Add likenesses and differences to your list.

Electrician   *Computer Programmer*

Both work with electrical devices
Both use diagrams in their work
The electrician fixes things but the programmer has to have someone else fix her machine.
The electrician goes out to work. The programmer works in an office.

TRAFFIC SYMBOLS →

Work with a group. Create some traffic signs that people all around the world could easily understand.

CURVING ROAD

FASHIONS ... of the Past

- Look in old newspapers, magazines, encyclopedias, or books to find pictures of fashions of the past.

- Discuss with your group the ways these fashions are different from today's fashions. How are they alike?

- Display some of your findings in a unique way to share with your class.

QUESTIONS ... ANSWERS ... QUESTIONS ... ANSWERS ... QUESTIONS

With a group, study a picture from <u>National Geographic</u> or <u>National Geographic World</u>. List all the details you can notice. Think of lots of questions about the picture. Now read the article and see which of your questions are answered. What things did you notice that the article did not even mention? What unanswered questions do you have?

Fairy Tale MAP

Make a map based on a story such as
Hansel and Gretel, Sleeping Beauty, or Little
Red Riding Hood. On your fairy tale map
trace the paths of travel of the main
characters in the story. See how unique and
interesting you can make your map. You
might wish to add unusual touches such as
mounting twigs in clay 🌱🌱 or making
milk carton houses for your map. 🏠

Luxuries . . . . Necessities

Cut pictures of lots of different products and
services from newspaper, magazines, or catalogs.
Talk about the products or the services. Decide if
they are luxuries or necessities. Glue them to
a poster or a large paper in the appropriate categories.

ALIKE   DIFFERENT

Look in a mirror with a classmate. Make a list of all the things you notice that are alike about the two of you. What things are different? Add to the list.

more Alike and Different

After you have thought about the problem above, try this one:

Do you know some things that are alike and different that you can't see in the mirror?

In this section you will find lots of ideas to extend and deepen children's understanding and interpretation of social studies concepts. You will want to choose some way for individuals to report and share the results of their work. Children learn a great deal from being exposed to the ideas of others. Since divergent thinking activities produce a wide range of ideas and ways of expressing them, children will encounter new thoughts that they have never been exposed to before. Upon these new ideas they will be able to build their own divergent thinking skills. The first part of this section features activities for you to use with individual children. In the second part the children are on their own; let them use the ideas introduced here independently.

history, geography, and political science

tasting party

Organize a tasting party. Ask each child to bring a food that reflects his national or ethnic origin. As students sample them, have each tell about the traditions of their food.

origins of household products

Have pupils speculate on how many countries would be represented if they chose 10 products from their closets, medicine cabinets, or pantry shelves. Now have pupils actually look at labels on 10 household products and find where they were made. Mark the origins of the products on a large map. Have pupils make generalizations about the places their different products came from. Are most foods from the United States? Why? Where are most items of clothing manufactured? Why?

time line

Demonstrate how students can make and display a time line representing the important events in their lives. Urge each one to make his time line in a unique way. Here

are some ideas for starters. Use clothespins and a clothesline or a fence and pin each important event in the right order on a clothesline.

Make a time line with adding machine tape, toilet tissue, masking tape on the sidewalk, or rocks on steps.

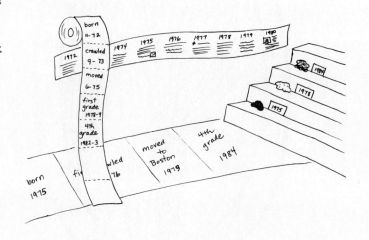

Children's time lines might make an interesting display for Parent's Day.

the good old days

Suggest that each child interview his grandparents or some other older person to find out what they did when they were children. Each student might ask questions related to the type of chores his grandparents did, afterschool activities, subjects learned in school, what school was like, clothing, cars, entertainment, or food. After the student conducts his interview, have him compare the "olden days" to the present. Encourage him to mention things that might have been fun and those things that he would not have particularly enjoyed.

historical fiction

After your pupils have finished studying a particular period of history, have each student compose a story set against that historical background.

if i had been that person . . .

Many children enjoy reading biographies of famous people. After a child has read a biography, have her record one or two of the high points in that person's life and tell how she would have reacted in each of those situations. If she had reacted differently, how might it have changed the course of history?

biographic maps

Speaking of biographies, what about making a biographic map? Have a student make a map and trace the famous person's travels on that map from birth until death. The student should draw pictures on the map to mark important dates.

how did it get its name?

Many interesting little tidbits can be found by investigating the historical background of place names. Ask your youngsters to pick the name of a familiar street, a town, or a river and find out how it got its name. Many of these places will be named for trees in that area; some might have Indian names or French names that reveal a characteristic or origin; still others might be named for famous people. After they have traced the names of their chosen places, have them each rename their places. Urge them to tell why they chose the new names.

sociology and anthropology

helping hands

Make a "Helping Hands" display. Have children trace around their hands. Print fingerprints on each finger. Use these methods:

- A stamp pad

- Food color on a damp paper towel

- Rub pencil lead onto paper. Rub fingertips into lead. Now print onto transparent tape. Stick tape to hand shape.

Let children examine and compare their fingerprints. Have each write ways to be helpful on hands. Arrange the hands on a bulletin board.

coats of arms

Make coats of arms or family shields. Let students design shield shapes and divide

them into several categories. Decide on
things the categories
might represent.
Students might use
things they're good
at, things they'd like
to improve, important

possessions, hopes for the future, greatest
accomplishments to date, and so on. Cut
pictures and words from the newspaper and
glue them to sections of the shield. This
activity could be extended to devising a
coat of arms for a person of another culture
or period of history.

checklists

Work with children to devise checklists
about themselves. Part of a list might look
like this:

What do you like to do after school?

☐ eat
☐ talk
☐ play sports
☐ read
☐ do homework

What's your favorite food?

_____

What do you do on Saturday morning?

☐ watch cartoons
☐ shop
☐ do housework
☐ play outdoors
☐ play indoors

The kids will use these checklists to
interview each other and exchange information. Count the number in each category and
graph the results.

feelings book

Encourage children to think about
emotions as they make a "Feelings" booklet.
Cut little squares of aluminum foil to look
like mirrors. Let children draw faces with
crayon on the "mirrors" to show emotions such
as happiness, sadness,
or anger. Encourage
children to write about
each emotion beside the
picture.

happy
Mom baked
a cake

sad
John kicked
me.

it's me!

Have students work in pairs and trace
their outlines on butcher paper or old
computer printout sheets, then have them
search newspapers and magazines for words or
pictures that describe them. Paste the words
and pictures onto the figures.
Students might include
things they like to think
about on the heads, things
they like to eat on the
stomachs, and so on.
Display the large figures
and encourage students to talk about an
item or two that they chose to paste on
their figures. Students can learn much
about themselves and others through this
activity.

A similar activity is to have students
divide each large figure
in two parts and display
positive qualities in
one half and qualities
they'd like to improve
in the other half.

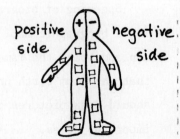

positive side   negative side

rock sociogram

Provide small rocks, paints, yarn, glue, and scrap materials. Encourage each child to decorate a rock to represent herself. Have each pupil initial her rock. Provide a log or a piece of driftwood and some clay for anchoring each rock on the log. Let each student anchor her rock near a friend's rock. The way children arrange their rocks might give you some interesting information about the social preferences of your students.

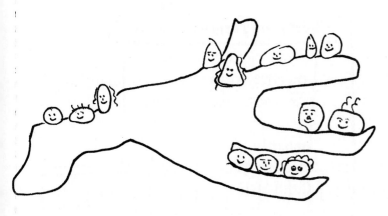

career education

job vocabularies

Different jobs use different vocabularies. Have students interview people with special jobs and find out some new words and their meanings. Compile, explain, and compare lists. For example, children might find these words associated with these jobs.

COMPUTER TECHNICIAN

input	debug
output	terminal
program	CPU

TRUCK DRIVER

route	cargo
CB	18-wheeler
pit stop	

Divergent Social Science Activities for Individual Children To Do On Their Own

Designing Ads

Design an ad for a product to be sold in the year 2000.

Product Investigation

People need to study products before they buy them. Look up a product in Consumer Reports or Penny Power. Study carefully what the report says. Tell which product you would buy and why.

Study the Ads

Find newspaper ads from big stores and small stores. List some similarities and differences of the two ads. Compare prices. Compare the sizes of the ads. Tell what might be good or bad about shopping at a big store or a small store.

Home Work

People do many jobs at home. Make a list of all the work that is done at your home. Interview some family members and add to your list. Tell who does which jobs. Compare lists with others in class.

Working Parents Mural

Draw pictures of your parents at work. Arrange your pictures as part of a class mural on work.

Eye Witness Report

Give an "eye witness" report of a particular event in history that you have been studying. Write about the moments that lead up to the event and people's reactions to it. For example, you might write about the first air flight and events before it. You could tell about your feelings as the plane rose from the ground.

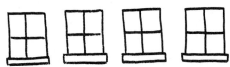

Poems of Slavery

Suppose you were a slave. Compose a poem telling about how you feel working all day in the field or the way you feel when your mother is taken away from you and sold to another master.

Folk Cure-Alls

Folks used to believe that if you tied a frog to your big toe, it would cure the chills and fever. A dirty sock tied around your neck was good for your sore throat. Suppose you were losing your hair. Invent a folk remedy for this problem.

Rain Making Charms

The southern black used to think that you could bring on a good rain by hanging a dead snake on the fence, turning a frog on its back, or sweeping cobwebs out of the house. Create your own rain making charm.

Family Members Working Together

What does each member of your family do to contribute to your family needs? What does your dad do? your mom? In what ways do you help out? List each family member and tell all of the ways they contribute to the family unit. How else might they work and cooperate to help the family?

The Sun In Alaska ☀

the sun is not seen in Barrow, Alaska from late November to late January. From early May to early August the sun does not set. Write a paragraph telling how these occurrences would change your life style.

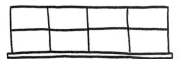

Greeting A Chinese Friend

Pretend you are a student from the U.S. meeting a Chinese student in China for the first time. She asks you to tell what America and the American people are like. What would you tell her?

Thanksgiving

Plan a thanksgiving feast. Make a list of the foods you will prepare and give your reasons for choosing them. Make a long list of things you have to be thankful for.

Grocery Mapping

Go to the grocery store with a parent. Pick out 10 products. Study the labels and find out where they were manufactured. Mark the places on a map at school.

Grocery Helpers

Think about the products you picked at the store. List all the people who helped to make or market those products.

Improving Products

Select one product from the grocery store. Name lots of ways to improve it. You might change its price, flavor, texture, packaging or other things about it.

Buenos Dias

People greet each other differently around the world. Find out some ways people say "hi", "good morning", or "hello" in different countries. Demonstrate these in class.

Sketching Talents

Draw a picture to show things you do really well. Draw another picture of things you wish you did better.

Political Jokes

Cut a picture from a newspaper or news magazine. Turn the picture into a joke by adding captions that are out of character. For example: In a picture of Prince Charles and Princess Diana, have Princess Diana say, "We're having soup tonight, dear. We'll have to eat light until the first of the month."

Family Memorabilia

Ask your parent to lend you a family keepsake. You may wish to search for a family memento in an attic or an old chest. Bring your family memento to class and tell about it. If you can't find a family keepsake, share a family story or tradition with your classmates.

Interviewing Authorities

Interview someone who enforces rules. You might talk to your teacher, principal, parent, a police officer, or a bus driver. Find out which rules are the hardest to enforce and why. Ask what might happen if rules weren't followed. Report your results to the class.

Advertise Your Services

Study some ads for services in the newspaper. Advertise a service that you usually do for family members. Maybe you help with the laundry or take out the trash. Write an ad for the services you provide and post it on the "Services" bulletin board.

Making Maps

Make a map to show friends how to get to your house. Try to show more than one route on your map. Add enough detail to your map so your friends won't get lost.

Budget Planning

Plan a budget based on your allowance. Be sure to set aside money for recreation, for special needs, and for savings.

Family Tree

Find out as much as you can about your relatives. Ask your mom or dad about your grandparents, your aunts and uncles, and your cousins. Use your information to make a family tree in an unusual way. You may draw a picture, make a family tree mobile, create a tree from a real branch mounted in a bucket of sand, or stitch your tree with yarn on fabric. Try your own idea.

Shoe Survey

People wear different shoes for different reasons — for fashion, protection, or warmth. Find out about shoes worn in different places. Invent new shoes. Draw pictures of them and describe their features.

BUILDING YOUR MIND POWER

We hope that encouraging divergent thinking activities with children in social studies has whetted your interest. Now it's time for you to design and carry out your own divergent thinking activities with the students in your class. This section has some suggestions to get you started thinking about some activities that will enrich your social studies curriculum. Work on these ideas and apply them one at a time in your classroom.

1. Observe another teacher conducting a social studies lesson. Take special notice of his presentation techniques, the learning activities, the questions asked, and the student and teacher responses. Now build on this lesson and revise it to incorporate divergent thinking. Use it with your class.

2. Plan and carry out a service project with your pupils. You may organize an endeavor similar to some of the following ones: a clean-up project; some type of service for older people, poor people, or young kids; or a project at the voting polls. Think of your own idea. Be original.

3. In social studies you are not only concerned with teaching content, but you should also focus on getting to know your students better. Brainstorm lots of ways of finding out more about your students. Here are some ideas for starters: reading about your pupils, case studies, observing students, reviewing health records, studying test data, making sociograms, talking to parents, talking to two or three students in your free time, and keeping anecdotal records. Now add some ideas to this list. Apply one or two of these methods to get to know your group better, or use some of your ideas on one or two students who need special attention.

4. Think of some resources that you used in social studies during the last month. Maybe you incorporated books, encyclopedias, filmstrips, and interviews. Brainstorm and make a list of additional resources that you might use. Promise yourself that you will include at least two or three of them during the next month.

5. Plan a field trip to a place you and your students have never been before. Be different. Have you thought of places such as the bank, the florist shop, or the hardware store? I'll bet your town offers some unique possibilities for exploration. Now stretch your mind a little further. Plan some divergent elements into your field trip. This one should be fun!

6. What is a unique and realistic way you could introduce the banking system and saving plans to your students? Don't be shy. Ask the bank for help. Get your students involved. One class we know of made cookies and sold them throughout the year and invested their money in a savings account that earned interest. At the end of the year, they took their savings out of the bank and had a special treat at the ice cream parlour. What is your idea? Try it out.

7. Plan a multisensory social studies lesson using divergent techniques. Does that sound hard? You can do it. Just think of some ways you can conduct a social studies lesson incorporating the sense of touch, taste, smell, hearing, or sight. Be sure to make use of more than one sense and to give your lesson a divergent slant.

8. Discussion is important in social studies. How could you change your room physically, or change your procedures or the classroom atmosphere to promote better, freer discussion with small and large groups? Brainstorm changes you might make. Ask your students to make suggestions. Choose one or two of these ideas and carry them out.

9. Select a social studies topic you don't teach often. For example, maybe you never get your class involved in economics or anthropology. Think of an activity related to the topic you have chosen. Carry out this activity with your students within the next ten days.

10. Suppose one of the children in your class is undergoing a crisis--something that will result in a major change in life style. This crisis could include events such as divorce, death, moving, or a major illness. What are some of they ways you can guide that child and help her cope with her crisis? In your planning don't forget to make use of other students. They could learn a great deal from this situation also.

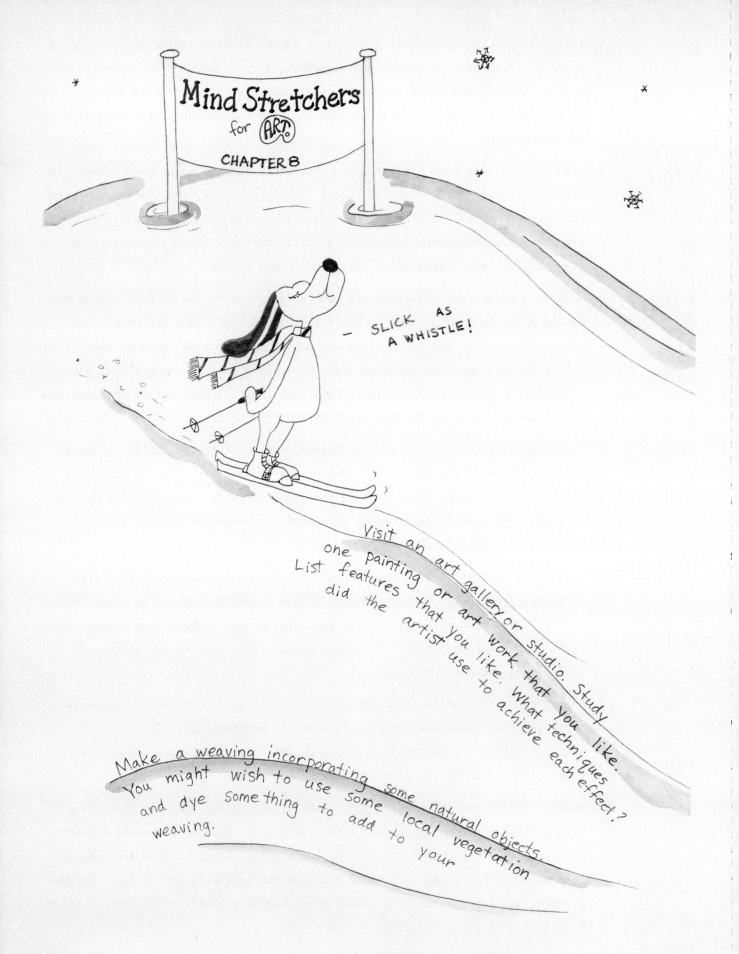

Mind Stretchers
for ART.
CHAPTER 8

— SLICK AS A WHISTLE!

Visit an art gallery or art work that you like. Study
one painting or art work that you like. What techniques
List features that you like. What effect?
did the artist use to achieve each effect?

Make a weaving incorporating some natural objects.
You might wish to use some local vegetation
and dye something to add to your
weaving.

Make a tiny work of art for dinner this week. You might design a special centerpiece or arrange food in an artistic way. Enjoy it!

Think over an art experience you've enjoyed. What gave you pleasure? Why? What art experiences have you wanted to try but never have? What kept you from trying them?

- HUMPH!

Art is perhaps the most inherently creative subject in the school curriculum. When art is taught in an atmosphere of freedom, children can use materials to make original designs and unique products that express their own individuality. Art activities that emphasize divergent thinking ensure that art work is creative—not just copies of someone else's ideas.

Sometimes art in the classroom is carried out in an assembly line manner with teachers giving explicit directions for each step of the art process and with the children's final products looking quite similar. Often art is shunted aside because of the busy classroom schedule and the heavy demands imposed upon classroom teachers. Many classroom teachers rarely use art with their children because it is messy and very time consuming and because extra money is not available for art supplies. When children experience art in an assembly line manner or only on rare occasions, they cannot experience the many benefits that art has to offer.

Art has many values. Children grow intellectually when they become involved in the art process. In art children have the opportunity to explore and solve problems. They search for answers and discover new ways to use materials and to refine methods. As they investigate and clarify their ideas, they find that there is no one right answer to every question. They learn to organize ideas in uncommon ways, thus refining their divergent thinking skills. Lowenfeld (1970, p. 4) states that the art experience is a "constant process of assimilation and projection," with children taking in a great amount of information through their senses, integrating it with their psychological selves, and expressing it in unique ways in forms that please them.

Because art is a sensory experience, it is very valuable in helping children develop perceptual and physical skills. Through art children develop eye-hand coordination, visual discrimination, an understanding of whole-part relationships, the ability to track visually and a recognition and understanding of symbols. All of these skills are basic to learning to read and to write. When children cut, weave, and color with crayons, they develop fine motor skills which are also essential for writing.

When children are involved in group art activities, they grow socially. They often talk and share ideas with one another as they work. They learn that many people have ideas that are different from theirs, that there is no one right way to paint or color a picture, and that each child has a right to her own point of view no matter how different it might be.

Experiences in art have emotional values. Art is a means of nonverbal communication. Through art children are often able to express feelings that they are unable to verbalize. Art provides children meaningful ways to communicate with themselves. The art process helps children to release their feelings. It helps them to develop an understanding of their relation to the world. When they complete successful art projects, children develop a sense of satisfaction and pride, thus building their self-concepts. Art is satisfying because it is a motor task; work with materials can stimulate the senses and relax children. Children often find great joy in the process of manipulating, experimenting, touching, feeling, and exploring art materials.

Art has much carry-over to the leisure time and occupations of adult life. People design original furniture, clothing, and needlework. They draw to decorate, enhance, and personalize all sorts of items including gifts and written materials. Such art endeavors provide adults with emotional satisfaction.

To facilitate a smooth flow with classroom art activities, teachers need to follow some basic guides. They should have an atmosphere of freedom in their classrooms. They should show an interest in children making them feel comfortable and accepted. Teachers need to remember that the emphasis in art should be on the art process, not the final product. The real value in art comes from the experience of exploring, manipulating materials, and creating something new and different.

Teachers need to be careful to make wise comments about children's art products. A great amount of bragging places emphasis on the product rather than the process. Factual comments are often more appropriate than evaluative comments. Encourage children in their art to work to please themselves, not the teacher. Treat each child's art with respect. Not only should teachers show interest in children by commenting on their art, they should also encourage and be responsive to the comments children make about their own art. Adults need to give instruction in skills such as cutting, mixing paints, or folding wherever they see a need. The creative process cannot flow where children are encumbered by a lack of skill. Patterns to copy or ditto sheets and coloring books to color in are inappropriate in a creative art environment. The basic purpose of divergent art activities should be to encourage children to produce their own ideas, not to copy someone else's.

Teachers should recognize and appreciate the stages of art that their children are in. Each child is different from others in the classroom and must be allowed to work on his own level and at his own particular pace. Finally, teachers need to use appropriate motivation to stimulate children to move into the art experience. They need to adequately prepare the materials, present them in a motivating way, and then leave children free to work without someone constantly talking or otherwise interrupting their thoughts.

Teachers can use many different motivational techniques to stimulate children's interest in art. Sometimes the art materials themselves are incentive enough to get children involved. Often just the presence of the teacher at the art table is motivating. Many times teachers can motivate children with verbal discussions that lead into the art experience. Storybooks and picture books or brief excerpts from books often serve as motivation for art. Field trips or various firsthand experiences often serve as catalysts for exciting art experiences. Teachers should make use of reproductions of famous paintings to motivate children. At times demonstrations showing the steps of an art procedure can be motivating.

The goal of art education, according to Lowenfeld (1957, p. 5), is to take children at their level of creativity and to extend their creativity in whatever areas it might be applied. Objectives of art education as set forth by the National Art Education Association[1] are very broad:

1. To develop each student's mastery of simple skills in expressing and realizing ideas in visual form--through familiarity with media that lend themselves to the expression and realization of ideas;

2. To develop in each student a positive self-image, a sense of personal confidence and willingness to deal with visual forms; to assume responsibilities for dealing with visual choices in areas of personal expression and the environment-at-large;

3. To develop in each student empathy and appreciation for the work of others; to build awareness that the arts honor the distinctive insight afforded through the expression of persons in other times and places;

4. To develop a beginning awareness of art forms as part of a larger tradition of man's achievements; to have students grasp the larger context of forms (past and present) that comprise the history of art;

5. And, perhaps most critically, to develop aesthetic awareness--the capacity to seek out the unusual, poetic, in short, those dimensions that enhance "the quality of life."

Since the art curriculum has many different areas, children's art experiences can be quite varied. Children can draw with pencils, crayons, chalk, or felt-tip pens. They can paint or make prints with tempera paint, finger paint, water colors, soap, or mud using various devices such as sponges, brushes, rollers, fingers, or sticks. The areas of cutting, tearing, and pasting offer many varied opportunities in art. Children can have interesting art experiences with sculpture and three-dimensional constructions. Many types of modeling materials such as clay, playdough, soap mixtures, or saw dust dough are available for sculpturing. Mobiles, stabiles, and box sculpture are among the many three-dimensional art experiences available to children. Children also enjoy weaving and sewing using many different types of materials from yarn, woven mesh sacks, and paper strips to objects in nature. In addition to manipulative experiences, a well-rounded art curriculum should also include many opportunities for children to develop a keen appreciation of art and a sensitivity to aesthetics.

---

[1]Pearl Greenberg, Chairperson, Art Education: Elementary (Washington, D.C.: National Art Association, 1972), p. 228.

Although art is basically an individual experience, large group art activities do have some advantages. In large group art experiences teachers can initiate class discussions prior to or after art experiences. Discussions of this sort allow children to brainstorm about things they can contribute to add variety to their art work. This sharing of ideas encourages a richer quality of divergent thinking in everyone because participants learn so much from each other. In this section you will find art activities that utilize a variety of skills, such as drawing, printing, cutting and pasting, sculpting, and weaving. You will also find activities that foster the appreciation of art. Use them as we have written them or vary them to fit the specific needs of your classroom.

drawing

cloud pictures

Clouds have many varied and beautiful formations. Here's a way to use the cloud formations to stimulate your children's imaginations and to help them develop an appreciation of the beauty found in clouds. Choose a day when the cloud formations are especially beautiful and frothy. Take your students outside and have them lie on their backs and observe the clouds. Encourage them to think of different objects that they might see suggested in the cloud formations. Then give each child a sheet of light blue construction paper and a piece of white chalk and ask him to draw a "cloud picture" including in his picture an object that he found hidden in the clouds. After the children have completed their pictures, let them share their pictures and see if the others in the group might be able to guess what is hidden in the clouds in each picture.

add-on pictures

This little divergent exercise should be lots of fun for your entire group. Gather a variety of art supplies—crayons, felt-tip markers, scissors, glue, scraps of colored paper, ribbons, lace, or whatever you wish to add. Seat your students in a large circle on the floor, and place the art supplies in the center of the circle. Give each student a plain piece of paper. Ask your students to put one mark on their paper using the available art supplies and to pass their paper to the right. They must take the piece of paper that they received from the person on their left and use the art supplies to add something to the mark on the paper. They might turn the original mark into a picture or incorporate it in a design that they make. They then pass the paper on to the person on their right, and the next person adds more distinguishing features to the picture. Keep passing the paper and adding to the original mark at least four or five times. Encourage your students to be original as they add features to the paper. They might wish to cut and paste new pieces onto the original sheet of paper, fold and glue on paper strips for three-dimensional effects, or use some other unusual techniques to add unique touches. Display the final products for all the students to enjoy.

dotted art

Give each of your students a plain piece of paper and a felt-tip pen. Ask them to draw twelve dots on their paper. Then let them create a design or a picture by connecting the dots or incorporating the dots in some way in their picture. Have a big supply of felt-tip pens or crayons for them to use. Encourage them to put a title on their pictures when they are finished.

classy quilt

Discuss possible themes for an easy patchwork quilt your class can put together. Choose a theme and have each student make a crayon drawing on a large (20 cm or 8 inch square) muslin square. Iron over each square with the iron set on "low." Stitch the squares together or have the students do it. Add a fabric border to your classy quilt and display it with pride!

Children might also draw on individual fabric squares, add borders, and take their squares home for wallhangings.

surrounded by sound!

Encourage each of your students to draw pictures of things that make sounds. Post the pictures all around the room. Hang sound pictures, such as pictures of birds and airplanes, on the ceiling. Display other pictures, such as pictures of people talking and household appliances, at eye level. Hang more pictures near the floor. You'll be surrounded by pictures of sound. Your students will be impressed by the large number of sound pictures they can draw.

colorful windows

After you have taught a lesson on color, let your students show what they know in a creative way. Students should cut an outline shape from black paper. Then have them cut out holes to make several little windows in the outline and trace their outline onto thin onionskin paper. Next have them color the sections on the onionskin paper using monochromatic color schemes, showing primary and secondary colors, or even using a free-form color wheel in their design. After students glue their outlines onto the onionskin paper, display the colorful creations on your window, perhaps grouping ones with similar color schemes together.

paper outline

color on onionskin

finished design

painting and printing

what can you paint on?

With your students, make a long list of kinds of paper you could paint on. Allow a few days for students to gather as many kinds of paper as possible. You might collect items such as

- computer paper or cards

- old sacks--colored, plastic, and brown

- shelf paper

- wrapping paper

- tissue paper

- egg carton cardboard

- box cardboard

- newspapers--regular sheets or colored funnies

what can you paint with?

Extend the possibilities for painting by brainstorming things to paint with. Focus a discussion at least two ways: What paints could we use? What could we apply paints with? Your students might respond with the following types of paint:

- fingerpaint

- shaving cream

- watercolor

- tempera paint

- acrylic paint

- mud

- white glue colored with food coloring

They might suggest items such as these to apply paint with:

- feathers

- sponges

- brushes

- bones

- sticks

- grass

- tree branches

- color swabs

- paint put in cleaned-out deodorant bottle

- flowers

Ask your students to help gather many items from their lists. Set out all the materials. Have students make a notebook of paintings done with at least 12 combinations of paint, paint applicators, and paper. They should label each sample in their notebooks. The possibilities are almost endless. This project will probably require several class periods to complete.

tints and shades

Colors to which white has been added are called tints. Colors to which black has been added are called shades. Try this activity to give your students an opportunity to explore the infinite variety of tints and shades that one color might have. Give each student paint brushes, water, paper and three small jars of tempera paint—one jar with black paint, one with white, and the other jar containing a color of her choice. Then let your students explore for a while mixing different amounts of white or black to their chosen color to get various intensities of that color. After they have an opportunity to experiment, ask each one to paint a picture using her chosen color and its various tints and shades. You might vary this activity by letting children add different amounts of yellow or blue to a selected color.

amalgamated art

Some art experiences are so basic and yet so much fun that children enjoy doing them over and over again. Many times children would like to add something different to the art lesson that the teacher has planned for the day. Why not take advantage of your student's creative tendencies? Have a day where you combine the materials and ideas from the past two or three art lessons. Encourage your students to try to come up with something new and different.

foggy mural

Foggy days can be inspirational for artistic endeavors. Be prepared for the next foggy day. Select a story or a few poems about the fog. When that day arrives, read your fog story or poems and draw your students into a discussion about the fog. Ask them questions such as "How does the fog make your feel?" "What do you do differently on foggy days?" "What did you see that looked different in the fog? How did it look?" Then tape a long sheet of butcher paper on the wall and ask your children to use crayons to draw pictures of out-of-door scenes around their town. Then mix two parts light gray tempera paint and three parts water. Let your students paint over their crayon-drawn street scenes with the gray tempera mixture to simulate the effects of fog.

cutting, tearing
and pasting

collage cafeteria

Ask each of your students to bring in a container of collage ingredients and a styrofoam food tray. Suggest that each student try to contribute something unique and unusual. She might provide such materials as wood shavings, small rocks, sewing scraps, or bits of leftover gift wrap and ribbon. Display all the collage materials on a long table. Call the display your "Collage Cafeteria." Invite each student to use her styrofoam tray, go through the collage cafeteria line, and select materials to make an interesting collage. Students can glue their materials to the styrofoam trays or to construction paper.

colored sprinkles

Here's a creative art activity with built-in success. Any sort of design is appropriate for use with colored sprinkles. Children use white school glue to "draw" designs on white or colored paper. Now the fun—pass around various containers filled with grainy ingredients to be sprinkled on. You might use old spice bottles with sprinkler tops. Fill them with sand, salt, cornmeal, or other grainy substances. Any of the substances may be mixed with a small amount of powdered tempera paint to add color to the glue designs. After sprinkling, children can shake any excess sprinkles onto' newspaper. The excess sprinkles can be poured back into the shaker containers.

yarn ornaments

Have students dip bits of yarn or heavy string into diluted white glue. A mixture of one part water and one part glue works well. The students then arrange the yarn into desired shapes on pieces of waxed paper.

They might want to interlock several pieces of yarn to make complex designs. Dry the ornaments overnight. Display them hanging in a window, on a holiday tree, or on a bare tree branch anchored in a flower pot.

masked dramas

Ask your students to bring nylon stockings, coat hangers, yarn, curtain trim, felt pieces, and scrap material from home. Add art supplies from the classroom to the collection. Encourage each student to make a mask by stretching a nylon stocking over a bent coat hanger. They can use scraps from home and art supplies from class to make facial features to glue on their nylon faces.

After they have finished their masks, let them work in small groups to use their masks as they put on impromptu plays.

sculpture and three-dimensional construction

decorate the ceiling

For a special occasion such as a holiday, a parents' night, or a class party, challenge your students to think of some unique ways to decorate the ceiling of your classroom. Provide the needed art materials, and let students carry out their ideas by hanging things from the ceiling or fastening little works of art to the ceiling.

natural sculptures

Clay and other natural materials make marvelously interesting little sculptures. Show children how to make imprints in oil-base or water-base clay with objects such as sticks, acorns, flowers, or shells. When the objects are carefully removed, they leave beautifully patterned indentations in the clay. Suggest also that natural objects can be stuck into a clay base and left there as part of the sculpture. Encourage children to experiment with several natural objects and a lump of clay. See what original designs they can invent.

sand painting

Ask children to bring in some clean, dry sand. Fill old coffee cans half full of sand. To tint some of the sand in the cans, pour in several milliliters of powdered tempera paint. Close each can with its plastic lid and shake gently. Let children "layer" different colors

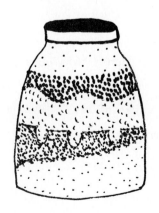

of sand in glass jars. Encourage them to
vary the patterns by tilting the jars to make
waves in the layers, or poking into the edges
of the layers with a toothpick or little
stick. When the jars are completely full of
layers of sand, close the jars tightly with a
lid. These little sand paintings make nice
gifts.

paper plate sculpture

Besides a picnic or quick meal, what else
do paper plates suggest? Ask your class to
devise lots of answers to this question.
Ask each student to bring four or five plain
paper plates to class. Let children cut or
bend them, draw on them, or apply paints and
glue to turn them into original sculptures.
See what sorts of things your class can
create. Some children we worked with
suggested

rock art

Ask your students this question: "What
are some possibilities for using rocks to
make little works of art?" They might
suggest things like these:

• paint on them

• glue them together

• imprint them in clay and make a plastic
cast

• crush them and make a mosaic of the
pieces

• rub them on the sidewalk to make a mural

See what your students suggest. Invite
each one to bring in a handful of rocks and
use them for an art project. If rocks are to
be glued together, super glue or epoxy glue
works well. Rocks can be effectively painted
with acrylic paint.

weaving and sewing

nature weavings

After discussing weaving with your
students, take them on a nature walk. Have
them look for objects in nature to weave with
or on. Pine needles, weeds, sticks, bark,
wild flowers, grasses and seed pods are great
materials to use for weaving. Students might
weave between the crook of a branch, on big
feathers, a bowed stick, driftwood, or any
other interesting object found in nature.
Let them select their own materials and make
a natural weaving.

colorful stitching

For students to be able to work skillfully with colors, teachers need to give them
lessons on color principles. Students need
to know the primary colors and the secondary
colors and that complementary colors are
opposite on the color wheel while analogous
colors are next to each other. (For a brush
up on color principles, see Clare Cherry's

book listed in the references.) After a few lessons on colors, have your students bring in yarn remnants from home. Supplement with more yarn, making sure that you have a wide array of colors. Give each student a small piece of natural colored burlap. Ask your students to choose one of the color principles learned in their art lesson as a theme for stitching on their burlap. If they choose "primary colors" as their theme, they will be working only with yarn of primary colors. If they select "analogous colors" as their theme, then they will stitch with one color of yarn and the colors closest to it on the color wheel. After they have finished stitching, have the students label their stitchings with the appropriate theme tag and display their art work for the rest of the class to see.

silly sock puppets

Encourage everyone in the class to make an original sock puppet. Show the children how they might attach button eyes and yarn hair, then stand back and let them create all sorts of sock animals, people, and creatures. Let children who finish early use a large box to make a simple stage. The children can

give brief impromptu puppet shows using their sock puppets and the stage.

art appreciation

a close look

Take an interesting reproduction of an art work to class. Study it carefully with your students. Encourage them to discuss the different colors that the artist used, the way the artist used light and shadows to achieve different effects, and the different lines or shapes used over and over in the painting.

After studying the painting from afar, give your students a chance for a bird's eye view. Cut a small hole (about 6 cm or 2 1/2 inches in diameter) in several pieces of paper. Place the papers near the painting and have each student come by sometime during the day, take a paper, and look through the hole in the paper and examine only a small portion of the painting closely. Ask them to notice details such as brush strokes and the colors the artist used. Have the students come back together and discuss what they observed with their closer looks. As a follow-up assignment, ask them to paint a picture incorporating some of the same techniques that the artist used.

guest artist

Invite a guest artist to demonstrate a technique in your classroom. When students actually see a proficient person engaged in an art process, they gain understanding and develop respect for both the artist and the type of art work. You may know a professional artist who might visit your classroom. If not, why not see if one of your students has a relative who could come? Children often relate well to a talented high school student, too. Prepare for your visitor by having your children make up questions to ask their guest artist. Have the guest artist work for several minutes explaining what she is doing and then show one of her finished works. After the artist has left, ask your students to write five details about what they learned from their visit with the artist. Let them discuss their observations with one another.

life and times . . . and art

Show several prints of an artist's work. Read a brief history of the life and times of the artist. Provide some historical background as well as personal details about how the artist lived. Next show prints again one at a time. Encourage the children to discuss how the artist's work reflects his life and times.

change it, improve it

Use prints, reproductions, or photos of especially striking pieces of art. You might use a print of Picasso's Three Musicians, Henry Moore's Reclining Figure, or da Vinci's Mona Lisa. Let your students discuss what they find pleasing about each piece of art. Then entertain suggestions about how each art

work might be changed to make it more pleasing to the student.

compare and contrast

Display prints of two famous artists' paintings side by side. If you can set the prints on easels, you will promote an "arty" atmosphere. Lead children in a discussion of similarities and differences in the two artists' work. You might compare and contrast works such as Chagall's In the Night and Gauguin's Portrait of a Woman, Picasso's Old Guitarist and Leger's The City, Miro's Dog Barking at the Moon and Seurat's La Parade, of Van Gogh's Starry Night and Monet's Water Lilies.

jungle scene

Study some prints of paintings by Henri Rousseau. Show the students examples of Rousseau's famous jungle scenes, such as The Dream and The Waterfall in which he paints lush green vegetation that looks something like huge houseplants. Let students create a large jungle scene much in the style of Rousseau. Have them make a large crayon-drawn mural on butcher paper showing plants and animals. Then have them add more color and texture to the jungle scene by finger-painting over the crayon drawings with a mixture of liquid starch and dry tempera paint.

ENCOURAGING DIVERGENT THINKING WITH SMALL GROUP ACTIVITIES IN ART

When children are involved in small group art activities, the teacher should keep the group size down to five children or less. By keeping group sizes small, all children can have free access to art materials. In small groups children can work together helping to steady a sculpture or balance a mobile. Small groups facilitate an informal sharing of ideas, a smooth flow of interaction, and acceptance of criticism. Since several heads are better than one, children working in small groups can use familiar ideas to generate new ones.

In this section you will find activities for you to initiate in small groups. You will also find activities addressed directly to the children. Activities addressed to children can be put on cards and placed on a table for students to pursue on their own. Be sure to laminate the cards before giving them to your groups in order to avoid the stains and spills of art supplies.

drawing

photographic adventures

When classroom pictures come in, take advantage of the situation for many classroom uses. Tape each student's picture close together on a piece of paper and photocopy the pictures. Make several photocopies of your students' pictures for future classroom uses. Here is one way to use these photo-copies in an art experience. Divide your students into small groups. Be sure that each group has a photocopied picture of each member of the group. Supply felt-tip mark-ers, crayons, old magazines, scissors, and glue. Let students cut out scenes from old magazines and add their own photocopied photograph as if they were the characters in the pictures. They might wish to draw their own adventures and add their photos. After each group has created its own "adventure," have the groups share their "adventures" with one another.

historical mural

Have groups of students choose a specific topic to show facts about a historical event or period. Ask them to draw a mural, perhaps adding glued-on sticks, grass, or sand. They might focus on topics such as home life in the 1850s, a native American village at the time of the first colonies, or a World War I battle scene.

window murals

Students often enjoy making decorations and hanging them in their classroom windows. Here's an art experience that adds a little unique touch to window decorations. Have your students cover the windows with a light coat of glass wax. If glass wax is hard to find, use a mixture of scouring powder and water. They may wish to paint over the glass wax with a thin coat of tempera paint. Then let students draw pictures on the glass wax with their fingers. You may encourage them to use a seasonal theme or a theme based on a unit of study.

painting
and printing

painting with ice cubes

Painting with brushes can be fun, but have you ever tried to paint with ice cubes? Place at the art table some paper, several small containers of dry tempera paint with spoons, a few containers of liquid tempera paint in squeezable containers with small holes for dispensing, washable felt-tip markers, and ice cubes. Ask your students to paint a picture using ice cubes for brushes. Avoid giving many instructions. Let students experiment and discover ways to spread the different colors. Encourage them to compare their findings and display their pictures.

marble painting

Marble painting is fun because it's easy and the results always look great. Have students cut colored and white paper to fit inside shallow pans or boxes of various shapes. Provide them with tempera paint in several sections of an egg carton. Each egg cup should have a spoon. The children dip a marble into a desired color of paint with the spoon then put the paint-covered marble carefully into the paper-lined box. Then they gently tilt the box and roll the marble around in it. As the marble rolls, it leaves a trail of paint. Students can make a multi-color design by allowing the paint to dry slightly, then using another color with the same procedure. Students will want to make several marble paintings—they're quick and easy. Encourage them to choose their best design and give it a title.

marbleized paper

Supervise a small group of students as they make pretty, elegant marbleized paper. Fill a cake pan or plastic tub with water. Spray two or three colors of oil-based spray paint on the water. Let students swirl the paint to create patterns. When they have a pleasing design, one student should lay a sheet of paper on top of the water, then carefully lift the paper out. After each

student has made at least one piece of marbleized paper, allow the sheets to dry overnight. Then have each student use her paper in a unique way—perhaps for a picture frame, as backing for a picture frame, for gift wrap, or as a book cover.

junk on junk

As an extension of the large group painting project using several kinds of things to paint with and many different kinds of paper, try this printing activity. Ask each student in a small group to bring at least one piece of discarded paper and two junk items to print with. Lay out all the contributed supplies on a table along with shallow trays of paint. Encourage the students in the group to select an interesting type of paper and print on it with the junk items they brought. Students can even print a border on their creations using small items. The print on the opposite page features marks made by a sponge scrap, some shells, a rock, and a leaf. Can you identify them? What might have made the border?

cutting, tearing and pasting

overhead art

Perhaps you have used our science activity exploring the transparent, translucent, and opaque qualities of various materials. Follow it up with this art activity. Let a group of three or four students work with the overhead projector in a corner of the room. Challenge them to create several pictures from materials such as colored acetate, waxed paper, thin fabrics, or scrap paper. They should arrange their materials on top of clear acetate. When they are satisfied with each arrangement they can affix the materials with a drop or two of rubber cement. The group should choose some music to play as they show their overhead art to the class. The children may want to make several pictures to illustrate a story, song, or poem, or they may simply create several designs to set a mood.

frame up I

Cover a large bulletin board with colored paper. Have pupils work in pairs. Give each pair about one meter (one yard) of yarn or rope and challenge them to arrange the yarn

to make a uniquely shaped frame. They may wish to tie a knot or bow in the yarn and let this be part of their design. They should pin the yarn in place on the bulletin board. Next the pupils should pin collage materials inside their frames to make pleasing designs. When the designs are finished, both the frames and collage designs may be stapled in place.

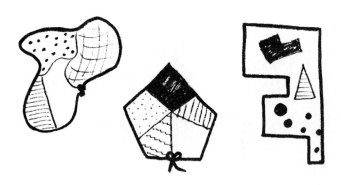

frame up II

Let students make smaller frames from about 30 cm (one foot) of yarn. They should work in pairs to arrange their yarn on top of construction paper. When they are satisfied with their designs, they should trace the outline of the shapes, cut out the shapes, and glue the yarn border back in place. Now students should design a little picture to go inside their frames. They might display their small frame-ups on the windowsill. You could lead them to discuss their solutions to problems in designing both small and large frame-ups.

theme collage

Talk with your pupils about art materials that could be sorted into two or more categories. They might sort fabric scraps into plain and patterned piles; divide paper bits into dark colors and light colors; or categorize collage materials into cloth, paper, wood, and plastic groups. Metal materials might be sorted as to whether they attract to a magnet or not. Divide the pupils in groups of four or five. Let each group decide on a sorting theme, then make a large collage in which the materials are sorted into groups.

sculpture and three-dimensional construction

scent it

For an interesting sensory experience, have small groups of children prepare a modeling dough recipe. Then add different scents to it. You might choose your favorite recipe or one of the following:

OATMEAL DOUGH
Mix 250 ml (1 c.) flour, 500 ml (2 c.) oatmeal, and 250 ml (1 c.) water in a bowl. Knead until pliable.

CORNSTARCH DOUGH
Heat 250 ml (1 c.) water and 750 ml (3 c.) salt for a few minutes. Slowly stir in 250 ml (1 c.) cornstarch. Knead the dough, adding a small amount of water if necessary.

Next let the children in each group add 2.5 to 5 ml (1/2 to 1 t.) flavoring to give the dough a pleasant scent. You might use oil of wintergreen, oil of cloves, lemon extract, vanilla, coconut extract, mint

leaves, toothpaste, or grated orange peel. Divide the different scented doughs among the groups. Let them discuss which scent they prefer and why. Finally, have each child mold a little sculpture from her scented dough.

playdough plus

Divide your students into groups of four or five. Tell them they will make playdough the next day and that each should bring a different ingredient to add to the dough to give it lots of texture. They might bring things such as sand, oatmeal, bird seed, sawdust, computer card bits, coffee grounds, or cornmeal. Let each group make a playdough recipe such as this one.

HOT WATER PLAYDOUGH
Measure and mix together in a bowl:
  600 ml (2 1/3 c.) flour
  250 ml (1 c.) salt
  15 ml (1 T.) powdered alum
Add and mix well:
  60 ml (1/4 c.) salad oil
Stir in:
  375 ml (2 1/2 c.) boiling water.
Mix or knead until smooth.
Add food color and knead again.

Divide the dough among the group members. Let each one add his texture ingredient. Then each student should sculpt and display a little figure from the textured playdough.

soap suds sculpture

Have a small group of children mix two parts of Ivory soap flakes with 1 part water in a large bowl. About 500 ml (2 c.) and

250 ml (1 c.) water will make plenty for four or five students. Have the children take turns beating the mixture with a rotary beater or an electric hand mixer. Add a small amount of food coloring or dry tempera paint if a colored sculpture medium is desired. When the mixture becomes very fluffy and stiff, children can mold and sculpt it into little shapes with their hands. They should work on a washable table top or on waxed paper. Soap suds sculptures will air dry in two or three days.

dryer lint clay

Could you imagine a modeling substance from dryer lint? This recipe recycles lint into an appealing clay that's just right in classroom modeling.

Stir together in a saucepan:
   750 ml (3 c.) dryer lint, firmly packed
   500 ml (2 c.) water
Stir in:
   175 ml (3/4 c.) flour
   2.5 ml (1/2 t.) oil of wintergreen
Cook on a hotplate, stirring constantly
   until it holds together and is thick.

Cool the dryer lint clay, then have students mold it into unique little shapes.

weaving and sewing

fabric collage

Ask students to bring in scraps of fabrics, and leftover bits of yarn, lace, and sewing trim. Have them work in groups of two or three to make fabric collages. They should sew fabrics and trims onto a piece of background fabric. Sewn-on buttons, pieces of rickrack, and ribbon add interesting details. Students can partially sew on fabric shapes, then lightly stuff them for additional texture. Display all the fabric collages when they are finished.

lotsa looms

Many different materials can be used to make simple looms or bases for sewing and weaving. Divide your students into groups of three or four and ask each group to bring things from home to make looms from or to weave on. The students might bring in berry boxes, coathangers, screen wire, or scrap boards with nails inserted. Allow an art period or two for experimentation with the different kinds of looms and weaving bases the students bring in.

OUR TOWN

Draw pictures of the stores in your town on small sheets of poster board. Tape the sheets of poster board together. Set it up to look like your town.

Drawing

Go around your school building. Look for lots of interesting textures. Cover them with thin paper. Rub back and forth over them with the edge of a crayon. Make a nice design. See if your classmates can identify some of the textures in your design. Can you find textures like wood grains, designs pressed in metal, or cracks in the floor?

Drawing

PLAID PICTURES

Brush some tempera paint onto paper. Use a comb to draw across the paint and make some lines. Now make more lines with the comb to create a plaid pattern. Can you make a whole plaid picture? How can you use some different colors in your plaid picture?

Painting

Dotted Designs

Work with your group. Punch lots of holes from different colored papers. Use both the punched out "dots" and the holey paper to make designs.

Cutting, Tearing, Pasting

Found Paper Collage

Cut and tear many small bits of colored paper from magazines and catalogs. Glue them on paper to make a creative design.

Cutting, Tearing, Pasting

tear

Experiment with Paper

cut out

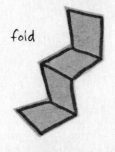
fold

List all the things you can think of to do with paper. Try them. Put your paper experiments together in some artistic way.

curl

fringe

Cutting, Tearing, Pasting

cut

glue

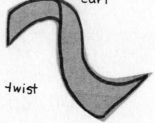
twist

Cardboard SCULPTURE

Work with two or three classmates to
cut cardboard into large, medium, and small
shapes. Cut a slit or two in each piece.
To make the slit, cut about half way through.
Build up the cardboard shapes to make a
unique kind
of sculpture.

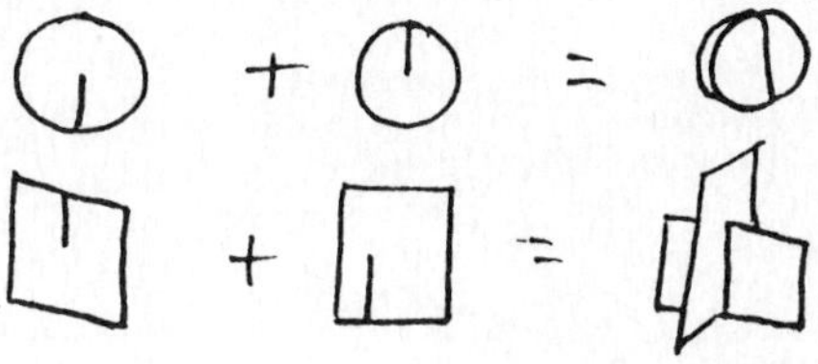

3 dimensional construction

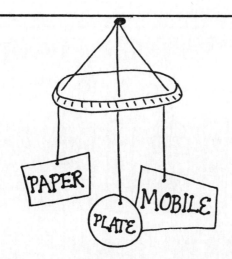

Work with your group to create a mobile.
Use a paper plate as the base. Add paper
shapes hung from strings. You might hang
things such as this on the mobile:

- pictures of foods
- geometric shapes
- holiday designs
- pictures of animals

Hang your mobile up in the hall

3-dimensional construction

EGG CARTON CREATIONS

Fasten egg cups together with pipe cleaners, wire, or toothpicks. Attach other objects to the cups. You might use fabric scraps, bits of paper, sequins, or thumb tacks. Make a new creation.

flowers   Martians   spider

3-dimensional constructions

* CARDBOARD CASTLES *

Collect cardboard tubes, small boxes, paper cones, and lace and gold trimmings. Work with your group. Use your materials to create a castle.

3-dimensional construction

ENCOURAGING DIVERGENT THINKING WITH INDIVIDUAL ACTIVITIES IN ART

The creative process is basically an individual process. Thus, your students will probably find a great deal of satisfaction from "creating" on their own. Many of the activities suggested in this section are introduced in large group settings and continue with students working individually. We recommend some activities for homework, others for classroom use. Encourage children to share their ideas and products with one another.

drawing

frosty sketches

Here's a way to make unique little pictures with a frosty look to them. Have children draw small crayon pictures on colored construction paper. They should make fairly heavy crayon marks, but be sure to leave some spaces unmarked. Help children mix a strong solution of epsom salts and hot water. In 500 ml (2 c.) hot water, dissolve 175-250 ml (3/4-1 c.) epsom salts. Let the children brush the epsom salt solution onto their crayon drawings. They should work on top of old newspapers and soak the drawings well with the epsom salt solution. When the drawings dry, they will be covered with pretty, frosty epsom salt crystals!

what's in a shape?

Challenge individual children to make several different designs based on a single shape such as a rectangle, triangle, oval, or bean shape. Each child can make a little accordian-folded booklet of her many designs.

The booklets look attractive pinned to a bulletin board for display.

logos

Post several logos in the art center. Encourage your pupils to find pictures of more logos and add them to the display. Have individuals design their own logos to represent themselves or to symbolize their school or grade.

batik

Let your students work on their own to create this batik-like effect. Have them color a picture or design on a piece of paper. Make sure they color heavily with the crayons to get a thick layer, then have them crumple their paper drawings to get many creases in the papers. After they have smoothed out their papers, they should paint a thick layer of tempera paint over the papers. Next have them put their papers in water to remove most of the paint. Some of the paint will remain in the cracks of the paper. Then students should smooth the paper out and let it dry. Encourage them to cut a frame from a pretty color of construction paper and to mat their pictures.

creative alphabets

Show the students several alphabets made up with common objects such as flowers, stars, or animals. You can find unique thematic alphabets in art books as well as needlepoint and cross-stitch books. Invite students to create their own thematic alphabets using little pictures of things that interest them. One student might design an alphabet incorporating little sketches of foods while another might use cars or sports equipment.

painting

rain drop paintings

On the next rainy day take some of your children to the window. Have them observe the rain, and talk about the way it makes them feel. Then ask each child to paint a rainy day picture. When the rain becomes a little drizzle, let her take a picture outside and expose it to the tiny drops of moisture. The light sprinkle of rain should make splatter marks and give her painting a real appearance of rain. After the picture has dried, each child may wish to add a few more details with crayons or felt-tip markers.

blow a picture

Provide several colors of thin tempera paint. Have the children put drops of paint on paper with a medicine dropper, spoon, or straw. Blow through a straw to move the paint around to form designs or creatures. Add features with a paint brush or felt marker if desired. Have children make up little stories or poems to go with their blown pictures.

lady bug's point of view

What would things look like from a lady bug's point of view? Make a minimural on a piece of shelf paper attached to the wall at eye level. Ask students who want to add to the mural to paint details on it showing what a lady bug's surroundings might look like.

cutting, tearing and pasting

popout cards

Make a few examples of popout greeting cards. These simple inventions turn an ordinary flat card into a cute, three-dimensional message. Cut two pieces of paper the same size. Work with one of them to make the popout part of the card. Gently crease the center of that piece of paper. Sketch a drawing using the crease as the center of your picture. Carefully cut around the top and bottom of the drawing leaving it attached with small pieces at each side. Pull the drawing outward and recrease it to stick out toward you. Color the picture and add a greeting. Close the card with the popout figure folded toward the opening of the card.

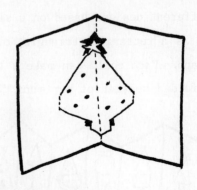

To make a cover for your card, paste the other paper to the popout card, gluing it only on the four corners. Add a design to the front of your card. Let children make some popout cards in their free time. Challenge them to see what different designs they can use with popout figures.

junk treasures box

Challenge your children to improvise a little art work from randomly chosen materials. Make a junk treasures box and invite students to contribute all sorts of reusable materials to the box. When the box is full, let each pupil draw just three junk treasures from the box. He must then choose just one more type of material—string, glue, paint, or crayons, for example—and complete his project.

styrofoam window hangers

Provide styrofoam trays, small sections of plastic drinking straws, cookie cutters, knives, other oddly shaped gadgets sharp enough to cut through styrofoam, and different colors of acetate or cellophane. Let each student cut the sides from around their styrofoam tray and cut the remaining piece of styrofoam into a shape that pleases him. Then he should cut designs from the center of the styrofoam tray with cookie cutters, small pieces of drinking straws, sharp-edged gadgets, or knives. After cutting away a design, the student attaches one or more colors of acetate or cellophane to the back of the styrofoam piece. He should then punch a hole in the top of the styrofoam piece and thread it with a piece of string so it can hang in the window. The sun shining through the acetate where

the styrofoam has been cut away will make a colorful effect.

nature collages

Nature offers so many beautiful specimens to enjoy. Why not encourage children to use their own creative genius and combine grasses, flowers, and leaves into an artistic nature collage? Each child paints a coat of liquid starch on a piece of waxed paper. Then she arranges small flat natural specimens on the waxed paper. After arranging the objects on the waxed paper, the student paints another coat of liquid starch over the specimens and places single layers of facial tissue on top of the design, smoothing out any bubbles in the tissue. She should then put her collage away and allow it to dry for two or three days. After the collage is dry, suggest that she spray it with a thin coat of hair spray. Let each student cut a "frame" from construction paper for her collage.

tree mosaics

When is the last time you stopped and looked up at the sky through the trees? Do you remember the myriad shades of green with the blue sky shining through? Give your students some time to go outside. Let them lie on the ground and look up at the sky through the trees. After they have had time to study the different colored leaves with the light playing on them, ask them to work on their own and create a picture showing the way the sky looks through the trees. Supply tissue paper in blue and a wide variety of greens. Mix a solution of half glue and half water. Each child can tear tiny bits of tissue paper and arrange them on the paper with some of the tissue overlapping. They should glue the tissue to the paper by painting over the tissue with a thin coat of the glue mixture. This arrangement of the tiny pieces of tissue paper will create a mosaic effect similar to the leaves through the trees.

punch-a-round

Have students draw a small simple shape on cardboard and cut it out, then lay the shape on top of drawing or construction paper. Place the shape and paper atop a smooth-textured carpet square. With a large nail, punch around the cardboard shape until there are enough holes to allow the shape to be punched out of the paper. Have students use both the punched-out shapes and "negatives" to make a design.

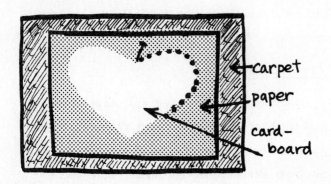

carpet
paper
card-
board

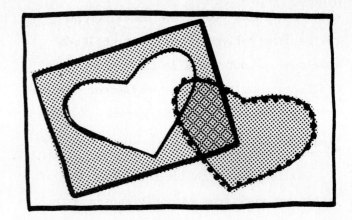

sculpture and three-dimensional construction

soap bar carvings

Here's a homework assignment that should receive favorable responses. Ask your students to take a large bar of soap and a paring knife and make a carving from it. Let them decide what they will carve. Remind them that the soap shavings can be placed in water and used for washing hands or dishes.

soaring sculptures

Sculpting with one's hands is quite an art, but even older elementary school children should be able to create some interesting effects with sculpting if they are given the right materials and a little guidance. Show your students how to bend coat hanger wire and how to tape cardboard and various lightweight objects to the coat hanger to get different effects. Show them how to mount the coat hanger in a wood or clay base. Then demonstrate how to dip strips of cloth in a mixture of plaster of paris and water and drape the strips over the coat hanger foundation. The plaster of paris will dry and leave a sculpture-like construction. After your students understand the steps in this sculpture technique, give them this assignment. Ask them to plan and build a sculpture that suggests flight.

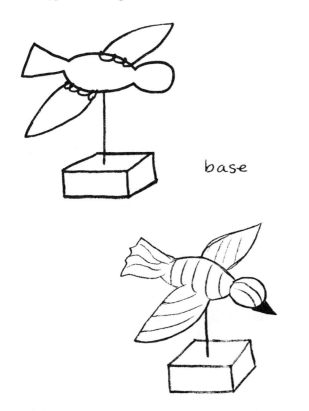

base

weaving and sewing

cross-stitched gingham gifts

Buy different colors of small checked gingham, colored embroidery thread, embroidery hoops, needles, and graph paper for your students to work with. Show your students how to draw a simple design on graph paper and how to mark x's in squares included in the design. Then demonstrate how to transfer a design from graph paper to gingham by drawing a simple outline on the gingham. Insert the fabric in an embroidery hoop and cross-stitch the design. After your students understand the technique, have them plan and make a little gingham gift to give to someone. They may decide to make a picture and frame it in a unique way, to make a cross-stitched pin cushion, a small pillow, or a little purse. Encourage your students to help each other and to share their ideas with one another.

string a necklace

How many ways can your students think of to make a necklace? Have them brainstorm and suggest ways. They might think of stringing dyed macaroni, short pieces of straw, clay dough beads, beads made from tiny, rolled up paper strips, or interesting shapes cut out of construction paper and strung with a needle on yarn. Solicit many suggestions. Then send your students off with the assignment of making a necklace by stringing unusual objects together. Encourage them to strive to make their necklaces different from the others and as pretty as they can.

petite pillows

Make a box of sewing scraps available for individual children to make tiny decorative pillows. Encourage them to make small simple shapes, to stuff their pillows lightly, and to decorate them with yarn and lace. The petite pillows can be personalized with initials. These tiny pillows make delightful gifts.

vine weaving

Show your students the basic techniques for weaving grape vine, honeysuckle, or other types of vines to make wreaths. Let your students discuss different things one might add to wreaths to make them pretty, different interesting shapes that they might achieve, or different things to make from vines besides wreaths. Then ask each student to work individually and design a unique weaving with vines.

dress your doll

Gather some old fashioned clothespins--one-piece wooden pins without springs. Make a thick dough of flour and water and shape it around the nob of each pin to form a head. Place the pins on a cookie sheet and bake in a 250°F oven and bake the clothespins until the heads harden. Let each student paint or draw facial features on the head of her clothespin doll and glue on yarn for hair. Provide needles and thread and fabric scraps for each student to use and sew a costume or outfit for her doll. The costumes could be futuristic, fanciful, or from a historical period or other country you are studying.

plaited projects

Plaiting or braiding is a simple form of weaving. It is easy to do, yet it can result in striking and unusual projects. If you have a student who is interested in weaving, let him collect scrap fabrics in the colors of his choice. Have him cut long strips of fabric about 2-3 cm (1 inch) wide and braid them together, using 3 strips at a time.

Encourage him to sew the plaited strips together to make a chair cover, wall hanging, rug, or whatever he desires to make. He may wish to sew in feathers, beads, or other objects to obtain special effects. Encourage each student to create a different and unique plaited project.

art appreciation

art observation book

Encourage your students to study works of art more closely. Select an interesting art reproduction or an actual work of art to share with your students. Make a class observation book. On each page write a different question related to the work of art. Here are some questions you might consider: "What do you see when you look at this work of art?" "What do you think the artist is trying to say?" "How does this work of art make you feel?" "What do you like about this work of art?" "What don't you like about this work of art?" Let your students observe the art work at their leisure and write answers to the questions in the art observation book.

in the style of . . .

Encourage individual children to choose and study the style of an artist. The student should try to draw or paint a picture in the style of the chosen artist.

art apprenticeship

Every community is filled with talented amateur artists and craft people. Ask for parents and other relatives of your students to volunteer to share their hobbies and artistic expertise with your students. Have each student decide on a new art talent about which she would like to learn more. She might wish to learn to paint, arrange flowers, make jewelry, or learn another new craft. Help each interested student find an appropriate teacher and set up a schedule for her apprenticeship. The period of apprenticeship may vary from 1 lesson to several lessons, depending on the "master's" available time, and the complexity of the skill being studied. As a culmination to the apprenticeship, each student should present to the class a final art project in her field of study.

Seashore Scene

Make a seashore scene using blue construction paper for a background. Paint glue thinned with water where the beach should be. Sprinkle sand on the wet glue. Use crayons, pens, or tiny seashells to complete the scene. Cover it with clear plastic wrap to create a watery effect.

three-dimensional construction

Salt Dough Ornaments

Instead of making traditional holiday symbols for Christmas or Hanukkah create a symbol of yourself to place on your mantle, window sill or tree. Sign your name and date on the back.

Salt Dough Recipe
200 mL flour (¾ c.)
125 mL salt (½ c.)

Mix flour and salt in a bowl. Stir in water a little at a time to make a stiff dough. Form into shapes. Bake at 80°C (200°F) for an hour.

Sculpture

Egg Cup Animals

Make an animal out of an egg cup from an egg carton. Add other materials to make an original little creature.

three-dimensional construction

Design A Flag

Design a new flag or coat of arms for a country or for yourself. Tell your class what some of the colors or symbols you used stand for.

Drawing

Nature Boat

Design and decorate a boat using objects from nature. You might use nuts, leaves, driftwood or other things. Try to make your boat unique.

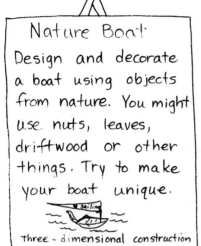

three-dimensional construction

Textured Drawings

See what happens when you draw with crayon over a screen wire. Try some more different effects drawing over plastic mesh.

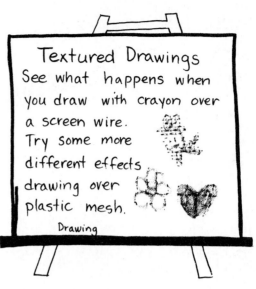

Drawing

Sandpaper Art

Rub natural materials onto sandpaper. Use berries, flowers, leaves or rocks. Rub them firmly onto the sandpaper. See what colors and textures result.

Drawing

Potato Planters

It's easy to make a little sculptured planter. Carve a potato with shallow cuts. Cut a thin slice off the bottom to make it stable. You might tint the cut surfaces with a little food coloring. Hollow out the potato to a depth of 1-2 cm. Fill it with dirt or cotton ball. Sprinkle on grass seeds. Keep it moist.

geometric

face

abstract

Three-dimensional construction

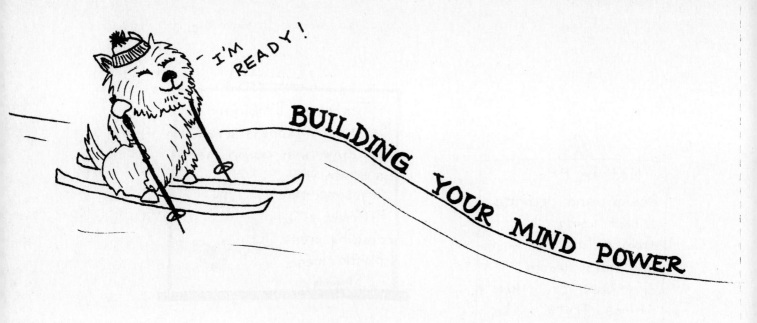

I'M READY!

BUILDING YOUR MIND POWER

Now that you have tried teaching divergent art activities in large, small, and individual settings, do you think that you are ready to plan some divergent thinking exercises for your own classroom? We have designed some exercises to help you begin using divergent teaching techniques on your own. Start out with the easier exercises and work up to the harder ones. Try to do at least one exercise a week for the next few weeks with your students.

1. How do you comment on your students' art work? Do you generally make vague comments such as these: "That's pretty!" or "How nice!"? For the next week think of ways to comment that might be encouraging and/or constructive. Be specific in your commands.

2. Find several books that you might read to your children and use as stimulation for an art experience. You might try <u>Discovering Colors</u> by David Alexander, <u>See What I Am</u> by Roger Divoisin, or <u>Going for a Walk with a Line</u> by Douglas and Elizabeth MacAgy. For other ideas see Appendix F in <u>Art in the Early Childhood Years</u> by Lendall Haskell. Use one book a week for the next month. Plan a way to use the book to motivate your students. Organize an art experience for your students as a follow-up.

3. Work on ways to organize the art materials in your classroom to make it easy for your children to get art supplies and to put them away.

4. Create a bulletin board on a famous artist. Have books available related to that artist and his or her art works. Assign your students to do some research about the artist, write questions for others to find the answers to,

and tack the questions on the bulletin board. Each student might hide the answer to his question on the back of the question for others to use as a self-check.

5. Think of some ways to involve children in new experiences that are highly sensory. For instance, you might try letting your children paint with pudding. Use two or three sensory experiences in your classroom in the next few weeks.

6. Plan a class visit to an art gallery, museum, or art studio. Plan an interesting art lesson to follow up your trip.

7. Take a very structured art activity--one that does not allow for much divergent thinking. Turn it into a very creative, motivating art experience.

8. Try a new motivational technique to stimulate your students in an art activity. See page 155 in the beginning of this chapter for a review of some different motivational techniques.

9. Line, shape, color, and texture are basic elements of art. Children learn about these qualities by continually being exposed to them. Take one of these elements. Plan an art lesson based on that element to help your children become more familiar with it.

DRIBBLING'S A CINCH WHEN YOU PUT YOUR MIND TO IT.

Put on some mood music --- something that really "sends you". Sketch to it.

Sing a message to someone. Whistle a tune to call your children. Sing a little ditty to wake them up. Tell some-one something in song.

MIND STRETCHERS
for
MUSIC

CHAPTER 9

Make up a song.
It can be very short.
Write the words and
tune. Record it
on your tape
recorder.

How long has
it been since you've
danced? When nobody is
looking, select some of
your favorite music.
Do a creative
dance to it.

SHOOTIN' BASKETS
REALLY
STRETCHES
YOU TOO!

Music is all around us; it is a vital part of our lives. We often wake up in the morning with a song on our minds that lingers throughout the day. We sing in the shower when no one is listening. We often hum a tune while we work. We turn on the radio to hear music when we get in the car. We shop to music in many stores. Many of us can be caught doing a little double step to a tune that catches our fancy. Some of us are more influenced by music than others, but we are all touched by music in one way or another.

Because music is an experience that most people enjoy, good music has the power to enrich our lives. Music is a flexible activity. It appeals to people of all ages and levels of maturity. A person can enjoy a beautiful musical experience alone, or music can be enjoyed by a large audience. Music can turn an ordinary experience into a vivid, meaningful one.

Not only does music permeate our lives, but it also has the potential for being a positive force in our lives. What are the values of music? Music is a language in its own right. It can be used to express the gamut of thoughts and emotions--from disgust, anger, and sorrow, to joy and jubilance. Through music we can express love and adoration. We worship with music. As we speak through the language of music we release our feelings and thereby maintain an emotional balance. For example, children often sing "mean" words to songs to express anger. They dance exuberantly around the room releasing excess energy and excitement; they hum or play quiet, rambling melodies to express pensive moods.

Besides its expressive and emotional assets, music can enhance our lives socially. Music has a unifying effect upon groups of people, drawing people from different backgrounds closer together. Group participation in music can lead to self-acceptance and acceptance of others in the group. Music has a place for all types of personalities. Shy people can participate comfortably and not feel as if they are standing out in the crowd. Aggressive people can blend into the musical experience and still be contributing members of the group.

With children music can play an important role in intellectual and perceptual development. Music educates our senses. Through music children develop spatial awareness, auditory discrimination, an understanding of whole-part relationships, and sequencing skills. All these skills add fluency to reading. They develop concepts related to time, rhythm, and pitch. When children learn to listen, they extend their vocabularies. Most importantly, music often fosters divergent thinking skills in children. Music can be used as an aid in developing all areas of the curriculum.

In spite of all of its assets, music usually is forced to assume a minor role in the typical school curriculum. Economic pressures and the cry for "Back to Basics!" have forced administrators to eliminate those so-called "frills," music and art. If music is taught at all, it is left up to the classroom teacher, who usually has very little training in teaching music. But music is not a frill. It is an <u>essential</u> if children are to have a rich, well-rounded background. Not only does music enrich and add fullness to children's lives, it also enhances learning abilities. Because it is such a valuable asset, music needs to be taught in the classroom. If music teachers are not provided, then classroom teachers must assume the responsibility. With little guidance, classroom teachers should be able to provide their students with an enriching, well-balanced music program. They should not need a special degree in music—just a lot of confidence, a little background knowledge, and a few resource books.

What is the overall goal of music in the classroom? Is it to perfect children's musical skills? No. The basic goal of classroom music is to enrich the lives of children.

What are the objectives of a well-rounded music program? One of the primary objectives is to help children enjoy music. Another objective is to help children learn to respond to music. The language of music has so many elements and moods, it can elicit a variety of responses, depending upon the personality and mood of the person who hears it. Still another objective of using music in the classroom is to help children develop a familiarity with, an understanding of, and appreciation of the basic elements of music. Since music is divergent in nature, teachers should use music to foster divergent thinking. Another objective for using music in the classroom is to help children develop intellectual skills and concepts that enhance learning in other areas of the curriculum.

What areas should be included in a well-balanced music program? When many people think of classroom music, they think only of singing; however, there are many other aspects of music that need to be included for a well-rounded music education program. Besides singing, teachers need to provide opportunities for rhythmic movement, creative movement, listening, and experiences where children can use instruments.

With children, singing is as natural as breathing, so all teachers need to begin with is a repertoire of a few songs to get children started. In selecting music, teachers may wish to tap resources from their past—old school songs, camp songs, or folk songs. Often by changing words or tunes, teachers can adapt songs to fit classroom needs. Since children are such natural changers and are so free with creating new words to old songs, teachers should encourage this creative tendency by giving them opportunities to compose original words or melodies in a variety of different settings.

Creative and rhythmic movements are two other areas teachers need to include in a well-balanced music program. Creative movement is very similar to rhythmic movement. In both experiences children are active; however, in rhythmic movement the emphasis is on responding to the rhythm of the music while in creative movement the emphasis is on responding to the music with their bodies in a creative way. Movement activities are flexible enough that they can be inserted almost anywhere in the classroom schedule. They need not require a great deal of classroom time.

A good music program would not be well-balanced without listening experiences. The primary purpose of listening experiences in music is providing opportunities for children to acquire aural skills, such as auditory awareness, auditory discrimination, auditory sequencing and memory, and helping children to develop an appreciation of music. A teacher can provide musical listening experiences in a variety of settings to achieve different purposes.

Activities focusing on instruments help to round out a good music program. Instruments add spice to musical experiences. Children need time to experiment and to create their own sounds with instruments. They need chances to make and use their own rhythm instruments, but they also need experiences using good quality commercially made instruments. Besides using the various instruments that might be available in the classroom, children need opportunities to actually see and hear instrumentalists play.

Singing, creative movement, rhythmic movement, listening, and experiences with instruments—these are the components of a well-rounded music program. You will find that many of the activities suggested in this chapter cannot be isolated in one particular area. They often blend into several areas, but this is one of the beauties of music. It is flexible and fluent and it meets many needs.

ENCOURAGING DIVERGENT THINKING WITH LARGE GROUP ACTIVITIES IN MUSIC

The music activities in this section are somewhat different from the traditional approach to music because they allow for considerable creativity on the part of the participants. These musical experiences let students express themselves divergently in words, melodies, rhythms, body movements, and pictures and symbols. Many of the activities use props such as scarves, food color, and flashlights to enliven and enhance musical exploration. After an introduction to some of the activities in a large group setting, many students will want to extend and refine their ideas in small groups or individually.

singing

dynamic singing

Have your students make cards representing musical symbols. They might have symbols such as "f," "ff", "p", "ritard", < > , or accelerando. Choose a student from the group to act as musical director. The director selects a familiar song for the rest of the group to sing. As the director holds up cards with the various musical symbols on them, the students must sing the song according to the particular symbol they see. For example, if the symbol is "f", they sing the song loudly. If the symbol is < > ,

they get louder then softer. Let students take turns being director, selecting songs for the the rest of the class to sing, and choosing symbols for them to follow.

add your own words

Have your students try this little song. Let them suggest words for the last line.

(Add your own words)

singing commercial

Divide your class into small groups of three or four. Let them make up a singing commercial to share with their classmates.

melodic poems

Select a simple poem. After your students have read the poem together several times to get the feel of the rhythm of the poem, ask them to compose a song to go with the poem.

complete the tune

Encourage your students to complete the tune of this old jump rope song. Have them suggest different ways to finish the song. Record their versions on a tape recorder. Let students select their favorite tune and write the notes for it.

I went upstairs to make my bed. I made a mistake and I bumped my head

rhythmic movement

body part copy cat

Brainstorm with your students about different body parts that they might use to create rhythms. They might suggest movements such as clapping hands, snapping fingers, patting thighs, stamping feet, tapping shoulders, and so on. Suggest that your students make up different rhythms for the rest of the class to copy using various combinations of body movements. For example, one student might start the rhythm

snap tap tap

snap tap tap

while snapping fingers and tapping shoulders.

stretchy rhythms

Sew together the ends of a yard of inch-wide elastic to make a circle. Have your students form a circle. Turn on some music that has a jivey beat or perhaps a flowing rhythm. Throw the elastic band to someone in the circle. That person steps out into the center of the circle and using the elastic band moves to the music. He thinks of as many ways as he can to use the band stretching it in front of him, behind him, underfoot or overhead. When that person finishes using the band, he throws it to another person, who steps into the center of the circle and moves with the elastic.

add a part

Select some music to play for your class. Ask them to move to the music using only one body part. Then at a given signal, have them dance using two body parts, then three, then four. Encourage them to experiment to see how many different ways they can move the body parts they are dancing with.

theme and variations

Begin this rhythmic exercise by clapping four even beats to the basic 4/4 rhythm.

One, two, three, four

One, two, three, four.

Everybody joins in. When someone has an idea for a variation on that basic 4/4 rhythm, she raises her hand and without losing the beat begins clapping her new rhythm. For example,

When others catch on, they follow the new rhythm. When someone else gets an idea, he raises his hand and begins clapping his new rhythm with others following. For example,

Let others continue creating rhythmic variations on the basic beat.

Just for fun let your class select two of the rhythms that they liked the best. Divide your class into three groups. Group one claps the basic rhythm:

Group two claps another rhythm:

Group three claps the other rhythm:

Have them clap their rhythms simultaneously. Then let each group think of another way to express their rhythm besides clapping. They may choose to use rhythm instruments, to click with their tongues, or to use other body movements. Have them express their rhythms simultaneously.

creative movement

dancing on air

When we consider dancing, we generally think of our feet being on the floor, but why must they be? Why can't we dance with our feet in the air? Try this idea with your children. Let them lie on their backs (on a towel if the floor is dirty) and raise their hips so that their feet are in the air. Play music and let them interpret the different moods with their feet. For variety, you might let them "dance" with partners by putting their feet together.

balloons

A good way to initiate creative movement in the classroom is telling stories and having children "become" the character or characters in the story. Try this idea using balloons as your theme. First, bring out a real balloon for the children to observe. Blow it up, bounce it, let the air out, and do all sorts of things with the balloon letting the children describe what they observe. Then it's time to begin your story. Ask the children to pretend they are balloons and to act out what they hear in the story. In your story you might pretend to blow the balloon up and let it get bigger and bigger as the children pretend to expand. You might pretend to let go of the balloon and watch it fly all over the room. Blow it up again a little at a time. Suggest that the balloon is about to pop. Clap your hands loudly as the balloon pops. You might pretend to put helium into it and let it float around on a string. Bounce the balloon and talk about its lightness. With the helium in the balloon you can tell a story about it getting loose and flying all kinds of places. Add you own ideas to the story to fit your mood and that of the children.

shirt on the clothesline

Here's another story for creative movement. Ask your children to pretend to be a shirt on the clothesline. You can talk about hanging the shirt on the clothesline one shoulder at a time as your children pretend to be the shirt. The sun shines as the shirt hangs loosely on the line. A gentle breeze begins to blow and the shirt flaps gently in the breeze. The wind becomes stronger, and the shirt flaps more vigorously. The wind becomes so strong that one shoulder of the shirt pulls loose from the clothespin, and the shirt flaps all the more violently in the breeze after becoming entangled. Finally, the rest of the shirt pulls loose from the clothespin, and the shirt falls to the ground.

themes to move by

Stories are good catalysts for initiating creative movement with children; however, one single theme is often enough to give a child an idea and to get him moving. Pick one of these themes and see what your children can do with it. Move like

- an alligator

- scissors cutting

- an old man with a cane

- syrup coming out of a bottle

- the beaters on an electric mixer

- catsup stuck in a bottle which finally comes out in a big blurp

Divide your students into small groups and generate other themes to move by. Ask them to write their ideas on slips of paper and to drop them in a can. When you have time for creative movement, draw some of these themes and have your students move creatively based on what the themes suggest.

living pictures

Select interesting pictures that suggest creative movement. To make the pictures sturdy and durable, laminate them. Scatter your pictures on the floor. Play music as the children march or walk around the room. When the music stops, each child must move and stand beside a picture. The teacher points to a child, who must make her picture come alive by moving creatively to express the picture that she is standing beside. The teacher then points to one or two others, who in turn make their pictures come alive. Then the teacher starts the music over again and the game continues.

scarf stories

Collect enough scarves for each student in your class to have one. Get your students to contribute scarves that are no longer used at home. Make up a story to start this activity. After you have carried it out once with your class, have your students make up stories. The rest of the students move their scarves to imitate what is happening in the story. For example, you might start the story like this: "On the way to school today I saw a large, beautiful bird gliding in the sky." The students must make their scarves glide as you tell the story. You might continue with, "The other birds were flapping their wings vigorously as they flew." The students flap the scarves to imitate the other birds. You might wish to create a corporate story for the students to move by. Various students could volunteer to tell about something that they saw on the way to school as the others move creatively with their scarves to interpret what is being said. Any story that has action in it should be appropriate for creative movement with scarves.

statues

Dim the lights in the classroom and play some music. Encourage your students to move freely to the music. Stop the music after a short period of time. When the music stops, each child must freeze in whatever position she happens to be in. Shine a flashlight on one person. The rest of the children may relax and assume their normal positions, but the person spotlighted must remain as still as a statue while the others offer suggestions as to what the statue looks like. After several suggestions resume the music and play the game again.

props for creative movement

Bring a variety of props to school and let your students use them in creative movement experiences. Keep them all in a big prop box where you can pull them out quickly when you need them. Here are some ideas of props you might collect:

- different types of hats
- colorful wide ribbon from a florist
- bells attached to flowing skirts
- scarves
- long sticks
- hula hoops made from plastic
- tubing
- canes
- umbrellas
- ropes
- balls

Encourage your students to contribute props for the prop box. When it's time to use the props, play music and let your students decide how to use the props in creative movement.

paper streamer shapes

Select a student to draw different shapes on the board while the rest of the class waves crepe paper streamers to make the shapes. Here are a few ideas of shapes they might draw:

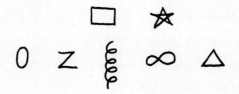

Let the students take turns drawing different shapes on the board.

creative movement wheels

When we move our bodies, there are three different aspects of our movement—space, time, and force. All movement takes place within a given area of space. Our movements last for specific amounts of time; they are fast or slow or moderate in speed (time). We move with a certain amount of force—with lightness or with strong exertive force. Bearing these different aspects of movement in mind, make four movement wheels out of pizza platters. One wheel is the movement wheel to designate the type of movement expected.

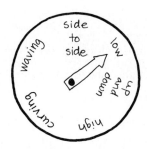

The next wheel is the wheel that designates the space the students are to move in.

The third wheel dictates the time or rhythm they are to move to.

The last wheel indicates the force with which they are to move.

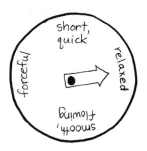

Spin the wheels and let them dictate how the students are to move.

Even though the different aspects of movement are dictated by the wheel, each student should be able to add something unique to the movement. Be sure to laminate each wheel before marking on it so you can vary the directions.

listening

describing music

Play a record of instrumental music. Ask students to listen carefully to the music and to think of all the adjectives that might describe it. After the music is over, ask them to brainstorm and share the descriptive adjectives that they thought of. Write their ideas on the board, categorizing the adjectives. Encourage flexible thinking. Help them think of categories that were little used or not used at all, and build on these categories. If the flow of ideas slacks, it might be appropriate to play the music again to stimulate new ideas.

sharing favorite songs

Let children share their favorite songs with one another. You might ask one or two children to bring their favorite records each day. When each child presents his music, ask him to tell the group why the music appeals to him. As the students listen to the music, ask them to record the mood that the music evokes in them or maybe to describe a picture that they "see" as they listen to the music. You might wish to encourage them to list all of the instruments they hear. Vary the way you ask your students to respond to the music.

colorful listening

Bring several flashlights to class. Cover the ends of each flashlight with a different color of clear acetate or cellophane. Darken the room and play a record for your students. Ask them to think of ways to respond to the music by using the colored flashlights. They might suggest using a red light going up the wall for music that goes up in pitch and using a blue light going down the wall for music that descends in pitch. They might choose to respond to the volume of the music, to the rhythm, or to various instruments. As they think of ideas, let them try them out as the music plays. This activity might be introduced in a large group setting and extended with a small group or an individual.

comparing art and music

Select a musical composition and a work of art from the same period (Contemporary, Impressionistic, Romantic, Classical, Baroque). Have your students carefully observe the piece of art and research its background and period. Let them listen to the music and research its background and period. Then play the music again and have them observe the piece of art. Ask your class to compare the music and the piece of art in as many ways as they can think of.

interpreting music with symbols

Listen with your class to a short record. Pick a very descriptive phrase in the music. Ask your students to suggest symbols that might describe what they hear in that phrase. Let them draw their symbols on the board. Their ideas for the same phrase will vary. For a staccato phrase they might draw symbols similar to the following:

. . . .　　　or　| |　| |

or　- ‾ - ‾

Then give each student several sheets of paper. Have each one draw symbols to represent selected phrases in the music. After the students have drawn their symbols, play the music again. Have them hold up the appropriate symbol for each phrase every time they hear that phrase repeated in the music.

ENCOURAGING DIVERGENT THINKING WITH SMALL GROUP ACTIVITIES IN MUSIC

When people think of classroom music, they often think of working in large group settings; however, musical experiences in small groups have advantages that large group situations lack. When children work in small groups, they are not as inhibited as they are in larger groups. Thus, they feel freer to be creative and to express their real feelings. In small group settings children have room to move. They have more chances to express themselves and to respond to each other's creative expressions. In this section you will find ideas that will provide children with many opportunities for creative musical expression in nonthreatening small group settings.

singing

creative lyrics

Encourage a small group of students to select a familiar song and rewrite the words to it. You might have to help them get started by suggesting tunes to use. Nursery rhymes and many songs in television commercials are easy to adapt. After your students have composed and practiced their new songs, ask them to sing them for the class.

mix 'n' match

Here's a variation on the previous activity. Help your students select the melody from one song and fit it to the words of another song. For example, try singing "Mary Had a Little Lamb" to the tune of "Row, Row, Row Your Boat." With a few slight rhythmic variations you can do it. After you show them how, let your students do their own mixing and matching.

rhythmic movement

classroom jingles

Divide students into small groups and show them how to compose jingles using people's names. Then ask them to write a jingle using the name of every person in

their group. For instance they might write

Look at Lucy
She's mighty goosey.

Here comes Al
He's my pal.

Hooray for Linda
She's getting slender.

After each group has composed their classroom jingle, let them chant it for their classmates. If they wish, have students in the class tap out the rhythms on rhythm instruments, while the group who composed the jingle chants the jingle.

clap your name

Have a small group of students take turns clapping out the rhythms of their names as they say each syllable. For example,

Ma - ri - mac   Ma - ri - mac
clap clap clap   clap clap clap

Ask each one to find another way to show the rhythm of his name rather than clapping it out. He might choose to snap it, pat his thighs to it, or stamp it out. Then challenge the group to take the names of each person in the group and to combine the names to make a group chant. They must clap as they chant each name. They may put the names in any order, repeat names or parts of names, use first names or full names, but they must use everyone's name. When they have finished

composing and practicing their chant, let
them chant and clap it for the entire class.

newspaper dance

Give one student a colored sheet of
newspaper from the Sunday comics section.
Hand each of the other students a regular
black and white sheet of newspaper. The
student who has the colored sheet of paper is
designated as the leader. The rest of the
group follows the leader as she uses the
paper to carry out the rhythm of the music
on a record. Stop the music after a short
period. When the music stops, the leader
hands her colored newspaper to someone else
in the group and takes that person's black
and white sheet. The person with the colored comic strip becomes the new leader of the
rhythmic dance as the music continues.

mouthy compositions

How many different sounds can you make
with your mouth? Let a small group of students experiment and see how many different
sounds they can come up with. Then ask them
to choose a few of those "mouth sounds" and
make up a rhythm combining the mouth sounds.
Let them record their rhythm on a tape recorder. After they have made "mouth sounds"
rhythms, have them experiment with different
"hand sounds" and "feet sounds."

keep the beat with body symbols

You will need to direct this activity in
the beginning until your students understand
it. After they catch on, they can play the
game on their own in small groups at any
time. Take a group of four or five people.
Ask each one to make up a symbol to represent
himself using a body rhythm. For symbols
students might choose body rhythms such as
pulling an ear, waving their fingers with
their thumb attached to their nose, or touching elbows together. Whatever symbol each
one selects, it must be short enough to do in
one or two beats. Everybody must remember
each person's symbol. Then the group is
ready to begin the game. Play a record with
a slow, steady, 4/4 march beat. Stand in a
circle. To start the game clap two times and
make your symbol. Then clap two more times
and make someone else's symbol. For example,

    clap, clap, pull ear (first person's
      1   2   3   4   symbol)
    clap, clap, touch elbows together (second
      1   2   3   4   person's symbol)

The person whose symbol you made now takes a
turn by first clapping and making his symbol
and then clapping and making someone else's
symbol:

    clap, clap, touch elbows together (second
      1   2   3   4   person's symbol)
    clap, clap, wave fingers over nose (third
      1   2   3   4   person's symbol)

The person whose symbol he made then takes a
turn and the game moves on with each student
keeping the beat.

creative
movement

human puppets

Have you ever pretended to be a puppet
dangling from strings? A puppet's movements
are stiff and stilted, and every motion is
determined by the puppeteer. Encourage your

students to practice being puppets. To add a little realism to the experience, get some 2.5 cm (1 inch) wide elastic and a bamboo pole about one meter long. Cut two short pieces of elastic about a half a meter in length and two longer pieces about a meter in length. Sew loops on both ends of each elastic piece--a small loop at one end that will thread on the pole and a larger loop on the other end of the elastic for hands or feet to fit into. Now thread the four elastic pieces on the pole with the short elastic pieces on the outside and the longer pieces on the inside. Have two children stand on chairs and hold the pole very high. Another child volunteers to be the "human puppet"; she puts her hands in the loops of the short elastic and her feet in the loops of the long elastic strips. Play some music that sounds like puppet music. "The Dance of the Puppets" from <u>The Small Dancer</u> (see bibliography) is an appropriate selection, but many other pieces of music would fit. When the music begins, the human puppet stretches and pulls on the elastic and moves stiffly to the music like a puppet. Let each child in the group have a turn at being a "human puppet."

footprint fun

Ask your students to draw and cut out their footprints. Tape the footprints in a circle on the floor spacing them close enough together so they are easy to step on. Then have your students suggest different ways we walk using as many different descriptive words as they can. They might suggest words such as <u>quickly</u>, <u>briskly</u>, <u>meander</u>, <u>dawdle</u>, <u>with a spring</u>, <u>limping</u>, or <u>prissily</u>. Have them write each description on a separate slip of paper and drop the slip in a can. One at a time a student pulls a slip of paper from the can and walks on the footprints in the way described on the paper. The others might wish to try to guess the word that was written on the paper from the way the person walks.

more themes to move by

Try these ideas to encourage children to move creatively. You may wish to develop each idea in more detail as the children move, or you may present the initial theme and have each student provide the details as she moves. Move like

• trees blowing in the wind

• a storm brewing

• a seed buried in the ground, pushing through the earth and unfolding into a beautiful flower

• elves bounding on mushrooms

• a dandelion seed floating through the air

• the waves of the ocean as they rush in and out

After presenting a few of these themes, ask the children to think of more themes to use for creative movement.

moving in outer space

Take three bamboo poles each about a meter in length. Ask six students to participate in an outer space walk. The students work in pairs, with one person holding each end of a bamboo pole with both hands. Ask your students to "freeze" at different levels while still holding the poles. Some might freeze quite close to the floor, others in a midway crouched position, while others might be reaching up high. Some of the poles might be crossing one another.

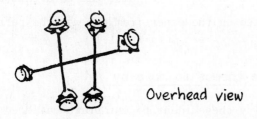

Overhead view

Play some electronic music that sounds a bit eerie or like outer space music. As the music plays, the students should begin to move as if they are moving in outer space, always holding the pole with both hands. They may weave in and out of the other poles, moving up and down, turning around and around, but they must always hold the pole with both hands. They must respond to and move with their partner, who is holding the other end of the pole.

listening

learning about the
basic elements of music

Take the basic elements of music—rhythm, melody, harmony, dynamics, form, and mood.

After studying some of these terms, let small groups of students select some of these terms, define them in their own words, and then tape record examples of the terms. They may put together a little skit using the tape recorder to demonstrate these elements of music. For example, melody is a sequence of tones. Harmony is a sequence of tones added to the melody to enrich it. Students may start out by recording examples of a melody played all alone. To demonstrate harmony, they may record examples of harmony being added to the simple melody. Let's think about another example. Dynamics is the loudness or softness of music, the gradual change in volume or accents in the music. With a tape recorder they may select and point out examples where dynamics are evident in the music. Encourage your students to be unique in planning their presentations. Ask them to present their demonstration to the rest of the class.

body interpretations of music

Play a record for your students, one that exemplifies contrasting dynamics, that is, several shifts between loud and soft passages. Ask your students to cup their hands around their mouths as if shouting every time the music is loud and to put one finger in front of their mouths when the music becomes soft. Ask them to suggest other body motions they could use to show the loudness and softness of the music. They might wish to clap with full hands when the music is loud and clap with only two fingers on each hand when the music is soft. Let them try out some of their ideas to the music. Select another record with varying pitches. Let students suggest ways to demonstrate the high pitches and the low pitches in the music. Have them try their ideas with the music.

fun with water glasses

Have a small group of students fill glasses with different levels of water and strike the glasses gently with a metal spoon. Let them experiment with the pitch by varying the levels of water in each glass. After they have had time to experiment making sounds, encourage them to take turns composing different tunes on the glasses. Then ask a student to pick a partner and make a simple tune of four or five sounds. The partner listens carefully and tries to reproduce that tune. Be sure that partners switch roles so that each person has a turn "composing" a tune on the glasses and each one has a turn listening and reproducing the tune.

instruments

rhythmic task cards

Let students work in small groups and write out task cards for their friends to decipher and play on rhythm instruments. First have them decide what symbol will represent each instrument. A drum might be represented with the symbol, "O". A triangle could be represented with a " ", rhythm sticks with "X", and so on. A student might write a task card that looks like this:

OOΔ OOΔ OOΔ

If someone played that task card, she would play

    drum, drum, triangle
    drum, drum, triangle
    drum, drum, triangle

Students can also make task cards for body rhythms. For instance, a snap could be represented by "6", a clap by "/", and " " could mean stomp feet. Thus, a task card with

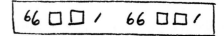

would mean

    snap, snap, stomp, stomp, clap
    snap, snap, stomp, stomp, clap.

In a small group, each student could hold up the task card he has written, and the rest of the students in the group could respond together.

invent an instrument

Kids are natural inventors. They often enjoy spending long periods of time inventing contraptions to overcome a problem that they have encountered. Present a small group of students with this problem. Ask them to invent an instrument that can make different pitches. There are many different possibilities—different thicknesses of rubber bands stretched with varying amounts of tension, a drum head loosened or tightened, or different lengths of metal pipe. Let your group come up with original ideas. Give them plenty of time to work on this project. Reward uniqueness.

SING ABOUT YOURSELF

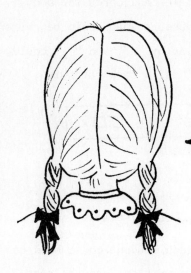

Sing a song to your group and tell them about yourself. Make up words to a song you already know, or make up your own tune.

Singing

IMITATIONS IN SONG

Can you sing like a BIRD?

a SEAL?

an OPERA STAR?

a CRICKET?

an AUCTIONEER?

a STREET VENDOR?

Singing

JUMP ROPE JINGLE

Make up a jump rope jingle.
Try jumping rope as you say it.

"Watch me jump. I'm a jumping dude. I can burn the ground up when I'm in the mood."

Rhythmic Movement

COPY MY "RHYTHM"

Let each person in your group select a rhythm instrument. Choose a leader. The leader plays a short rhythm on his instrument for the rest of you to copy. After the leader has had several turns, switch leaders.

Rhythmic Movement

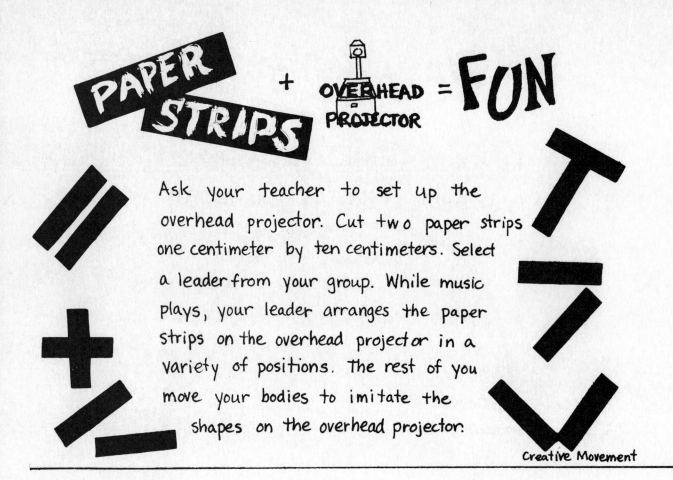

PAPER STRIPS + OVERHEAD PROJECTOR = FUN

Ask your teacher to set up the overhead projector. Cut two paper strips one centimeter by ten centimeters. Select a leader from your group. While music plays, your leader arranges the paper strips on the overhead projector in a variety of positions. The rest of you move your bodies to imitate the shapes on the overhead projector.

Creative Movement

MOVE A Partner With Your SOUND

Work with a partner. Make sounds like these:

JUMPY sounds

LOUD sounds

soft sounds

smooth sounds

HIGH SOUNDS

LOW SOUNDS

See if your partner can move to interpret your sounds. Switch places to make and interpet more sounds.

Creative Movement

SHADOW DANCING

Ask your teacher to set up an overhead or filmstrip projector. Turn on your favorite record. Stand in front of the light and do a shadow dance to the music. Observe your shadows on the wall as you dance. Now make your fingers dance. Experiment to see how many different shadows you can cast using only your fingers.

Creative Movement

MIRROR IMAGES

Select a partner. One of you pretends to be a person moving in front of a mirror, while the other pretends to be the image reflected in the mirror. See how closely you can make your movements match. Switch roles and try it again.

Creative Movement

SEA SHELL SOUNDS

Hold a big shell to your ear. What do you hear? Show the people in your group what the sound you hear reminds you of by moving your body. As they watch you moving, let them try to guess what you heard. Pass the shell to someone else. Let him listen and move!

Listening

NATURE'S SOUNDS

"tap tap"

"squeek"

Go for a nature walk with your group. Each one of you bring back an object that makes an interesting sound. Get together with your group and experiment with the sounds your objects make. Combine some of your sounds in an unusual way to "compose" an interesting musical composition.

"crinkle, rustle"

"tick-tick"

"THUD"

Instruments

STORMY MUSIC

Work with your group to compose some stormy music. You might use the piano as one of the instruments, but use other instruments also. What could be the thunder? lightning? raindrops? wind?

Instruments

Background Music

Read or make up a story. To make your story more vivid, choose instruments to play for background music as you tell the story.

You might choose drums, rattles, xylophones, tambourines, or you might branch out and create your background music with other objects.

Instruments

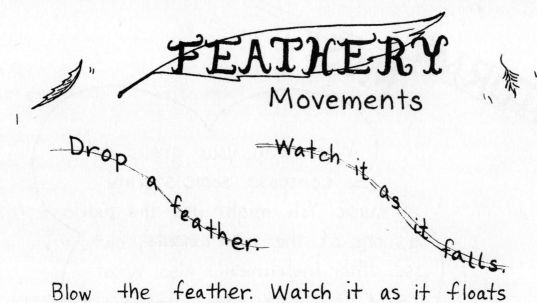

FEATHERY
Movements

Drop a feather. Watch it as it falls.

Blow the feather. Watch it as it floats gently on the air currents. Pretend to be that feather. Move the way the feather moves. Experiment doing different things with the feather and trying to move like it moves.

Creative Movement

ENCOURAGING DIVERGENT THINKING WITH INDIVIDUAL ACTIVITIES IN MUSIC

Classroom music generally flows better in large and small group settings than individually. Many times students encourage and spur one another on when they work in groups; however, there are times when an individual needs to be all alone to experience music deeply and to respond truthfully, fully, and accurately to his emotions. In this section you will find activities that allow children time to be alone, to think, to experience music in depth. Our individual music activities will allow children to experiment expressing music divergently on their own. Quite often these activities will begin with motivational large group discussions before they require the child to work alone. In many of the activities the individual begins working alone and ends by sharing what he has learned with a group.

singing

singing telegram

Here's a unique music assignment that students can work with on their own. Let students study about telegrams and how they are sent. Discuss how the costs for telegrams are figured by the word and how each sentence ends with the word "stop." Tell them briefly about singing telegrams and the different occasions for which they are used. Then ask each student to make up a singing telegram for one of her friends.

telephone songs

Did you ever realize you could compose a fancy tune based on your telephone number? Here's what you do. Find middle C on the piano. Put the numeral "1" on that key with a grease pencil or by taping on the numeral. Take every key starting with middle "C" going through "D" above high "C" and number each one consecutively 1-9. The key below middle "C" should have the numeral "0."

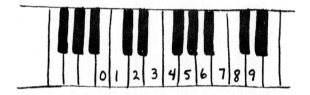

Suppose your phone number is 234-6398. Go to the piano and play these numbers, singing each number as you play. Play it over and over and arrange the numbers rhythmically to please you. You might wish to add other notes after you have played and sung these first seven notes to give your song a finishing touch.

After you have experimented making a song out of your own telephone number, show your students how to do it. Ask them to make up a song using their own telephone numbers. Encourage them to sing the numbers as they play them in order to develop a keen sense of pitch. Individual students might enjoy choosing other telephone numbers and making up songs.

creative movement

listen, look and mime

People who pantomime are called mimes. Discuss mimes with your children and explain how they tell a story without saying a word. Mention that mimes must be very observant in order to give accurate presentations. Let your students experiment pantomiming and guessing what each one is acting out. Then give your students an assignment. Ask them to go outside alone sometime during the day and sit for five minutes observing the things around them and listening carefully to the sounds they hear. Ask each one to plan a mime based on something she observed during that five-minute period and to present that mime to a small group of students.

listening

listening to music i don't like

Encourage children to talk about types of music they like and types they dislike. With the help of your students, bring in a variety of different records. Give each student the following assignment to complete within the week: "Pick some kind of music that you don't especially enjoy. Listen carefully to it and to other records like it if they are available. Can you think of reasons this kind of music might appeal to others? Write about it." After all the students have completed their assignment, let them share the music they choose and what they wrote about it in small groups.

stories based on music

Find the record <u>Peter and the Wolf</u> by
Prokofiev. Tell your children the story.
Encourage them to listen to the music and
to follow the story in their minds as they
listen, then provide a variety of music for
your students to listen to. Include some program music--music that tells a story--in your
supply of records. Ask a student to select a
record, listen to it, and write a story based
on what the music might be saying. Encourage
that student to illustrate the story.

television homework

Most of the students in your classroom
watch television at night. Why not work in a
little creative listening assignment for them
to carry out while they are watching? Ask
them to listen to the background music played
on their favorite television shows. Have
them listen carefully and make a list of all
the different musical instruments they hear.

instruments

pick an instrument

Let each student pick an instrument to
study. Have a wide variety of books on musical instruments available. Ask each student
to find out about the instrument chosen and
locate a record that gives an example of that
instrument playing. Ask each one to report
to the class in an interesting and unique way.

composing music

Many teachers have pianos in their
classroom just collecting dust. If you
happen to be one of those teachers, take advantage of this situation. Who knows? You

might have a promising composer in your classroom just waiting to be awakened and motivated.
Here's what you do. Number the keys on the
piano from the "B" below middle "C" to the "E"
above high "C" with the numerals 0-10.

See the activity "Telephone Songs" on page
209 for more detail. Ask each child to write
a series of numbers 0-10, making sure that
the series ends on the numbers one or eight.
After the child has written his series of
numbers, have him play his music on the piano
by matching the numbers he has written to the
numbers on the keys of the piano. Ask him to
adjust his numbers if needed in order to
improve his tune.

This activity may be carried out in
another way. The student may play a short
series of notes on the piano and write down
the corresponding numbers to those notes on
a card so that others can play it.

instrumental designs

For a different kind of homework, give
this assignment. Ask students to design their
own rhythm instruments using objects around the
house. Encourage them to think hard in order to
make an instrument that might be different from
anyone else's in the class. They might combine
and alter objects such as coat hangers, bottle
caps, cans, embroidery hoops, bells, or combs.
Ask them to give their instruments descriptive
names. After the students have brought their
instruments to class, let them play their
instruments all together to accompany a
record.

instruments from a grab bag

Make a big collection of junk items--
popsicle sticks, plastic lemons, tennis
balls, bells, rubber bands, small boxes,
paper, dried beans, cans, and sticks. Put
your objects in a big bag. Let each student
draw three objects from the bag. They must
work together combining the three objects to
create a rhythm instrument. They may use
other items from the classroom if they need
them. Encourage each student to be creative
in designing the instrument.

background sounds

Here is an assignment for your students
to work on individually. Have each student
search for objects to make the following
background sounds:

- Someone falling down a staircase
- A giant walking through a house
- A creaking door
- A snake slithering through dry leaves
  (a snake does make a sound)

Encourage each student to "compose" three
other background sounds of her own choosing.
Let the student play the background sounds
for others to see if they can guess what the
sounds represent.

playing with the symphony

Have serveral different recordings of
instrumental music for your students to listen to. Let each student select his favorite
recording and listen to it until he becomes
familiar with the music. Let him create some
new dimension to the sound of the music. He
may want to accompany the music with a rhythm
instrument of his choosing, with an object
that he put together to obtain a unique
effect, or with a body sound. Encourage
him to use an "instrument" that adds to the
beauty of the music.

copy the rhythm

Ask each student to watch someone in
action--someone walking, rocking, working,
dancing, or playing. Let each student choose
an action, then encourage that student to
select an appropriate rhythm instrument and
accompany the action observed.

harping harmony

"Have you ever seen a homemade harp?"
"What might you use to make the sound of a
string instrument?" "How could you vary the
pitch?"

After asking the students many questions
about stringed instruments and brainstorming
about materials to use, give each student a
musical homework assignment. Have him construct a harp--one that is different from any
homemade instrument he has ever seen. After
the students have completed the assignment
let each demonstrate his instrument before
the class. Let the students vote on the most
versatile harp, the most original harp, and
the most beautiful sounding harp. Let them
think of other categories for recognition and
make awards to be handed out.

Divergent MUSIC Activities
for individual students to do on their own

Imitate the Sound
Sit very quietly. Listen to all the sounds around you. Try to imitate the sounds you hear. How closely can you duplicate them?

Show the Beat
Listen to some music. How many different ways can you move your body to the beat of the music?

Moving Creatively
How many ways can you walk, sit in a chair, run, slide, or move from one side of the room to another?

Musical Report
Find out about the life of a famous composer. Show your results in a unique way.

Silly Sounds
Create sounds that are funny, sounds that are mournful, scary, or harsh. Can you think of other kinds of sounds to make? Get with two friends. Combine your sounds in a "sound trio".

Music To Paint By
Listen to some beautiful music. Paint what the music sounds like as you listen.

Shapes and Letters
Using your body how many geometric shapes can you make? How many letters of the alphabet can you make?

Tambourine Experiments
What can you do with a tambourine? Experiment. See how many different ways you can play it.

- 1 - 2 - 3 - 4 !

Building Your Mind Power

Now that you've had an opportunity to use divergent music activities with your students in various settings and group sizes, you should be ready to create a few divergent music activities on your own. These ideas should give you a little workout with divergent thinking. Take the ideas presented below and try them one at a time in your classroom.

1. Make up a story for your students. Ask them to move creatively to it and act it as you tell it. For ideas see "The Shirt on the Clothesline," p. 193.

2. Take time to let children listen to a few different types of music. Let them discuss how these compositions make them feel. Follow up this discussion with some classroom activity based on their responses.

3. Find a creative way to introduce a new composer to your class.

4. Plan some rhythmic movement activities to use with your class. Be creative. Use a different rhythmic movement activity every day for a week.

5. Plan an interesting way to bring some live music into your classroom. You may wish to use parents, fellow teachers, high school students, friends, or you may take your class on a visit. Plan a motivating introduction and a unique follow-up.

6. Music is often a neglected art in the classroom. Find a creative way to blend music with one of the subjects you teach every day. Do it at least once a week for a semester.

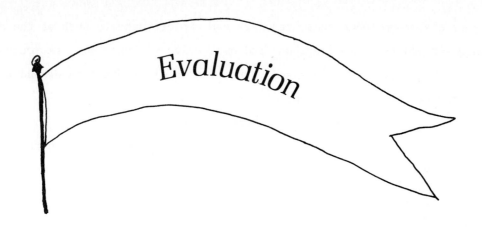

Evaluation

10

Observation and evaluation are vital educational processes. These processes are important because they help teachers understand themselves and their students, and they provide insight related to the quality of their programs. Evaluation techniques help teachers see themselves objectively. Observation and evaluation can provide guidance in day-to-day planning. These processes also help teachers make long-range plans wisely. Children benefit from observation and evaluation, too. By using these techniques, teachers can identify children's interests and needs and assess their progress. Through observation and evaluation teachers can gain clearer understanding of their programs. They are able to pinpoint strengths and weaknesses. Without observation and evaluations, teachers could not set realistic goals and judge whether or not they have reached them. To benefit from observation and evaluation procedures, educators need to know how to evaluate properly. Teachers should evaluate frequently rather than spasmodically. The items they include in their observation and evaluation instruments should focus specifically on their program goals and objectives. Educators should make their instruments easy and short enough to complete quickly. Since most classrooms include students with a wide range of abilities, teachers should strive to include items with varying levels of difficulty.

Evaluation Questions for Teachers

Through evaluation, teachers can gain insight into their own personal development. They can judge their effectiveness as leaders of divergent thinking in the classroom. In evaluating their classroom techniques, teachers can explore aspects such as the classroom atmosphere they set and their motivational and evaluative techniques. Ask yourself the following questions to help you understand yourself as a divergent thinker and as a facilitator of divergent thinking in the classroom.

Personal Development

1. Have you done any divergent thinking on your own since you read this book?

2. In what situations did you apply divergent thinking? Did you use your skills to solve family problems, economic problems, relational problems with adults outside the family, or did you use your skills in other ways?

3. How frequently do you use divergent thinking skills? Do you find that you use your skills more frequently since reading this book?

4. What techniques did you use to develop your divergent thinking skills? Did you use the exercises in this book, or did you develop your skills independently?

5. Are you now comfortable and confident in using divergent thinking? Do you find it fun and challenging, or is it a problem for you?

6. Do you see an improvement in your life as a result of divergent thinking? How has your life improved?

Classroom Atmosphere

1. When you use divergent thinking activities in your classroom, do the students seem to contribute their ideas freely?

2. Do you use divergent thinking for different purposes in the classroom? Consult your lesson plan book and see if you have incorporated divergent thinking as you introduce or conclude topics of study. List some ways you have used divergent thinking as an integral part of your work on various topics. How have you used divergent thinking exercises just for fun? Have you encouraged students to use their divergent thinking skills to solve social problems?

3. As you ask divergent thinking questions, do you use ones that your students can relate to? Describe some examples.

4. Do you vary the lengths of time spent on divergent thinking in your classroom?

5. How do you vary your routines for sharing answers to divergent thinking questions?

6. Have you built up a tolerance for periods of silence as children develop answers to divergent thinking questions?

7. How well have you adapted to the role of listener in the divergent thinking process? Describe some ways in which you have improved your listening skills.

8. List some ways in which you respond to and encourage students' answers to divergent thinking questions.

9. How do you encourage students to respect and value each other's ideas?

10. What are some techniques you use when students "get stuck" or run out of ideas in the divergent thinking process?

11. List several specific ways in which you help students to improve and refine their divergent thinking skills.

The Teacher as a Motivator

1. Do you display enthusiasm when you interact with your students?

2. Are you willing to participate in classroom activities?

3. Do you allow your students ample time and freedom to interact with each other?

4. Who does the most talking and planning in divergent thinking experiences in class--you or the students? Do you trust students to work independently in groups or alone, or do you constantly interrupt them?

5. Do you use a variety of motivational techniques, such as good questions, demonstrations, guests, field trips, and unusual materials or objects? List several motivational techniques you have used successfully.

6. Do you gather appropriate material to get high quality divergent thinking experiences started?

The Teacher as an Evaluator

1. What have you learned from observation of your students working together? Who participates freely? Who needs encouragement before participating? Who plays the roles of leader and follower? When do students play these roles?

2. Have you used observation and evaluation items that reveal students' interests and experiences? What have you learned?

3. Have you used observation and evaluation items that help to pinpoint specific problems that students have? What changes have you made as a result of what you have learned?

4. How do you share the results of your observations and evaluations? What kinds of praise and encouragement do you give? How do you guide students to improve? Do you give specific criticism? Do you give clear suggestions for overcoming problems?

5. Do you ask questions that focus on your goals and objectives?

6. What changes have you made in your program as a result of your observation and evaluation activities?

Evaluation Questions for Students

Observation and evaluation techniques help teachers to become aware of student participation and to assess their progress. Through observation and evaluation teachers gain understanding of their students' attitudes toward divergent thinking. Teachers learn about students' strengths and weaknesses related to divergent thinking skills. Teachers use many different settings and techniques to promote divergent thinking in the classroom. Observation and evaluation can help teachers find which settings and techniques are most effective with their students. Consider the questions below. They should help you understand how well your students are developing in their divergent thinking skills.

1. Have your students progressed in their abilities to think divergently? How do you know? Can you identify specific students who seemed unable to use divergent thinking skills in the beginning but who have shown unusual progress?

2. Do your students seem enthusiastic about using divergent thinking skills? Give examples.

3. To what divergent thinking experiences did your students respond most positively?

4. At what points do your students seem to have difficulty with divergent thinking?

5. Do your students seem to generate more creative ideas in large group settings, in small group settings, or when they work alone?

6. Which students seem to prefer oral forms of divergent thinking? Which ones seem to enjoy responding in written forms? Which students seem to freely express themselves in nonverbal forms, such as art, drama, music, or creative movement?

7. Do the same students generate ideas all of the time, or is there a wide spread of participation? If the same students seem to be dominating the classroom discussions, what techniques do you use to get more students to participate?

8. Do your students seem to be building on each other's ideas, or do they mainly work from their own ideas?

9. Do your students present a variety of ideas from different categories, or do they generally stay in the same category when producing ideas?

Evaluation Questions About Divergent Thinking in Educational Programs

This section includes some specific questions to help you focus on the nature of divergent thinking and your expertise in motivating students to use divergent thinking in the classroom. Use the following questions to help you determine how well you have dealt with divergent thinking in your program.

Thinking About Brainstorming

1. How do you present problems for brainstorming in order to encourage students to contribute many ideas?

2. How well do you withhold criticism until students have generated many ideas?

3. Do you accept and value fanciful and unusual answers?

4. As a part of brainstorming do you encourage students to combine ideas and to build on each other's ideas?

5. What procedures do you use to help students to evaluate the relative merits of answers or ideas?

Thinking About Fluency

1. Do you encourage students to contribute many different answers to problems or questions?

2. Do you allow enough time for students to generate many answers?

3. On the average, has the number of student responses to questions increased since you first began divergent thinking activities?

Thinking About Flexibility

1. How do you make students aware of many different categories of possible responses to questions or problems?

2. Do you encourage flexible thinking by introducing new categories for answers or encouraging students to do so?

3. Describe some methods you have prepared in advance so that you can suggest different categories for your students to explore.

4. Have your students started to introduce new categories of answers independently? List some examples.

5. In general, has the number of categories of answers to divergent thinking questions increased in your classroom?

Thinking About Elaboration

1. How do you encourage students to elaborate on their answers to divergent thinking questions? How do you motivate your students to elaborate on each other's answers?

2. Do you encourage elaboration in several forms? Describe examples of your students elaborating by drawing, writing, talking, or other means.

Thinking About Originality

1. What cues do you use to promote original thinking? List some ways you ask questions. You might include phrases such as "Try to get an answer no one else could think of" or "Make something really unusual."

2. What different ways do you try to encourage originality? Do you encourage students to branch off from other's ideas, build their own ideas "from scratch," or combine several ideas to make new original ideas?

3. Describe some ways you have provided opportunities for students to compare their ideas and determine which ones are really unique, original, and unusual.

Divergent thinking can be challenging. It can offer new perspectives to both children and adults. Divergent thinking can open up people's lives to many new possibilities and adventures. We hope you have seen that divergent thinking is not limited to one small facet of learning but can apply to all areas. As you practice divergent thinking, remember to stop and evaluate often. Only then can you refine your skills, improve, and grow.

REFERENCES

ALDOUS, John, "Family Background Factors and Originality in Children," 1970 (ERIC Document Reproduction Service No. ED 080187).

ANDERSON, Richard C., "Shaping Logical Behavior in Six- and Seven-Year-Olds," 1964 (ERIC Document Reproduction Service No. ED 001232).

ARONOFF, Frances Webber, Music and Young Children. New York: Holt, Rinehart and Winston, Inc., 1969.

BAYLESS, Kathleen M. and Marjorie E. RAMSEY, Music: A Way of Life for the Young Child. Saint Louis: The C.V. Mosby Company, 1978.

BEAVEN, Mary H., "My God, There Are Trees in Texas!", Elementary English, 53, no. 5 (May 1975), 695-700.

BENNETT, Albert B. and Leonard T. NELSON, Mathematics: An Informal Approach. Boston: Allyn and Bacon, 1979.

BERRETTA, Shirley, Comparative Effects of Play on Creative Thinking: The Immediate Influence of Art, Drama, and Playground Experiences on Children (Doctoral dissertation, University of Southern Mississippi, 1971). Dissertation Abstracts International, 35, 05, 2981.

BESEMER, Susan P. and Donald J. TREFFINGER, "Analysis of Creative Products: Reveiw and Synthesis," Journal of Creative Behavior, 15, no. 3 (third quarter 1981), 158-78.

BIRKENSHAW, Lois, Music for Fun Music for Learning. Toronto, Canada: Holt, Rinehart and Winston of Canada, Limited, 1977.

BITTER, Gary and Jerald L. MIKESELL, Activities Handbook for Teaching with the Hand-Held Calculator. Boston: Allyn and Bacon, 1980.

BLATT, Gloria, and Jean CUNNINGHAM, It's Your Move: Expressive Movement Activities for the Language Arts Class. New York: Teachers College Press, 1981.

BLOOM, Benjamin S., ed., Taxonomy of Educational Objectives, Handbook I: Cognitive Domain. New York: Longmans & Green, 1956.

BLOOMFIELD, Dorothy, Young Math Activity: Measurement. New York: Thomas Y. Crowell, no date.

BRITTAIN, W. Lambert, Creativity, Art, and the Young Child. New York: Macmillan Publishing Co., Inc., 1979.

BROWN, Rosellen, and others, eds., The Whole Word Catalogue. New York: Virgil Books, 1972.

CALLAHAN, C.M. and J.S. RENZULLI, "The Effectiveness of a Creativity Training Program in the Language Arts," The Gifted Child Quarterly, 21, no. 4 (Winter 1977), 538-41.

CARIN, Arthur A. and Robert B. SUND, Teaching Science Through Discovery (4th ed.). Columbus, Ohio: Charles E. Merrill, 1980.

CARLSON, Deborah Lynn, "Space, Time, and Force: Movement as a Channel to Understanding Music," Music Educators Journal, September, 1980, 52-55.

CARLSON, Ruth Kearney, Enrichment Ideas (2nd ed.). Dubuque, Iowa: Wm. C. Brown Company, 1976.

CHASE, Linwood W. and Martha T. JOHN, A Guide for the Elementary Social Studies Teacher (3rd ed.). Boston, Massachusetts: Allyn and Bacon, Inc., 1978.

CHENFELD, Mimi Brodsky, Teaching Language Arts Creatively. New York: Harcourt Brace Jovanovich, Inc., 1978.

CHERRY, Betty Steinbarger, A Strategy for Developing Creative Thinking (Torrance Model) in Trainable Mentally Retarded Children Through a Program of Attention and Concentration and Open-Ended Methods. Dissertation Abstracts International, 33, 9-A, 4975.

CHERRY, Clare, Creative Art for the Developing Child. Belmont, California: Lear Siegler, Inc./Fearon Pulishers, 1972.

CLAGUE-TWEET, Claudia, "The Effects of the Implementation of Creativity Training in the Elementary School Social Studies Curriculum," Journal of Creative Behavior, 15, no. 1, (first quarter 1981), 70-71.

CLIATT, Mary Jo Puckett, Criteria for the Selection of Music Activities for Young Children. Unpublished Ph.D. dissertation, University of Mississippi, 1975.

CLIATT, Mary Jo Puckett, Jean M. SHAW, and Jeanne M. SHERWOOD, "Effects of Training on the Divergent Thinking Abilities of Kindergarten Children," Child Development, 51, no. 4 (December 1980), 1061-64.

CLIATT, Mary Jo Puckett, and Jean M. SHAW, Junk Treasures. Englewood Cliffs, New Jersey: Prentice-Hall, Inc., 1981.

COLE, Henry P., "Exemplary Curricula as Vehicles for Facilitating Creativity," Journal of Research and Development in Education, 4, no. 3, (Spring 1971), 23-28.

Consumers Union, Consumers Report. Mount Vernon, New York: Consumers Union of the United States, Inc. Published twelve times yearly.

Consumers Union, Penny Power. Mount Vernon, New York: Consumers Union of the United States, Inc. Published six times yearly.

COODY, Betty. Using Literature with Young Children. Dubuque, Iowa: Wm. C. Brown Company, 1979.

COODY, Betty, and David NELSON, Successful Activities for Enriching the Language Arts. Belmont, California: Wadsworth Publishing Company, 1982.

COODY, Betty, and David NELSON, Teaching Elementary Language Arts: A Literature Approach. Belmont, California: Wadsworth Publishing Company, 1982.

CULLINAN, Bernice E., and Carolyn W. CARMICHAEL, eds., Literature and Young Children. Urbana, Illinois: National Council of Teachers of English, 1977.

DAFFRON, Martha Ruth, The Influence of Selective Factors on the Divergent Thinking Abilities of Fourth Grade Children. (Doctoral dissertation, Mississippi State University, 1971), Dissertation Abstracts International, 32, 07, 3780.

DAVIS, Gary A., "Teaching for Creativity: Some Guiding Lights," Journal of Research and Development in Education, 4, no. 3 (Spring 1971), 29-33.

DAVIS, Terry and others, "A Comparison of Achievement and Creativity of Elementary School Students Using Project vs. Textbook Programs," Journal of Research in Science Teaching, 13, no. 3 (May 1976), 205-12.

DE MILLE, Richard, Put Your Mother on the Ceiling. New York: Viking Press, 1967.

DEVITO, Alfred and Gerald H. KROCKOVER, Creative Sciencing. Boston, Massachusetts: Little Brown and Company, 1976.

EMERSON, Peggy and Cindy LEIGH, "Movement: 'Enchantment' in the Life of a Child," Childhood Education (November, December, 1979), 85-87.

FARLESS, James W., "Indices of Classroom Creativity," 1974 (ERIC Document Reproduction Service No. ED 106372).

FEELINGS, Muriel, Moja Means One: A Swahili Counting Book. New York: Dial, 1971.

FELDHUSEN, J.F., S. HOBSON, and D.J. TREFFINGER, "The Effects of Visual and Verbal Stimuli on Divergent Thinking," The Gifted Child Quarterly, 19, no. 3, (1975), 205-9.

FORMAN, Susan G., "Effects of Socioeconomic Status on Creativity in Elementary School Children," Creative Child and Adult Quarterly, 4, no. 2 (Summer 1979), 87-92.

FORSETH, Sonia Daleki, "Art Activities, Attitudes, and Achievement in Elementary Mathematics," Studies in Art Education, 21, no. 2, 1980, 22-27.

FRANK, Marjorie, If You're Trying to Teach Kids How to Write, You've Gotta Have This Book. Nashville, Tennessee: Incentive Publication, 1979.

FRANKLIN, B.S. and P.N. RICHARDS, "Effects on Children's Divergent Thinking Abilities of a Period of Direct Teaching for Divergent Production," British Journal of Educational Pyschology, 47, no. 1 (February 1977), 66-70.

FULTS, Elizabeth Ann, The Effects of an Instructional Program on the Creative Thinking Skills, Self-Concept, and Leadership of Intellectually Gifted Elementary Students (Doctoral dissertation, North Texas State University, 1980). Dissertation Abstracts International, 40, 7-A, 2931.

FUYS, David J. and Rosamond Welchman TISCHLER, *Teaching Mathematics in the Elementary School.* Boston: Little, Brown and Company, 1979.

GAITSKELL, Charles and Al HURWITZ, *Children and Their Art: Methods for the Elementary School.* New York: Harcourt Brace Jovanovich, 1975.

GALLAGHER, James J., *Teaching the Gifted Child.* Boston: Allyn and Bacon, 1964.

GERBER, Linda L. and B. Joan E. HAINES, *Leading Young Children to Music: A Resource Book for Teachers.* Columbus, Ohio: Charles E. Merrill Publishing Company, 1980.

GOOR, Amos, and Tamar RAPOPORT, "Enhancing Creativity in an Informal Educational Framework," *Journal of Educational Psychology,* 69, no. 5, 1977, 636-43.

GRAHAM, Al, *Timothy Turtle.* New York: The Viking Press, Inc., 1946.

GREENBERG, Pearl, Chairperson, *Art Education: Elementary.* Washington, D.C.: National Art Education Association, 1972.

GUILFORD, J.P., *Creative Intelligence in Education* (Conference Report). Los Angeles: Division of Research and Guidance, Los Angeles County Superintendent of Schools Office, 1958.

GUILFORD, J.P., "Creativity," *American Psychologist,* 5, no. 9 (September 1950), 444-54.

HADDON, F.A., "Primary Education and Divergent Thinking Abilities," *British Journal of Educational Psychology,* 41, no. 2 (June 1971), 136-47.

HARLAN, Jean, *Science Experiences for the Early Childhood Years*, 2nd ed. Columbus, Ohio: Charles E. Merrill Publishing Company, 1980.

HASKELL, Lendall L., *Art in the Early Childhood Years.* Columbus, Ohio: Charles E. Merrill Publishing Company, 1979.

HERBERHOLZ, Barbara, *Early Childhood Art.* Dubuque, Iowa: Wm. C. Brown Co., 1979.

HOLLANDER, Sheila K., "The Effect of Questioning on the Solution of Verbal Arithmetic Problems," *School Science and Mathematics,* 77, no. 4 (December 1977), 659-61.

HUNT, Tamara, and Nancy RENFRO, *Puppetry in Early Childhood Education.* Austin, Texas: Nancy Renfro Studios, 1982.

HUNTSBERGER, J., "Developing Divergent-Productive Thinking in Elementary School Children Using Attribute Games and Problems," *Journal of Research in Science Teaching,* 13, no. 2 (March 1976), 185-91.

HURWITZ, Abraham B., and Arthur GODDARD, *Games to Improve Your Child's English.* New York: Simon & Schuster, 1969.

JACOBSON, Willard J., and Abby BERGMAN, *Science for Children.* Englewood Cliffs, New Jersey: Prentice-Hall, 1980.

JOHNSON, Jerald Eugene, <u>Creative Teaching:</u> <u>Its Effect Upon the Creative Thinking</u> <u>Ability, Achievement, and Intelligence of</u> <u>Selected Fourth-Grade Students</u> (Doctoral dissertation, McNeese State University, 1974), <u>Dissertation Abstracts International</u>, 35, <u>07</u>, 4132.

JONES, Cynthia, and Dorothy RICH, "Success for Children Begins at Home: Thinking," 1973 (ERIC Document Reproduction Service No. ED 113053).

KENNEDY, Leonard M., <u>Guiding Children to</u> <u>Mathematical Discovery</u>. Belmont, California: Wadsworth, 1980.

KHATENA, Joe, "Teaching Disadvantaged Preschool Children to Think Creatively with Pictures," <u>Journal of Educational</u> <u>Psychology</u>, <u>62</u>, no. 5 (October 1971), 384-86.

KING-STOOPS, Joyce, <u>The Child Wants to Learn</u>. Boston: Little, Brown, and Company, 1977, 54, 55.

KNAPP, Clifford E., "Environment: Children Explore Their School, Their Community, Their Values," <u>Instructor</u>, <u>81</u>, no. 6 (February 1972), 62+.

KOCH, Kenneth, <u>Wishes, Lies, and Dreams--</u> <u>Teaching Children to Write Poetry</u>. New York: Vintage Books, 1970.

KOHL, Herbert and Judith Kohl, <u>The View from</u> <u>the Oak</u>. San Francisco: Sierra Club Books, 1977.

KRAMER, Klaas, <u>Teaching Elementary School</u> <u>Mathematics</u>. Boston: Allyn and Bacon, 1978.

LAMENT, Marylee McMurray, <u>Music in Elementary</u> <u>Education</u>. New York: Macmillan Publishing Company, Inc., 1976.

LEEPER, Sarah Hammond, Dora Sikes SKIPPER, and Ralph L. WITHERSPOON, <u>Good Schools for Young</u> <u>Children</u>. New York: Macmillan Publishing Company, Inc., 1979.

LIST, Lynn, <u>Music, Art, and Drama Experiences</u> <u>for the Elementary Curriculum</u>. New York: Teachers College Press, 1982.

LOVELL, Hugh, and Charlotte HARTER, <u>An</u> <u>Economics Course for Elementary School</u> <u>Teachers</u> (2nd ed.). Portland, Oregon: Center for Economic Education, 1975.

LOWENFELD, Viktor, and W. Lambert BRITTAIN, <u>Creative and Mental Growth</u>. New York: The Macmillan Company, 1970.

MCLAUGHLIN, Roberta, and Lucille WOOD, "The Small Dancer," <u>The Small Music Series</u>. Glendale, California: Bomar Records.

MANSFIELD, Richard S., and Thomas V. BUSSE, "The Effectiveness of Creativity Training Programs," <u>Childhood Education</u>, <u>50</u>, no. 6 (Summer 1974), 53-56.

MAXIM, George W., <u>Methods of Teaching Social</u> <u>Studies to Elementary School Children</u>. Columbus, Ohio: Charles E. Merrill Publishing Company, Inc., 1978.

MEEKER, Mary, "Measuring Creativity from the Child's Point of View, Journal of Creative Behavior, 12, no. 1 (Winter 1978), 56-63.

MILLER, Jean Harbaugh, The Effectiveness of Training on Creative Thinking Abilities of Third Grade Children (Doctoral dissertation, University of Alabama, 1974), Dissertation Abstracts International, 35, 11-A, 7032.

MORRIS, William, ed., The American Heritage Dictionary of the English Language. Boston: Houghton Mifflin Company, 1971, pp. 384, 385.

National Council of Teachers of Mathematics, Arithmetic Teacher. This professional journal is published nine times yearly.

National Geographic Society, National Geographic. Washington, D.C.: National Geographic Society. Published twelve times yearly.

National Geographic Society, National Geographic World. Washington, D.C.: National Geographic Society. Published twelve times yearly.

National Science Teachers Association. Science and Children. Washington, D.C., published ten times yearly.

NAUMANN, Nancy L., Creative Teaching of Reading to Promote Children's Creative Thinking (Doctoral dissertation, Boston University, 1980), Dissertation Abstracts International, 41, 05, 1987.

NICHOLS, Eugene D. and Merlyn J. BEHR, Elementary School Mathematics and How to Teach It. New York: Holt, Rinehart, and Winston, 1982.

NICKSE, Ruth S., and Richard E. RIPPLE, "The Use of Creativity Training Materials With Special Children: A Report of a Feasibility Experience," Child Study Journal, 1, no. 4, (Summer 1971), 175-85.

PECK, Judith, Leap to the Sun. Englewood Cliffs, New Jersey: Prentice-Hall, Inc., 1979.

PEPLER, Debra J., and Hildy S. ROSS, "The Effects of Play on Convergent and Divergent Problem Solving," Child Development, 52, no. 4 (December 1981), 1202-12.

PETTY, Walter, Dorothy C. PETTY, and Marjorie F. BECKING, Experience in Language: Tools and Techniques for Language Arts Methods. Boston: Allyn and Bacon, Inc., 1981.

PUCKETT, Newbell N., Folk Beliefs of the Southern Negro. New York: Dover Publications, Inc., 1969.

RATHS, Louis B., and others, Teaching for Thinking: Theory and Application. Columbus, Ohio: Charles E. Merrill Publishing Company, 1967.

RICHARDSON Jr., Lloyd I., Kathy L. GOODMAN, Nancy Noftsinger HARTMAN, and Henri C. LE PIQUE, A Mathematics Activity Curriculum for Early Childhood and Special Education. New York: Macmillan, 1980.

RIEDESEL, C. Alan, <u>Teaching Elementary School Mathematics.</u> Englewood Cliffs, New Jersey: Prentice-Hall, Inc., 1980.

RISING, Gerald R., and Joseph B. HARKINS, <u>The Third "R" Mathematics Teaching for Grades K-8.</u> Belmont, California: Wadsworth, 1978.

ROOKEY, Thomas J., and Francis J. REARDON, "The Interdependence of Creative Attitude and Creative Ability," 1973 (ERIC Document Reproduction Service No. ED 075515).

ROSENBAUM, Dave, <u>Assessment of Divergent Thinking in Children: Effects of Task Context, Race, and Socio-economic Status</u> (Doctoral dissertation, New School for Social Research, 1973), <u>Dissertation Abstracts International</u>, 34, <u>07</u>, 3507.

RUNKLE, Aleta, and Mary LeBow ERIKSON, <u>Music for Today: Elementary School Methods.</u> Boston: Allyn and Bacon, 1976.

RYAN, Frank L., <u>The Social Studies Sourcebook: Ideas for Teaching in Elementary and Middle School.</u> Boston, Massachusetts: Allyn and Bacon, Inc., 1980.

SANDERS, Norris M., <u>Classroom Questions: What Kinds?</u> New York: Harper & Row, 1966.

SCOTT, Norval C., Jr., and I.E. SIGEL, "Effects of Inquiry Training in Physical Science on Creativity and Cognitive Styles of Elementary School Children," 1965 (ERIC Document Reproduction Service No. ED 003700).

SHARPE, Lawrence W., "The Effects of a Creative Thinking Skills Program on Intermediate Grade Educationally Handicapped Children," <u>Journal of Creative Behavior,</u> <u>10</u>, no. 2 (1976), 138-145.

SHAW, Jean M., "Learning On the Run," <u>Early Years</u>, <u>9</u>, no. 7 (March 1979), 46-47.

SILVERSTEIN, Shel, <u>A Light in the Attic.</u> New York: Harper & Row, 1974.

SILVERSTEIN, Shel, <u>Where the Sidewalk Ends.</u> New York: Harper & Row, 1974.

SIMON, Marylu Shore, and Judy Moss ZIMMERMAN, "Science and Writing," <u>Science and Children,</u> <u>18</u>, November-December, 1980, 7-9.

SISK, Dorothy Ann, <u>The Relationship Between Self Concept and Creative Thinking of Elementary School Children: An Experimental Investigation</u> (Doctoral dissertation, University of California, Los Angeles, 1966), <u>Dissertation Abstracts International,</u> 27, <u>08</u>, 2455.

Special Education Students Handout, "Suggestions for Teaching the Gifted," University of South Florida, no date.

SPIER, Peter, <u>Fast-Slow, High-Low: A Book of Opposites.</u> New York: Doubleday, 1972.

THOMAS, Nancy G., and Laura E. BERK, "Effects of School Environment on the Development of Young Children's Creativity," <u>Child Development,</u> <u>52</u>, no. 4 (December 1981), 1153-62.

TORRANCE, E. Paul, Creativity. Belmont, California: Fearon, 1969.

TORRANCE, E. Paul, "Creativity and Infinity," Journal of Research and Development in Education, 4, no. 3 (Spring 1971), 35-41.

TORRANCE, E. Paul, "Examples and Rationales of Test Tasks for Assessing Creative Abilities," Journal of Creative Behavior, 2, no 3 (Summer 1968), 165-78.

TORRANCE, E. Paul, "Priming Creative Thinking in the Elementary Grades," The Elementary School Journal. 62, no. 1 (October 1961), 34-41.

TORRANCE, E. Paul, Torrance Tests of Creative Thinking. Lexington, Mass.: Personnel Press, Inc., 1969.

TORRANCE, E. Paul, "The Minnesota Studies of Creative Behavior: National and International Extensions," Journal of Creative Behavior, 1, no. 2 (Spring 1967), 137-54.

TORRANCE, E. Paul, What Research Says to the Teacher: Creativity in the Classroom. Washington, D.C.: National Education Association, 1977.

TRESSLT, Alvin. The Mitten. New York: Lothrop, 1964.

TURNER, Pauline H., and Mary Ellen DURRETT, "Teacher Level of Questioning and Problem Solving," 1975 (ERIC Document Reproduction Service No. ED 105997).

VICTOR, Edward, Science for the Elementary School, 4th ed. New York: Collier Macmillan Publishers, 1980.

VIORST, Judith, Alexander and the Terrible, Horrible, No Good, Very Bad Day. New York: Atheneum, 1972.

WALLACH, M.A., and N. Kogan, "Creativity and Intelligence in Children's Thinking," Transaction, (January/February 1967), 4, no. 3, 38-43.

WALSH, Huber M., Introducing the Young Child to the Social World. New York: Macmillan Publishing Company, Inc., 1980.

WALTER, Nina Willis, Let Them Write Poetry. New York: Holt, Rinehart, and Winston, 1966.

WANKELMAN, Willard F., Philip WIGG, and Marietta WIGG, A Handbook of Arts & Crafts. Dubuque, Iowa: Wm. C. Brown Co., 1975.

WEITZMAN, David, My Backyard History Book. Boston, Massachusetts: Little, Brown, and Company, 1975.

WEZEL, Peter, The Good Bird. New York: Harper & Row, 1964.

WHITMAN, Nancy C., and Frederick G. BRAUN, The Metric System: A Laboratory Approach for Teachers. New York: John Wiley, 1978.

WILLIAMS, Frank E., Classroom Ideas for Encouraging Thinking and Feeling. Buffalo, N.Y.: D.O.K. Publishers, Inc., 1970.

WILLIAMS, Frank R., "Teaching for Creativity: Continuing Process," _Instructor_, 81, no. 4 (December 1971), 42-44.

WISEMAN, Ann, _Making Things: The Handbook of Creative Discovery_. Boston: Little, Brown, and Company, 1973.

WRIGHT, Beverly A., "Common Characteristics in the Educational Backgrounds of Highly Creative Children and their Preferences Regarding Classroom Behavior," _Journal of Creative Behavior_, 15, no. 1 (Fourth quarter 1982), 283-84.

YAWKEY, Thomas D., and others, _Language Arts and the Young Child_. Itasca, Illinois: F.E. Peacock Publishers, Inc., 1981.

ZAVATSKY, Bill, and Ron PADGETT, eds., _The Whole Word Catalogue 2_. New York: McGraw-Hill Paperbacks, 1977.

TOPICAL ACTIVITIES INDEX

	page no.	Recommended Level		Recommended Group Size		
		lower	upper	large	small	individual
ART						
<u>Drawing</u>						
Cloud Pictures	157	•		•		
Add-On Pictures	157	•	•	•		
Dotted Art	158	•	•	•		
Classy Quilt	158	•	•	•		
Surrounded by Sound!	158	•		•		
Colorful Windows	158		•	•		
Photographic Adventures	165		•		•	
Historical Mural	165				•	
Window Murals	165	•			•	
Our Town	170	•			•	
Texture Search	170	•	•		•	
Frosty Sketches	175	•				•
What's In a Shape?	175	•	•			•
Logos	175		•			•
Batik	175	•	•			•
Creative Alphabets	175	•	•			•
Design a Flag	181		•			•
Textured Drawings	182	•				•
Sandpaper Art	182	•				•

	page no.	Recommended Level		Recommended Group Size		
		lower	upper	large	small	individual
Painting and Printing						
What Can You Paint On?	158	•	•	•		
What Can You Paint With?	159	•	•	•		
Tints and Shades	159	•	•	•		
Amalgamated Art	160	•	•	•		
Foggy Mural	160	•	•	•		
Painting with Ice Cubes	165	•	•		•	
Marble Painting	166	•	•		•	
Marbleized Paper	166		•		•	
Junk on Junk	166	•	•		•	
Plaid Pictures	171	•	•		•	
Rain Drop Paintings	176	•				•
Blow a Picture	176	•				•
Lady Bug's Point of View	176	•				•
Cutting, Tearing, and Pasting						
Collage Cafeteria	160	•	•	•		
Colored Sprinkles	160	•		•		
Yarn Ornaments	160	•	•	•		
Masked Dramas	161	•	•	•		
Overhead Art	167		•		•	
Frame Up I	167		•		•	

	page no.	Recommended Level		Recommended Group Size		
		lower	upper	large	small	individual
Cutting, Tearing, and Pasting						
Frame Up II	167		•		•	
Dotted Designs	171	•	•		•	
Theme Collage	167	•	•		•	
Found Paper Collage	172	•			•	
Experiment with Paper	172	•	•		•	
Popout Cards	176		•			•
Junk Treasure Box	177		•			•
Styrofoam Window Hangers	177		•			•
Nature Collages	177	•	•			•
Tree Mosaics	177	•	•			•
Punch-A-Round	178		•			•
Sculpture and Three Dimensional Constructions						
Decorate the Ceiling	161		•	•		
Natural Sculptures	161	•		•		
Sand Painting	161		•	•		
Paper Plate Sculpture	162	•	•	•		
Rock Art	162		•	•		
Scent It	168	•			•	
Playdough Plus	168	•	•		•	

	page no.	Recommended Level		Recommended Group Size		
		lower	upper	large	small	individual
Sculpture and Three Dimensional Constructions						
Soap Suds Sculpture	168	•			•	
Dryer Lint Clay	169	•			•	
Egg Carton Creations	174	•	•		•	
Cardboard Castles	174	•	•		•	
Soaring Sculptures	178		•			•
Soap Bar Carvings	178	•	•			•
Seashore Scene	181	•	•			•
Egg Cup Animals	181	•	•			•
Salt Dough Ornaments	181		•			•
Nature Boat	182	•	•			•
Potato Planters	182	•	•			•
Weaving and Sewing						
Nature Weavings	162	•	•	•		
Colorful Stitching	162		•	•		
Silly Sock Puppets	163	•	•	•		
Fabric Collage	169	•	•		•	
Lotsa Looms	169		•		•	
Cross-Stitched Gingham Gifts	179		•			•
String a Necklace	179	•	•			•

	page no.	Recommended Level		Recommended Group Size		
		lower	upper	large	small	individual
Weaving and Sewing						
Petite Pillows	179		•			•
Vine Weaving	180		•			•
Dress Your Doll	180	•	•			•
Plaited Projects	180		•			•
Art Appreciation						
A Close Look	163		•	•		
Guest Artist	163	•	•	•		
Life and Times... and Art	164		•	•		
Change It, Improve It	164	•	•	•		
Compare and Contrast	164	•	•	•		
Jungle Scene	164	•	•	•		
Art Observation Book	180	•	•			•
In the Style of...	180		•			•
Art Apprenticeship	181		•			•
LANGUAGE ARTS						
Oral Language						
Questions, Questions, Questions	28	•	•	•		
Getting to Know You	28	•	•	•		
What Would You Do Questions	28	•	•	•		
Window Peeking	29	•		•		
Divergent Chatter	29		•	•		

Oral Language

	page no.	Recommended Level		Recommended Group Size		
		lower	upper	large	small	individual
Questions About Pictures	29	•	•	•		
Telephone Conversations	29	•	•	•		
Junky Conversations	29	•	•	•		
A Different Kind of Homework	29	•	•	•		
Unlikely Matches	30	•	•	•		
Loving Questions	30	•		•		
Ole Mo's Dog	30		•	•		
String Stories	35		•		•	
What Happened Before?	35	•	•		•	
Classy Conversations	35	•	•		•	
Mini Stories	39		•		•	
Peanut Tales	39		•		•	
Class Interviews	41	•	•		•	
Using Stories That Have No Words	47		•			•
Pretending Pillow	48	•				•
Dreamscapes	52		•			•
Guess Who I Am	52	•	•			•
Learning Through Interviews	53		•			•

	page no.	Recommended Level		Recommended Group Size		
		lower	upper	large	small	individual
Listening and Reading						
Poems We Love	30		•	•		
Talking About Listening	30	•	•	•		
Tell the Story's End	31	•	•	•		
Inflections and Interpretations	31		•	•		
Name Acrostics	31	•	•	•		
Scavenge for Nouns	31	•	•	•		
Compound Words	31	•		•		
Cartoons Convey Meanings	31		•	•		
New News	31	•	•	•		
Soft Sounds	36	•	•		•	
Puppet Show	40	•	•		•	
Tape Recorder Fun	46	•	•		•	
Listening Walk	46	•	•		•	
Machine Sounds Inventory	45	•	•		•	
Favorite News Personalities	41		•		•	
Descriptive Adjectives and Adverbs	48	•	•			•
Word Blurbs	48		•			•
Takeoffs on Good Books	48	•				•

	page no.	Recommended Level		Recommended Group Size		
		lower	upper	large	small	individual
Listening and Reading						
Guess Who I Am	52	•	•			•
Unique Book Reports	53	•	•			•
The Listening Game	53	•	•			•
Writing						
Rhyming Race	32	•		•		
Comparing and Contrasting with Words	32	•	•	•		
Expanding Kernel Sentences	32	•	•	•		
Color Walk	32	•		•		
Creative Writing Tasks	33	•	•	•		
Mystery Pictures	33	•	•	•		
Relay with a Beginning and an Ending	33	•	•	•		
Writing Haiku	34	•	•	•		
More Creative Writing Tasks	34	•	•	•		
Writing Lists	34	•		•		
Braille Writing	34			•		
A Classroom Newspaper	36		•		•	
Goofy Tales with Odd Adjectives	36	•	•		•	

| | page no. | Recommended Level | | Recommended Group Size | | |
		lower	upper	large	small	individual
Writing						
Writing Cinquains	36		•		•	
Elderly Pen Pals	37	•	•		•	
Writing Myths	37	•	•		•	
Roll the Dice and Spin a Tale	37		•		•	
Code Messages	47	•	•		•	
Cubs Win Over Phillies	43	•	•		•	
Riddle Tree	43	•			•	
Funny Words	44	•	•		•	
These Are a Few of our Favorite Things	44	•			•	
Rebus Messages	38		•		•	
Letters to Write	49	•	•			•
Things to Write About	49	•	•			•
Shades of Meaning	49	•	•			•
The Problem Jar	50	•	•			•
A Special Gift	50	•	•			•
Creative Writing Assignments from Old Calendars	50	•	•			•
Idea Box of Similes and Metaphors	51	•	•			•
Recycled Newspaper	51	•	•			•

	page no.	Recommended Level		Recommended Group Size		
		lower	upper	large	small	individual
Writing						
Hidden Treasure	51	•	•			•
Interesting Noise	52	•	•			•
Sticky Homework	51		•			•
Class Notes	52		•			•
Observing Nonverbal Language	53		•			•
How Do People See You?	51		•			•
The Listening Game	53	•	•			•
Tombstone Rubbings	51	•	•			•
Drama						
Silent Talk	38	•	•		•	
Prop Box	38	•			•	
Soap Operas	42	•	•		•	
Dramatic Book Reports	42	•	•		•	
MATH						
Relationships						
Patterning	60	•		•		
The Category Zoo	60	•		•		
Relationships Galore	67	•			•	
Really Big and Small	84	•	•			•

	page no.	Recommended Level		Recommended Group Size		
		lower	upper	large	small	individual
Numbers and Operations						
Count It Off	60	•		•		
Patterns and Functions	60	•	•	•		
Always Smaller	61		•	•		
Brainstorming About Numbers	61	•	•	•		
Budgeting	61	•	•	•		
Spinner Math	61	•	•	•		
Number Families	61	•		•		
Fraction Family Flowers	62		•	•		
Productive Practice	62	•	•	•		
Palindrome Play	62		•	•		
Comparing Texts	67	•	•		•	
Ancient Numerals	68		•		•	
Prime and Composite Patterns	68		•		•	
Ratios from the Yellow Pages	68		•		•	
Piggy Banks	69	•			•	
Calendar Creations	74		•		•	
Number Cubes	73	•	•		•	
Mathematics Card Games	73		•		•	
Domino Dynamite	76	•	•		•	

	page no.	Recommended Level		Recommended Group Size		
		lower	upper	large	small	individual
Numbers and Operations						
Holey Math!	76	•	•		•	
Cataloging	80	•	•			•
Folding Paper	80	•	•			•
Puzzle Corner	80		•			•
Number Collage	81	•	•			•
Number Diary	81	•	•			•
Dart Boards	84	•	•			•
Percent Collage	84		•			•
More Dart Boards	85		•			•
Problem Solving						
Problem Formats	63	•	•	•		
Miniproblems	63	•	•	•		
A Kilometer Walk	63	•	•	•		
Picture Problems	69	•			•	
Math Adventure Stories	69		•		•	
Fit the Problem to the Equation	69		•		•	
Problem Solving with Diagrams	74		•		•	
Road Map Math	81		•			•

	page no.	Recommended Level		Recommended Group Size		
		lower	upper	large	small	individual
Graphing, Probability and Statistics						
Sampling Techniques	63		•	•		
Graphing Gadgets	63	•	•	•		
Groovy Graphs	64	•	•	•		
Graph-A-Car	69	•	•		•	
Probability Bag	70		•		•	
Circle Graphs	85		•			•
Geometry and Measurement						
Cubic Centimeters	64		•	•		
Hot 'n' Cold	64	•		•		
Model Students	64		•	•		
Brainstorming About Measurement	65		•	•		
Geoboards for Tots	65		•	•		
Look Around You-- Geometry Style!	65		•	•		
Balancing Act	70	•	•		•	
Same Volumes, Different Masses	70		•		•	
Holey Math!	76	•	•		•	
Build With Cubes	77	•	•		•	
Mirrors and Symmetry	78	•	•		•	
Axis of Symmetry	78	•	•		•	

	page no.	Recommended Level		Recommended Group Size		
		lower	upper	large	small	individual
Geometry and Measurement						
Big Figures	75	•			•	
Toothpick Geometry	75	•	•		•	
Tangrams	77	•	•		•	
About As Long As	79	•			•	
Even Split	82	•	•			•
Wallpaper Patterns	82	•				•
Plotting Practice	82		•			•
Same Area Many Shapes	83		•			•
Same Perimeter, Different Areas	83		•			•
The "Metric Me" Book	83	•	•			•
Just One Decimeter Tall!	85		•			•
As Long As a Meter	86	•	•			•
Geometry Rubbings	86	•				•
Stair Studies	86		•			•
Depends on How You Look	87	•	•			•
Big Volumes	87		•			•

	page no.	Recommended Level		Recommended Group Size		
		lower	upper	large	small	individual
Calculators and Computers						
Calculator Usage	65		•	•		
Input, Output	66		•	•		
Ideas for Flow Charts	66		•	•		
To Calculate or Not to Calculate-- That Is the Question	71	•			•	
Largest Answer	70	•			•	
Calculatin' Pairs	71		•		•	
Computer Responses	71		•		•	
Programming Play	71		•		•	
The Smiley Face and Other Simple Pictures	72		•		•	
Flow Chart Comparison	72		•		•	
Calculator Challenge	79	•			•	
MUSIC						
Singing						
Dynamic Singing	190		•	•		
Add Your Own Words	190	•	•	•		
Singing Commercials	191		•	•		
Melodic Poems	191		•	•		

	page no.	Recommended Level		Recommended Group Size		
		lower	upper	large	small	individual
Singing						
Complete the Tune	191	•	•	•		
Creative Lyrics	197	•	•		•	
Mix 'n' Match	197		•		•	
Imitations in Song	203	•			•	
Singing Telegram	208		•			•
Telephone Songs	209		•			•
Imitate the Sound	211	•	•			•
Silly Sounds	212	•	•			•
Rhythmic Movement						
Body Part Copy Cat	191	•		•		
Stretchy Rhythms	191	•	•	•		
Add a Part	191	•	•	•		
Theme and Variations	191		•	•		
Classroom Jingles	197		•		•	
Clap Your Name	197	•	•		•	
Newspaper Dance	198	•			•	
Mouthy Compositions	198	•			•	
Keep the Beat with Body Symbols	198		•		•	
Jump Rope Jingle	203	•	•		•	
Copy My Rhythm	203	•			•	
Show the Beat	211	•	•			•

244

	page no.	Recommended Level		Recommended Group Size		
		lower	upper	large	small	individual
Creative Movement						
Dancing on Air	192	•		•		
Balloons	192	•		•		
Shirt on the Clothesline	193	•		•		
Themes to Move By	193	•		•		
Living Pictures	193	•	•	•		
Scarf Stories	193	•		•		
Statues	194	•	•	•		
Props for Creative Movement	194	•		•		
Paper Streamer Shapes	194	•		•		
Creative Movement Wheels	195		•	•		
Human Puppets	198	•	•		•	
Footprint Fun	199	•	•		•	
More Themes to Move By	199	•			•	
Moving in Outer Space	200	•	•		•	
Paper Strips and Overhead Projector Fun	204	•	•		•	
Move a Partner with Your Sound	204	•	•		•	
Shadow Dancing	205	•	•		•	
Mirror Images	205	•	•		•	
Feathery Movements	208	•			•	

	page no.	Recommended Level		Recommended Group Size		
		lower	upper	large	small	individual
Creative Movement						
Listen, Look, and Mime	209	•	•			•
Moving Creatively	211	•	•			•
Shapes and Letters	212	•				•
Listening						
Describing Music	195	•	•	•		
Sharing Favorite Songs	195	•	•	•		
Colorful Listening	196	•	•	•		
Comparing Art and Music	196		•	•		
Interpreting Music with Symbols	196		•	•		
Learning About the Basic Elements of Music	200		•		•	
Body Interpretations of Music	200	•	•		•	
Fun with Water Glasses	201	•	•		•	
Sea Shell Sounds	206	•	•		•	
Listening to Music I Don't Like	209		•			•
Stories Based on Music	210	•	•			•
Television Homework	210		•			•
Imitate the Sound	211	•	•			•

247

	page no.	Recommended Level		Recommended Group Size		
		lower	upper	large	small	individual
Biology						
Testing Variables for Plant Growth	94		•	•		
Original Ice Cream Recipes	94	•	•	•		
Sandpile Greenhouse	104	•			•	
Seed Sort	105	•			•	
Name Your Own Thing	108		•		•	
Design a Pot	113	•	•			•
Natural Dyes	114		•			•
Nature Symmetry	116	•	•			•
Tree Trunk Patterns	118	•	•			•
ANIMALS						
Inquiries About Animal Products	95	•	•	•		
Creatures of the Sea	95	•	•	•		
Creative Bird Watching	95		•	•		
Bird Feeder Invention	104	•			•	
Animal Information	106	•	•		•	
Design a Better Bug Trap	106		•		•	
Animal Senses	117	•	•			•
If I Were a Worm	117	•	•			•
Pet Poems	116	•				•
Scent Test	117		•			•

	page no.	Recommended Level		Recommended Group Size		
		lower	upper	large	small	individual
Biology						
ANIMALS						
An Insect's Point of View	117	•	•			•
HUMAN						
Sensory Handicaps	95	•	•	•		
The Foot Bone's Related to the Ankle Bone ...	95		•	•		
X-Ray Exam	96		•	•		
Delectable Dinners	105	•			•	
Foot Feelings 1	107	•	•		•	
Foot Feelings 2	107	•	•		•	
Stomach Curealls	108		•		•	
Careful Look	116	•	•			•
Fingerprint Designs	116	•				•
MISCELLANEOUS						
A Close Look at Physical Properties	99		•	•		
Pudding Creations	114	•				•
Add-On Bulletin Board	114		•			•

	page no.	Recommended Level		Recommended Group Size		
		lower	upper	large	small	individual
Environmental Science						
INTERRELATIONSHIPS						
Life Chain	96		•	•		
Interrelation- ships	96		•	•		
The Great Iceberg Melt	96		•	•		
House Detectives	109		•		•	
Pollution Evidence	118	•	•			•
ROCKS						
Rock Recipes	96	•	•	•		
Rocks and More Rocks	97	•	•	•		
Crystal Pictures	114	•				•
WEATHER						
Rain Walks	97	•		•		
Making Weather Instruments	97		•	•		
Pondering Clouds	118	•	•			•
UNIVERSE						
Sun Fun	97		•	•		
Mini Moon Craters	98	•	•	•		
Solar System	98		•	•		
Spacey Sortie	98		•	•		

	page no.	Recommended Level		Recommended Group Size		
		lower	upper	large	small	individual
Environmental Science						
UNIVERSE						
Life on Another Planet	99		•	•		
Planets Beyond Pluto	119		•			•
Constellation Creations	118		•			•
ENERGY						
Reducing Energy Consumption	98		•	•		
Draft Meter	114	•	•			•
MISCELLANEOUS						
More Add-Ons	115		•			•
Science Processes						
Buttons 'n' Bones	102	•			•	
Alike and Different	102	•	•		•	
The Eclectic Mystery Boxes	103	•	•		•	
Testing Ads	113		•		•	
Dramas About Discoveries	112		•		•	
Paper Clip Perusals	119	•	•			•

	page no.	Recommended Level		Recommended Group Size		
		lower	upper	large	small	individual
Physical Science						
AIR						
Soap bubbles	99		•	•		
Parachute Designs	119	•	•			•
HEAT						
Candles, Whale Oil, and Peanuts	100		•	•		
Solar Cooker	112	•	•		•	
LIGHT						
Transparent, Translucent, and Opaque	100	•	•	•		
Sun and Shadows	103		•		•	
Shadow Shows	103		•		•	
Fantastic Flashlights 1	111	•	•		•	
Fantastic Flashlights 2	111	•	•		•	
WATER						
Dissolving Test	100	•	•	•		
The Great Water Transfer	110	•	•		•	
Power Boats	115	•				•
Shell Boats	115	•				•
MACHINES						
Mystery Machine Box	101	•	•	•		
Machine Collage	101		•	•		

	page no.	Recommended Level		Recommended Group Size		
		lower	upper	large	small	individual
Physical Science						
MACHINES						
Machines Help Us	115	•	•			•
MAGNETISM AND ELECTRICITY						
Repellattract	101	•	•	•		
Sparks 'n' Shocks	110	•	•		•	
SOUND						
Sounding Boards	101		•	•		
Design a Phone	109	•	•		•	
Noisy Pictures	119	•				•
MISCELLANEOUS						
Marble Capers	100	•	•	•		
Gravity Gabble	101		•	•		
Rusty Research	102	•	•	•		
SOCIAL STUDIES						
Sociology and Anthropology						
Conserve, Conserve Conserve	128		•	•		
Wood Carriers in Ethiopia	130		•	•		
"Roots"	127		•	•		
Blindfold Walk	127	•	•	•		
Secret Buddies	127	•	•	•		

	page no.	Recommended Level		Recommended Group Size		
		lower	upper	large	small	individual
Sociology and Anthropology						
Hot Springs Cooking and Bathing	128		•	•		
A City Under the Sea	129	•	•	•		
Family Mementos	129	•	•	•		
More Consequences	127		•	•		
Living Style of Eskimos	129	•	•	•		
Arty Artifacts	126	•	•	•		
The Great Time Machine	129		•	•		
Working Together	126	•		•		
Rules, Rules, Rules	126	•	•	•		
Travel Memories	129	•	•	•		
Comparative Family Studies	135		•		•	
Holidays in Foreign Countries	135		•		•	
Information Bank	136		•		•	
Games Around the World	135		•		•	
Helping the Handicapped	135	•	•		•	
Alike--Different	141	•			•	

	page no.	Recommended Level		Recommended Group Size		
		lower	upper	large	small	individual
Sociology and Anthropology						
More Alike-- Different	141	•			•	
Traffic Symbols	138	•	•		•	
Coats of Arms	143	•	•			•
Checklists	144	•	•			•
It's Me!	144	•	•			•
Feelings Book	144	•				•
Helping Hands	143	•				•
Rock Sociogram	145	•	•			•
Home Work	146	•				•
Folk Cure-Alls	147	•	•			•
Rain Making Charms	147		•			•
Family Members Working Together	147	•				•
Thanksgiving	147	•				•
Buenos Dias	148	•	•			•
Sketching Talents	148	•	•			•
Family Memorabilia	148	•	•			•
Family Tree	149	•	•			•
Shoe Surveys	149		•			•

	page no.	Recommended Level		Recommended Group Size		
		lower	upper	large	small	individual
History, Political Science, and Geography						
Changes	142	•		•		
Solving Mysteries from the Cemetery	130		•	•		
Now and Then	130		•	•		
Consequences	128		•	•		
Life in a Different Environment	128		•	•		
The History of My Name	130	•	•	•		
Who Am I?	131	•	•	•		
Imaginary Trips	134		•		•	
Passports	134		•		•	
Maps, Maps, Maps	134	•			•	
More Mapping and Modeling	135		•		•	
Antique Fantasy	134		•		•	
Local Folklore	133		•		•	
Classroom Calendar	133	•	•		•	
Fashions of the Past	139		•		•	
Questions ... Answers	139	•			•	
Time Capsule	137		•		•	

	page no.	Recommended Level		Recommended Group Size		
		lower	upper	large	small	individual
History, Political Science, and Geography						
Flag Designs	137		•		•	
Fairy Tale Map	140	•			•	
Origins of Household Products	142		•			•
Tasting Party	142	•	•			•
Historical Fiction	143		•			•
How Did It Get Its Name?	143		•			•
The Good Old Days	143	•	•			•
Time Line	142	•	•			•
If I Had Been That Person	143	•	•			•
Biographic Maps	143		•			•
Eye Witness Report	146		•			•
Poems of Slavery	147		•			•
The Sun in Alaska	147		•			•
Greeting a Chinese Friend	147	•	•			•
Grocery Mapping	148		•			•
Political Jokes	148		•			•
Interviewing Authorities	149		•			•

	page no.	Recommended Level		Recommended Group Size		
		lower	upper	large	small	individual
<u>Economics and Career Education</u>						
Old and New Jobs	132		•	•		
Family Economy	131	•	•	•		
Label Search	131	•	•	•		
Truck Collage	132	•		•		
Search the Classified Ads	133		•	•		
Bartering	132	•	•	•		
Assembly Line	136	•	•		•	
Ways Public Servants Protect Us	136	•	•		•	
Improving Community Operations	136	•	•		•	
Yellow Pages	136	•	•		•	
More "Ads"	136		•		•	
Job Research	138		•		•	
Luxuries ... Necessities	140	•	•		•	
Job Vocabularies	145		•			•
Designing Ads	146		•			•
Product Investigations	146		•			•
Study the Ads	146		•			•

	page no.	Recommended Level		Recommended Group Size		
		lower	upper	large	small	individual
<u>Economics and</u> <u>Career Education</u>						
Working Parents Mural	146	●				●
Grocery Helpers	148	●	●			●
Improving Products	148	●	●			●
Advertise Your Services	149		●			●
Budget Planning	149	●	●			●

259